Go-Go Speaks: The Heartbeat of a Culture

Jill Greenleigh

Jill Greenleigh

Cover Design by Nate Lucas at Asterisk WDS

Edit by Sarah Godfrey

Line Edit and Format by Pooja Yadav

ACKNOWLEDGMENTS

IT'S TIME TO PUT PEOPLE ON DISPLAY (Also Known as) ACKNOWLEDGMENTS

There are quite a few people that I'd like to thank for their encouragement, motivation, confidence in me to facilitate this work of love, and those who created this music that beats in our hearts.

I need to start out by thanking my family- My Grandparents Julius and Bernice Shapiro and Arthur and Frances Greenleigh for demonstrating to me the person that I wanted to be- using whatever it takes to help people when I was presented with an opportunity. My parents Steve and Judy Greenleigh for their patience and love, especially my dad who has been behind me pushing me when I was ready to give up and my Mom watching over me from above. To David, Suzanne, Lily and Evan Greenleigh and my special Aunt Lynn Shapiro. Thank you all.

Next, before anyone else, I need to thank the incomparable Sarah Godfrey for keeping me focused, on track and getting me over the finish line. You are an amazing motivator, therapist and, of course, editor.

My team Nate Lucas at Asterisk WDS and editor Pooja Yadav. I couldn't have done this without you.

There would be no book without the music, so I thank Chuck Brown, James "Funk" Thomas, "Big" Tony Fisher, Timothy "Teebone" David, Gregory "Sugar Bear" Elliott, and all of the members past and present of Rare Essence, Trouble Funk, Chuck Brown and the Soul Searchers, Experience Unlimited, Ayre Rayde, Peacemakers, AM/FM, Reality Band, Junkyard Band, Legacy Band, High Potential and Shear Madness and all of the bands that came out to keep the beat alive creating their own sound, their own lane and their own catalog.

A special dedication going out to Mark "Godfather" Lawson, "Little Benny" Harley and the entire Harley Family, Ivan Goff, "Outta Site" Mike

3

Hughes, Al Winkler, Maurice "Moe" Shorter, Alona Wartofsky and my Beta Readers Bobbie Westmoreland and Steven Coleman.

I have to thank my foundation, the friendships that have carried me through most of my life- Leslie Cohen, Gena Johnson, Yolanda Van Horn, Sharon McDonald Johnson, Sandra Edwards Ward, Tami Taylor Polcak, The Harris Family, my Town and Country Family, my Silver Spring Crew, Vincent Coleman and my 5-year old best friend Derek "DJ" Deane who always keeps a smile on my face and probably the first 5-year old to be thanked in a book.

I would be remiss if I didn't give a special thank you to Davey Shark aka Db Sharks the Celebrities Favorite, formerly of the Get Fresh Crew, who pushed me and believed in me when I didn't believe in myself, who wouldn't take an excuse or "no" for an answer. "Get the book done and then talk to me!"

Most of all, I want to thank they entire Go-Go Community and all those who continue to preserve, enhance, protect and continue the legacy- all of the musicians, clubs and venues, promoters, managers, security, clothing designers, podcast hosts and owners, Kato Hammond and Nico Hobson, Malachai Johns, DJs and producers, sound engineers, the best photographer to document the history ever- Thomas Sayers Ellis, Ron Moten and the Go-Go Museum and the fans.

I also want to thank you, the reader, for having an interest in this book. I hope this inspires someone to pick up an instrument or a pen.

TABLE OF CONTENTS

Preface

My career in Go-Go started when I was a student at Towson University in the late '80s. I had a roommate from Southeast D.C., K Street, to be exact. Her name was Angie Green. We were both heavily into Go-Go and decided to create a company called "Tri-Gold Productions." We weren't exactly sure what we were going to do, but we knew it would be something!

The very first thing that we did was a campus event in 1988. We partnered with a fraternity on campus and put on a show with Little Benny and the Masters, Legacy Band, and Show (from Montgomery County, MD), The Pretty Boys (including Khalid Keene from K.O. Productions), and a white rap artist from Gaithersburg, MD called MC Kool Breeez, who was a childhood friend of mine named Rick "Gene" Edwards. The show turned out well and introduced me to Legacy Band and Show.

Legacy was a group of guys from Kennedy High School in Silver Spring (with some members from Northwood High School and Duke Ellington School of the Arts sprinkled in). After that campus show, they asked me to manage them. I had some managerial experience, but not in music. I understood business, though. I have been working various jobs since I was 14 years old. Somehow, we all made it work. I booked the band in venues all over Montgomery County. They even played at Cheiry's in D.C., one of the popular Go-Go venues at the time.

Here I was, this young 20-year-old trying to make things happen. Meanwhile, my parents were more confused when I became involved in Go-Go. Even though I grew up in a diverse neighborhood in downtown Silver Spring, Maryland, and went to a private school with kids of all different races and ethnicities, they didn't get my interest in the music. When I got into the business side of Go-Go, they didn't know what to make of it. I was in college, and they wanted me to focus on my studies.

They didn't get it even when I was eventually published as a writer. I remember the first time my work was featured in *RapMasters* magazine. I had been visiting New York, and I went up to a magazine stand on 86th Street in Manhattan and bought every copy of *RapMasters* they had. I was super excited to return home and share this with everyone I knew. I showed the magazine to my family and let them know how thrilled I was, but the air was soon let out of my tires.

My family has been nothing but encouraging during the writing of this book – attitudes change, and people change. But at the time, it hurt so badly because here I was, published in a national magazine with an assignment to write a regular column, the Washington/ Baltimore music report, and my family did not share my enthusiasm. They weren't against Go-Go culture or the people in it. It just was something that was not relatable or understandable to them.

Not only did my family not approve, but I felt people wouldn't want to work with me because how could I, as a young white lady, possibly know anything about Go-Go? Still, I was fortunate enough to have some fantastic mentors and friends in Go-Go who took me under their wing. I soaked up everything I could about the music business, like a sponge, from great people like Mr. Busey (manager of The Pumpblenders), Moe Ziegler (owner of Cheiry's and manager of Physical Wunder), promoters Dave Rubin and Joe Clark, and Howard Teller (manager of Little Benny and the Masters).

During my last semester at Towson, I started working with Ivan Goff at his Big City Records. Ivan was a musical genius in his musical ability and production work. And they were unstoppable when Ivan teamed up with Kent Wood, producer and former member of both EU and Rare Essence. During that time, Ivan released several records on The PumpBlenders, Go-Go Lorenzo, Pure Elegance, and "Goin' Hard Ivan Goff featuring Chuck Brown," including his many projects. Big City had also previously released two wildly popular albums and staples of the genre, "Cat in the Hat" by Little Benny and the Masters and "Go Ju Ju Go" by EU.

During this time, WOL-AM, one of the most prominent D.C. radio stations, had a dedicated Go-Go show hosted by Keenan "Konan" Ellerbee. The show catered to the youth in the city. But around 1990, WOL owner Cathy Hughes decided to end the show, which many people saw as a disservice to the kids that needed the music and the guidance of "Big Brother Konan." We also were witnessing many other things going on that could have very well led to the demise of Go-Go: no other radio stations in the area were playing Go-Go as part of their regular rotation, and local officials were trying to shut down the clubs that catered to the Go-Go crowds, claiming that the music instigated violent behavior.

In response, people from the Go-Go community formed a group called The D.C. Committee to Save Our Music. Musicians, managers, record labels, and even the son of a city council member joined, along with others impacted by these changes. We stepped up and worked hard to find a solution.

The Committee collected signatures on a petition to prove that Konan's Go-Go program was essential to the community. We then marched from Hechinger Plaza in Northeast down to the WOL studio on H Street in Northeast to deliver the signed petitions to Ms. Hughes. We also held a forum in the D.C. Council chambers with guest speakers and other luminaries. Cathy Hughes did not budge on her stance, and the group shortly disbanded, but another group, The Go-Go Coalition, formed in its place and continued to fight to keep Go-Go alive and thriving in D.C.

Around the same time, I met two gentlemen, Malcolm Alexander, and Mark Bretzfelder, who published a street music paper called "Straight from the Street." It was an excellent vehicle to inform people about the goings-on of bands and musicians, upcoming shows, and other happenings. The great thing about it was that, at the time, all the popular rap artists and other musicians of the day were constantly in D.C. to perform for the students at Howard University, especially during Howard's homecoming, where there were parties galore.

I had started writing for "Straight from the Street," first about The Committee and the march, then as a staff writer and soon, Senior Editor. I spent a lot of time with those groundbreaking groups of the time: Public Enemy, Run DMC, Super Cat, and a lot of the other Def Jam artists. The regional representative for Def Jam for the Mid-Atlantic Region was Thomas Lytle, and he always ensured that I got all the interviews I wanted. I also got to interview a lot of Sony/Columbia artists, as well, thanks to Mike Archie. Bo Sampson was my "go-to" at MCA.

"Straight From the Street" was a steppingstone for me—it allowed me to get my feet wet, so to speak. In the late 80s, I attended a music business conference representing "Straight from the Street" and sat next to BethAnn Hardison, a well-known model scout and the mother of Kadeem Hardison (Dwayne Wayne from "A Different World"). Thanks to her and a music executive friend, Terry Moorer, I was introduced to Kate Ferguson, editor of *RapMasters* and *Word Up!* Magazines. She asked me immediately to do a piece on Go-Go, and then we would "see how it went." It went well because I was assigned to do the Regional Music Report for Washington and Baltimore. I don't have to be the one to tell you that Washington music and Baltimore music are two entirely different things, but it was an amazing opportunity, and I did it for quite a few years. I also wrote many stories for both *RapMasters* and *Word Up!* on the significant artists of the time, from Public Enemy, Onyx, and Cypress Hill to Chante Moore and everyone in between.

I was also writing for *Page One* magazine out of Florida and did some specials for *Dance Music Authority* overseas, to name a few.
After all this hoopla subsided, I was burned out and drained mentally and physically. I was a perfectionist, and that took a toll. I stepped away from the day-to-day, thinking it would be temporary, but it lasted about a decade. I did some behind-the-scenes, like writing bios, and kept in touch with my friends in the industry.

But in 2010, when Little Benny passed away, I realized how short time was. I attended his funeral, heartbroken because I hadn't seen him for some time. Right around that time, I got hooked up with an online outfit called Examiner.com, where I was the D.C. Local Music Examiner. My first story was about Benny. I wrote more than 100 more pieces after that, all on local artists in the DMV. I continued until they shut down the platform, and just like that – poof! – everything I had written was gone. Thank God, I had printed them all out.

In 2011, in an effort to throw a memorial show to mark the first anniversary of Benny's passing, Mark "Godfather" Lawson, Benny's good friend and former bandmate in Rare Essence and Little Benny and the Masters, asked me to help him with a band that he would be putting together. We decided to have a memorial dinner at Marygold's, where I had it catered for Benny's family and other luminaries that he worked with during his career. After dinner, there was a show that was open to the public. It was spectacular. And not one person asked for a dime, which shows the character of the people who performed that night. They donated their time for rehearsals and the performance to do this for Benny.
Although people still ask, I don't think I would ever get back into management again. The late nights of Go-Go don't appeal to me at my age.

But I was thrilled to be asked to work on the radio show "The Heartbeat

Conga Hour" in 2013 and produced some of those shows. The "Honor" shows were my favorite because I firmly believe in giving people their flowers while they are here to enjoy them. Honoring James Funk of Rare Essence and Proper Utensils, Timothy "Teebone" David of Trouble Funk, drummer extraordinaire Ricky Wellman, and the Tiger Flower/G Street/ CD Enterprises Crew of Excellence – Darryll Brooks, Carol Kirkendall, and Gerald Scott – were among my favorites.

I was also fortunate enough to be honored by The Heartbeat Conga Hour on August 9, 2016, when I received a lifetime achievement award for journalism. I was also given another award in June of 2018 for women behind the scenes.

After 30-plus years in Go-Go, I thought it was time to compile some of the stories – both the ones I lived and the ones I've heard over the years – in one place. I called it "Go-Go Speaks: The Heartbeat of a Culture" because I wanted to share some uncut, unfiltered thoughts about Go-Go music and culture that people have been kind enough to share with me over the years.

A lot has changed over these many years. Go-Go has gone from being blamed for a rise in violence in the 1980s to having Washington, D.C. Mayor Murial Bowser sign a bill in 2020 recognizing that Go-Go music is the official music of Washington, D.C. As a matter of fact, in 2018, the NBA secured the twenty-third G League team to be owned by the NBA and named this Washington, D.C. team The Capital City Go-Go, even utilizing a conga in the logo.

What you'll read here only scratches the surface of Go-Go. You may ask why certain people may not be quoted- people choose their priorities, but it wasn't for lack of trying as I wanted to hear from everyone. Some people just weren't available. With the many people involved in Go-Go over the years, we know it is impossible to speak with all of them.

This book is something that I have been contemplating for the past 7 years and is for those who have no idea what Go-Go is and for those who helped create the genre. For those who think you know all there is to know on the subject, you will find that this fills in the blanks for some of the things that we have only heard about- straight from the "horse's mouth." The Go-Go Community tells the story in its own words and voice. I realized it was either time to do it or let it go. So, here it is.

Jill Greenleigh

Introduction: How Chuck Brown Created a Sound and Captivated a City

The first time I ever heard Go-Go music was Chuck Brown and the Soul Searchers. I was 11 years old. I was on the school bus, Bus 82 to be exact, traveling to Town and Country Day School in Wheaton, Maryland, a suburb of Washington, D.C. "Bustin' Loose" came on the radio. Usually, one of the older kids or our bus driver, "Catfish," brought a pocket radio for a daily groove session.

As a young white girl, it was unbelievable to me when everyone on the bus started to sing along with Chuck. On the school bus that day, we were one. This song was completely different from what typically came from the small, white tabletop radio in my house. I heard Don McLean singing "Miss American Pie" at home and had impromptu dance sessions with my mother and brother to Elton John's "Crocodile Rock."

"Oh, when we are one, I'm not afraid, I'm not afraid!"- Chuck Brown

Bus 82 provided door-to-door transportation to the students who lived in the Upper Northwest corridor of D.C.—I grew up in downtown Silver Spring, Maryland, which bordered D.C., so I also rode this bus. Town and Country was a very diverse private school, and I was one of just a few white children on this bus. I was exposed to Chuck Brown, Parliament-Funkadelic, The Isley Brothers, and all the other funk and soul acts popular then. Imagine an 11-year-old Jewish kid singing along to "Amen" by The Impressions. These sounds would mold me musically for the next 43 years.

One of my very best friends at the time, and to this day, Gena Johnson, also rode this bus. As youngsters, we became tried and true Chuck fans (and Go-Go fans)— decades later, we still are. Simply, Chuck Brown provided the soundtrack to my life, and hers, and legions of others—the kids on Bus 82, as well as people around the entire D.C. metropolitan area, across the country, and worldwide.

"Keep what you got until you get what you need. You've got to give a lot

just to get what you need sometimes, y'all."- Chuck Brown

Chuck was played at every one of our birthday celebrations, and we would celebrate with him during his annual birthday show every August at the 9:30 Club. He was with us at New Year's celebrations—sometimes by CD, other times live, when the "lavish buffet" at the hotel where he was playing consisted of pigs in a blanket and not quite enough champagne to go around for the customary midnight toast. The countdown to 12 was always off by 10 seconds or so, but it didn't matter because we were with Chuck.

He was with us in the summertime while we sat outside eating crabs and drinking beer, when we were in our early 20s buying wine coolers from Sam's Beer and Wine on Georgia Avenue, at our holiday parties, and while we were laying on the beach in the Dominican Republic celebrating our 40th birthdays. Gena and I even sat on the wall of the Malecon in Havana, Cuba, playing Chuck from our iPods for anyone who would listen. Chuck was always with us. As long as he was with us, we remained, in our minds, as ageless and timeless as he was.

"Whatever you do, big or small, do it well or don't do it at all."- Chuck Brown

As I matured and began my writing career, I had ample opportunity to speak with Chuck and develop an excellent relationship with him. As humble as he was, he was still larger than life! From his pigeon-toed stance to his toothy grin and big smile, he made everyone feel like family. He raised not only his own kids but generations of fans and musicians, some affectionately calling him "Pops."

He taught us life lessons that we will carry with us forever. He taught us that a smile can get you almost anywhere, but hard work and the right combination of people can get you to the Grammys. He taught us that you will rarely have an enemy if you go through life being kind and encouraging. He taught us that if you can take a bad situation, learn your lesson from it, and strive to be a better person, you will have abundant success. He taught me about jazz and blues legends through his interpretations of "Run Joe," "Go-Go Swing," "2001," "Misty," "Moody's Mood," and so many more. He taught me that it is ok to cover a tune but make sure you add your spin to it so it's more than a regurgitated version of the original. He was a genius.

14

"Chuck Baby don't give a f**k!"- Chuck Brown

As Gena and I aged into our late 30s and 40s, schlepping down to the Safeway Barbeque Battle to see Chuck took a little more effort. We were always instantly transported back to when we were on bus 82 or in our early 20s at Rock Creek Park with a massive spread of crabs and beer. It didn't matter because whatever grown-up issues we were going through, Chuck was there, and temporarily, everything was ok.

"If I ever get my hands on a dollar again, I'm gonna squeeze on it till the eagle grins."- Chuck Brown

The day that Chuck passed away, May 16, 2012, at 75, Gena and I had a conversation. We talked about our experiences and how lucky we were to have grown up in Washington, D.C., and have Chuck in our lives. Gena said, "Go-Go is the rhythm that makes your body move, and no one did it better than Chuck. There's always a party when Chuck is playing. He makes sure the audience has a good time. He was a great musician, whether he was playing Go-Go or jazz. It's about the music with him. He always gives the audience something to groove to. There is no flashy stage production necessary. He IS the best."

"Sho ya right!"- Chuck Brown

My last conversation with Chuck was at the Go-Go Awards in 2011. We were happy to see each other and hugged. After speaking for a few moments, his daughter KK walked by. He asked me, "Jill, have you ever met my daughter, KK?" I told him that I had not. He introduced us with that warm smile of his. "I am so proud of KK," Chuck beamed. That was our last conversation. KK and one of Chuck's sons, Wiley, have stepped in with some of the other Chuck Brown's Band members and have kept the brand and legacy alive. After all, Chuck Brown is the Godfather of Go-Go.

"When I step on stage, I forget all about my age. I think about you, 'cause I love to see y'all groove!"- Chuck Brown

On Thursday, May 31, 2012, luminaries, politicians, grandparents with their grandchildren, and the thousands of fans that Chuck raised converged on the Walter E. Washington Convention Center—the only place large

15

enough to accommodate the crowd expected for the Godfather's funeral. And you better believe that Gena and I were both there, too. We were in the company of thousands of other people of all races and ages, paying respects to the man that kept us so young, for so long, by sharing his gift. As we celebrated his life that day – and it was truly a celebration – we also said goodbye to a part of our childhoods when we said goodbye to Chuck. Even though he has passed on, we still listen to his music, "Bustin' Loose," in particular, at our cookouts and celebrations. And whenever we reminisce about our good times with Chuck, I'm still transported back to Bus 82, an 11-year-old singing with her friends for one more day.

Chapter 1: Go-Go Music: What's It All About?

My career in Go-Go started when I was a student at Towson University in the late '80s. I had a roommate from Southeast D.C., K Street, to be exact. Her name was Angie

What exactly is Go-Go? Go-Go is three things. *The* Go-Go is a venue, as in Smokey Robinson's "Goin' to a Go-Go." Go-Go is a culture. Go-Go is a genre of music.

In January 1993, I was asked to write an article about Go-Go in *Word Up!* Magazine. *Word Up!* titled the article, "Music That Makes You Go-Go - What's It All About?" (Remember, this was from 1993, 30 years ago). Below is the text from the article, one of the first national magazine stories about the music. If you're unfamiliar with Go-Go, it defines and looks into the music and culture during its early decades.

Go-Go, a descriptive name for dance music unique to Washington, D.C., is a non-stop live party. It is also a lifestyle for most young African American adults in the D.C. area. This distinctive music is rapidly gaining national acclaim due to nationwide exposure from Go-Go bands such as EU ("Da Butt") and Rare Essence ("Work the Walls"). But there are many other Go-Go bands, and there is a very unique history behind this powerful force called Go-Go.

In this funky form, as we know it today, Go-Go was started by the legendary Chuck Brown and the Soul Searchers. The drummer, Ricky Wellman, kept the beat strong between tunes while the band decided what to play next, and the audience went wild. The non-stop rhythm grew more complex as the rhythm section added congas, backed up by drums, cowbells, and tambourines.

The strong percussion sound is the trademark that defines Go-Go from any other music. It is the percussion that gets the feeling going. It is also the sound of the timbales, cowbells, and congas as trumpets, trombones, saxophones, and synthesizers which incorporate jazz, funk, and soul, flavored with an ongoing dialogue between the dance floor and the

17

band. There is no other music form that incorporates every format of music style but gets powerful energy from audience chant participation.

Many talented bands work in and around Washington, D.C., but this is the original Go-Go. A few of the major record labels were interested in bands such as EU, Junkyard, Rare Essence, and Trouble Funk, but these major labels were not quite sure how to market Go-Go on a national level without changing the sound. It couldn't be marketed in its true form. Once you have heard the authentic, percussion-driven sound, it would be agreed that there is no Go-Go unless it is true Go-Go.

Chuck Brown, the "Godfather of Go-Go," has been able to take various forms of music, from the "2001" theme to Louis Jordan's "Run Joe" to calypso, reggae, and blues, then mix it with the Go-Go sound and interpret this music through the Go-Go beat which then exposes the "younger generation" to hits of the past, but with a flavor all its own. This is different from replicating the original song, note for note.

People nationwide and overseas audiences started to take notice of Chuck Brown and the Soul Searchers which helped to land them a record deal in 1971, producing their first hit, "We the People." This was followed by "Bustin' Loose," "Go-Go Swing," "Run Joe," and "We Need Some Money."

Besides being popular in the United States and Europe, Chuck Brown and the Soul Searchers were also very successful in Japan. Go-Go secured its overseas acclaim with live performances, product sales, and music licensing. Chuck Brown and the Soul Searchers also significantly impacted the creation of other bands, Rare Essence and Trouble Funk, to name two.

Trouble Funk watched Chuck Brown closely as they met as Howard University and University of the District of Columbia music students. They liked what they saw in Chuck Brown's foundation and are celebrating international success. Trouble Funk was also featured in the movie Good to Go, with "Drop the Bomb" and "Let's Get Small," two of the hits that brought them the taste of international success and the attention of Island Records.

After the group was signed to Island Records in the early 1980s, they released "Still Smokin.'" Changes in their personnel and several outside

18

projects changed their style. Island hired Bootsy Collins to produce an album for Trouble Funk. The two styles did not match. Trouble Funk has returned to their roots, getting closer to the original sound, and several original members are back to make the group a continuing success.

Another group that Chuck Brown inspired is Rare Essence. Back in 1976, as elementary school students at St. Thomas Moore in Southeast D.C., the original members of Rare Essence, John "Big Horn" Jones, Quentin "Footz" Davidson, Andre "Whiteboy" Johnson, and Michael "Funky Ned" Neal, decided they also liked what they heard and saw and put a band together. These youngsters liked how Chuck Brown kept the beat going between the songs and elaborated on that to come up with the style that dubbed Rare Essence "The True Inner City Groovers."

With hits such as "Body Moves" and the hit album, Live at Breeze's Metro Club, Rare Essence is known as D.C.'s number-one band. Recently, the remix of their hit "Lock It," remixed by Hurby Azor, was featured on the Uptown/MCA soundtrack for the movie, Strictly Business. This gained Rare Essence national exposure and the attention it deserved, leading to a national distribution deal with Relativity Records.

Rare Essence's hit, "Work the Walls," had been on the charts for weeks and quickly rising. The video "Work the Walls" could be seen on every major video show (BET, Yo! MTV Raps, Video Jukebox, etc.). Their next step was re-releasing "Lock It" in the original Go-Go form that true Go-Go fans appreciated.

Another band that rose to a high level of success is Experience Unlimited, also known as EU. EU has been together since the 1970s with many personnel changes. Gregory "Sugar Bear" Elliott, the primary force behind the group, with his trademark, "Owww!" is the only remaining original member.
"Da Butt," a national hit and dance craze, brought EU into the mainstream eye. Spike Lee caught an EU performance at the 9:30 Club in Washington, D.C., and was so impressed with what he saw he featured them in the movie School Daze. EU was also featured on the Salt N' Pepa cut and video, "Shake Your Thang," and that is Sugar Bear's "Owww!"

The Junkyard Band was formed in 1980. With an average age of 11, these kids hailed from the Barry Farms Public Housing Projects in Southeast Washington, D.C. The lack of financial resources did not stop them. They were so determined to form a band that they searched their neighborhood for anything that resembled a musical instrument in sight and sound. These creative young men created instruments from paint cans, plastic buckets, boxes, bottles, and sticks and began to make music as the Junkyard Band.

The members of the Junkyard Band began having rehearsals and played anywhere from street corners in downtown Washington, D.C., to the prestigious Kennedy Center and Apollo Theater. The uniqueness of the band being so young, coupled with their drive and talent, Junkyard Band landed a deal with Def Jam Records in 1985. They released one of the most popular Go-Go recordings to date, "Sardines," and they were featured in the movies, Tougher than Leather and D.C. Cab. They are still one of the busiest bands on the circuit over 40 years later.

Two all-female Go-Go bands dominate the roster as well- Pleasure and Precise. Pleasure was around for several years before Precise. Pleasure was the pioneering group. They caught the eye and interest of hip-hop producer, Hurby "Luv Bug" Azor, who was responsible for Salt N Pepa's success. During Azor's interest, some of the group's members left to form the band Precise. Then some of the members of Pleasure and Precise left to become the band for Salt N Pepa.

Along with the many pioneers of Go-Go, there were also many other Go-Go bands as well representing the genre, including Hot Cold Sweat, Northeast Groovers, Shear Madness, AM/FM, The Peacemakers, Ayre Rayde and Little Benny and the Masters, to name a few.

Finally, these records and performances have allowed D.C.'s own Go-Go to have fans worldwide- from Europe to Japan to Africa, and this institution is still going strong.

Spotlight: The Venues

The venues are an essential part of the history of Go-Go since it is best experienced live. There were different types of venues, from high school gymnasiums to rec centers, outdoor venues, and regular night clubs. But wherever you went, you knew that it would be a party. Whether the place held 10 people or 4,500 people, you were in for a great night if the right band was playing. It is important to mention these venues because there have been many places where Go-Go has flourished over the years, in MD, D.C., and VA. Many venues have come and gone, but these are just a few that will never be forgotten in the fans' minds and captured on PA tapes.

Amazon, Anacostia Park, Anthem, Aqua, Atlas Theater, Babylon, Barnetts, Black Hole, Boyds Park, Brown's, Bumpers, Bus Stop, Byrne Manor, Calvert County Armory, Capital Centre, Capital Lounge, Carter Barron, Celebrity Hall, CFE, Chapter III, Cheiry's, Classics, Club Distinction, Club 4, Club La Baron, Club U, Cross Creek, Crystal Skate, Deno's, East Alco Park, Eastside, Echo Stage, Emory Park, Evans Grill, Fast Eddie's, Felicities, Firestation 1, Frederick Armory, Glenarden, Half Note, Heart and Soul Café, Highland, Howard Theater, Ibex, Ibiza, Icebox, Jimmy's Lounge, Kaywood Theatre, Kilamanjaro, LaFontaine Bleue, La Gamma Ballroom, Lamont's, La Pearl, La Pena, Legends, Lincoln Park Rec, Mad Chef, Magic Room, Martini's, Masonic Temple, Maverick Room, Metro Club, Mirage, Mirrors, Moonlight Inn, MSG, Neon, Northeast Gardens, Northwest Gardens, Oak Tree, Odyssey, Panorama Room, Paragon II, Patapsco Arena, Piney Branch Rec, Presidential Arms, RFK, Ritz, Rhythms, RSVP, Safari Club, Sandy Spring Rec, Showmobile, Silver Spring Armory, Society Lounge, Southeast Gardens, Sugar Kane Palace, Taj Mahal, Takoma Station, The Burgundy Room, The Room, The Scene, Tradewinds, Triples, Upper County Rec, Utopia, Washington Colosseum, Wheaton Rec, White Oak Armory, Wilmer's Park, WUST, Zulu Cave, 5 Sisters, 909 Spot, 9:30 Club, 94th Aero Squadron

Chapter 2: What Is Go-Go to You?

Ask 100 different people to define Go-Go, and you'll get 100 different answers, but a few words will come up repeatedly: culture, life, love, heart, soul, home. I asked various people – musicians, record executives, music collectors, DJs, and fans – to answer two questions: *what is Go-Go,* and *what's your favorite band?* From the answers below, you can see that Go-Go goes much deeper than music.

Responses are listed in alphabetical order.

Alan Amsterdam, Owner of Capitol Hemp
Go-Go is, to me, an art form native to Washington, D.C., that broadened my horizons in my musical tastes and got me moving completely differently from my metal/hardcore background. I would go see hardcore bands in the '80s that also billed Go-Go bands and was blown away by them!!! 2 completely different music styles playing together. It was magical!! It was one of the only times growing up that 2 different groups (hardcore and Go-Go) hung out, and both groups started enjoying each other's cultural offerings. D.C. hardcore with an angry anti-establishment angle and Go-Go with a feel-good, enjoy-the-moment, get up and dance (move your body!!) feeling that was incredible. The musicianship from both types of music was stellar, but the Go-Go scene was filled with charismatic musicians who owned the stage, brought the city together, and became a staple in my music playlist. I feel fortunate to have grown up in Washington, D.C., at that particular moment in time. My favorite band: Chuck Brown. No one, in my opinion, embodied the spirit of Go-Go more than Chuck. When I saw him play with his band, I was always blown away by the energy, music, and his charisma. He was one of a kind and makes me smile and want to dance every time I hear one of his songs (his Thievery Corporation collab was phenomenal, and I watch that video all the time)!!

Stephanie Asbury, Fan
Go-Go is like being transported by a time machine back in time and being able to dance through my high school memories. Two of my favorites are Rare Essence and JYB.

Damon Atwater, Musician

Go-Go: a strong feel of music that can sound off but be completely on. Go-Go to me is like FUNK, within the accents. Even the musical approach, Go-Go is a genre of Love, Broad Understanding, Courage, and Determination, but mostly the ability to learn. Go-Go is the only genre where you literally have to go in and remake an entire song. Even the words can be changed over time. I know my dad is [Northeast Groovers drummer] "Stomp Dogg," but I've always been a "Backyard Band" fan because Backyard Band embodies our genre. What do I mean? Okay, when listening to Backyard everything I generally clean, from the mix to the musician syncopation. Some bands don't swing either enough, or they'll overswing or simply just play straight, which isn't Go-Go with swing being needed. You also have to be able to feel the music as well.

Wendell Bacon, Musician

Go-Go is a continuation of percussion between songs where the beat never stops. Favorite band: Suttle Thoughts from 1996-2002.

Donald Donnie Ray Barnes, Vocalist

Go-Go saved me from me, so it means a whole lot to me!! Favorite band: No fav. I love all of them!!!

Michael Benjamin, Musician (Reality Band, Soul'A Movement)

Go-Go, to me, is the blend of percussive music—unscripted, improvisational, and spiritual. My favorite band is easy: Rare Essence, but not today's Rare Essence. I would say up to 1987.

Darryll Brooks, Concert Promoter CD Enterprises

Go-Go, to me, is the heartbeat of my city. It's a release. It's a pleasure. It's a stress reliever. And after a hard day, a hard week, you go somewhere and just relax, get funky and sweaty, and let that tension out. It's a relaxer and it's turned into a whole lot since I started. But it's like a familiar face.

I used to go when I was in High School, college, and when I got out. It's a place to dance, socialize, cabarets, cotillions. It's barbeques at the beach. I came up on Young Senators, Chuck Brown. I used to manage Black Heat. That was the first band I ever managed. And I would go on the road with them, and they were playing "No Time to Burn", and this different product, and they would put their percussion break in there, and it worked every time. And I watched Chuck perpetuate that and perfect that to such an extent that it was addictive. And it got so addictive where that Chuck was basically preaching, testifying, giving testimony, guidance, and education, history lessons through their music in the midst of keeping people mesmerized on the dance floor as you were throwing out from whatever distractions or prejudice or stuff you were going through way before heavy drugs got into our culture. We may have had a little liquor. But it wasn't to the extent of the drug da jour. It was that safe haven. That's what it was to me.

And then, it was always fun to present it because the whole purpose of having concerts was the gathering of bodies, enjoying the interaction and socializing and making memories, etc., so that also gave me a certain kind of pleasure or happiness just seeing people having fun. I think the thing that George Clinton called it was "JuJu." It was some tribal beat. Well, guess what? It IS a tribal beat. I know that a great deal of the African Americans were born and bred and ended up living in Washington, D.C. came from The Carolinas, came from Virginia, which were basic slave plantations and where the drum and escape and trying to raise families was their plight and the church, through gospel music, though the Pentecostal church, the Baptist churches, and the African American Episcopal churches messages come through the sermon and also comes through the music. There happen to be some groups in D.C. that did that very tastefully in reference to giving positive messages to the community and to people who enjoyed it, and then I think our educational system with high school and jr. high school bands, drill teams because they were basically grooming kids in D.C. to work for the government. Those were the kinds of jobs that were basically being offered, office jobs and military. They had ROTC. I learned how to shoot a rifle in Spingarn. I don't know if they do that today, but I'm just telling you that's where I first shot a rifle in high school. It just tells you the times you're in and what it means, so to me, it's like what reggae means to Jamaica, what country music means to people in Tennessee, that's what Go-Go means to me. That's my comfort. That's my briar patch, as Brer Rabbit would say. I'm home.

And I don't care where I am if I hear Little Benny in the background, I'm pumped! If I hear Chuck in the background, I'm pumped! If I hear Sugar Bear, I'm pumped! All day long! If I hear that, I will stand up and shake my ass because that was my relief. I can't really say I have a favorite band because it's like saying, " do you have a favorite kid? How? Chuck took me to Japan and took me to Holland. Black Heat took me all through the South. Sugar Bear, we played in Philadelphia together on the road.

Who else? Rare Essence? I was involved with them for a minute and worked with Ms. Mack and Annie Mack, and here's something- We had the opportunity to promote the Jacksons, and we didn't have the money. The guy wanted like $25,000 deposit, and we didn't have that kind of money in the bank, so it was Rare Essence, Ted Hopkins (Manager of EU), Annie Mack, and a few others, and they came to our office with paper bags. We sat on the floor, counted the money, and ended up sending the deposit, and in the tradition of Carol and Darryll, they were our partners on the show. So, they had a piece of the Jackson's show that we did. So, it's like, how am I going to have a favorite? These are my people. This is my family. We had to tell people to stop bringing money because when Ted put the call out, and Annie Mack put the call out, other people in the street who knew us said, "I want to be down. I'll help." And people kept coming to the door- Y'all need some more money? No! No more money! We're good. We can take it from here.

Timothy Brown, aka Recording artist Father MC
Go-Go to me is real feel-good music! Go-Go to me represents peace, harmony, and soul.

Adrienne "Dre Dre" Burkley, Vocalist, Manager (HORU)
The beginning stages of Go-Go were a combination of rap music carried out with a percussion drive. It borrowed cover tunes from the R&B/soul, funk, and jazz genres and added an African and Latin percussion beat to its undertone to create a unique sound. It also brought forth audience involvement by way of call-and-response. As for today's Go-Go music, it is majority cover tunes from any genre, still seasoned with the percussion drive without as much audience involvement. The best way to get the best experience with this Washington, D.C.-created genre is to experience it "live." My favorite group in the early era was Rare Essence, with close runners-up Experience Unlimited (EU) and Trouble Funk. My favorite Go-Go group today is my own - HORU Music Experience and Vybe.

Keith "Keebee" Campbell, Manager, Promoter
Go-Go is the music of my LIFE!! Favorite band: RARE ESSENCE

Kwame Coleman, Fan
Go-Go is a D.C.-based genre that combined African and Latin percussion rhythms with funk (in the early day). Then it combined those rhythms with hip-hop. It is called Go-Go because of the long musical set with no stoppage between songs. My favorite band is the original Rare Essence.

Because not only were they filled with highly skilled musicians, but also the two "x-factors" they had: Little Benny and Jungle Boogie. The way they ignited the crowd with their showmanship is unmatched to this day.

Steven Coleman, Musician

Go-Go is a musical expression of the real Washington, D.C. Favorite band: Chuck Brown and the Soul Searchers (the originators).

Vincent Coleman, Musician

What does Go-Go mean to me? Go-Go is the irresistible extra funky beat originated by the drummer Ricky "Sugarfoot" Wellman of Chuck Brown and the Soul Searchers. Go-Go music is a non-stop party. My favorite Go-Go artists?

1. Grace Jones "Slave to the Rhythm"
2. Chuck Brown and the Soul Searchers "We Need Some Money," "Run Joe," "Bustin' Loose"
3. Trouble Funk "Pump Me Up"
4. Rare Essence "Lock It," "Body Moves," "Take Me Out to the Go-Go"
5. Experience Unlimited "Future Funk," "EU Freeze," "Da Butt"
6. Little Benny & the Masters "Who Come to Boogie"
7. Hot Cold Sweat "Meet Me at the Go-Go"
8. Northeast Groovers "Booty Call"
9. Huck A Bucks "The Bud"
10. BLACK ALLEY CRANKS!

Whop Craig/ Wisdom Speeks, Musician

Go-Go is a feeling. It's in you. Once it's in you, you understand it; once you understand it, it's not going anywhere. That's Go-Go to me. It's a certain vibe. You know Go-Go when you hear it. You know someone who's not playing it at all when you hear it. Music is music to me. How you move it around is totally on you. Go-Go Music… you had Go-Go girls back in the day, and those were white chicks. The word "Go-Go", you can still go to a Go-Go in LA. In fact, they have Whiskey A Go-Go, a club in LA called Whiskey A Go-Go. Whatever Go-Go is to D.C. is one thing. Whatever Go-Go is to Pop culture is another thing. Whatever Go-Go was in the 50's was a thing. Whatever Smokey Robinson called Go-Go, that's what it was to him. So, I can't really define what it is or how it's to be played, but I know when I feel it, that's Go-Go right there to me.

Timothy "Teebone" David, Musician

Go-Go is a feel that is created by a 1/16 heavy swing on the beat. If that swing isn't there, the Go-Go feel isn't right. Many drummers think it's the tempo, but it's the swing. Like Chuck Brown said, "It don't mean a thing if it ain't got the Go-Go Swing." My favorite group, of course, is Trouble Funk.

Derrick Leon Davis, Musician, Former Prince Georges County Councilmember

What is Go-Go? At the root, it's the warmth and comfort of "the pocket" or the electricity inspired by a tight "socket," living inside a melodic groove inspired by our gospel, jazz, R&B, rock, and funk roots. It's head-bobbin', foot-tapping, feet-beating music born and raised (up) in Washington, D.C., and its suburbs (affectionately dubbed "The DMV"). It's hard to "copy" because it's a feeling, an innate sorta sixth sense of rhythmic, percussive timing and syncopation nurtured over the years. You may think you know it when you hear it, but it ain't Go-Go until you "feel it"! Which Band!?! After my Ayre Rayde Family, E.U.! I love all my creative brothers and sisters who safeguard, preserve, and keep our art form growing, from Essence to Be'la Dona, Vybe to M.O.B.

Wayne Davis, Musician

Go-Go is the sound of the city. It's a groove consisting of tight African rhythms on drums, congas, tambourine, and cowbell, mixed with call-and-response, solid chords with funky bass, and colorful guitar complimented by jazzy horns. All this is mixed into a tight pocket and released at the click of the sticks! By the way, my favorite band used to be Rare Essence now I don't have one.

LeAnthony Day, Fan

Go-Go is LOVE. My favorite band is Northeast Groovers and Experience Unlimited, and Sugar Bear.

Valeria Day, Fan

Go-Go is home! I can be in any city anywhere on earth and hear a beat, and I am immediately taken to a place – no, *transported* home. I have been on a street corner in Atlanta with my students and forgotten who I am and who I'm with at the drop of a beat. When it's a bad day at work, it is usually Go-Go that calms me. it is home. Backyard is my favorite band.

Robert J. Dean, Fan

Go-Go isn't just a style of music like jazz or country-western, but it is a way of life. Go-Go is D.C. Go-Go isn't just a beat in D.C. It is the way we walk and talk, and it is also the way we live. Chicken wings and mumbo Sauce, the music, the dancing, and eeeerrrrything we do. Go-Go Forever!!! Favorite band: Chuck Brown and the Soul Searchers

Martin Doneghy, Fan

First and foremost, I believe that one who has never been to a Go-Go can never understand what Go-Go is. And I mean *been*. Like '80s, '90s, and '00s too. If you never saw the plethora of main players still doing it (or those we've lost—RIP Chuck, Benny, and too many more) back when they were prime teens and 20-plus-year-olds, then chances are you can only learn Go-Go...not FEEL it. Praise is due to those carrying on the traditions, but those who have been there know. Ibex, Paragon, Cherry's, Caveyard, Black Hole, Malcolm X Park, The Ha'ad (Howard Theatre), The Coliseum on blazing hot summer nights or Super Timmed up in winter with parkas...no matter what...those yesterdays can't be re-created, not by the seniors still crankin' out faves, nor by the youth blowin' up the spots around the DMV today. Go-Go is a Maxell cassette. Go-Go is cowbells and congas. Go-Go is stories shared of moments that are gone. The groove remains the same. But it is a Time and an Era...where the pulse of today has traveled very far from the heart that started the beat. To get the full-blown anaphylactic shock, one has to have been there then. Sadly, for me, it is a time gone by. That's Go-Go. You didn't ask me to define Go-Go music (yet, lol). Favorite band: Who do you blame when your lips just go Rare Essence, Rare Essence, Rare Essence, Rare Essence!!!

Ron Duckett, Manager, Promoter

Go-Go is the spirit of our region. My favorite band: Trouble Funk, is my ALL time favorite.

Butchie Farrell, Promoter

Go-Go, to me, is a style, a groove, a movement, a community that comes together to listen to good music, fellowship, and fun. My favorite bands are RE and EU.

Leon "Funkregulata Celo" Ferguson, Radio DJ

Go-Go is an expression through music. More than any other part of the band, the drums drive the narrative of the pulse of the city. The urban part of the city. It's our expression. It makes us feel good. It's going to get your name called out, shouted out by the lead talker who is James Funk or Chuck Brown. Or someone shouting you out and your neighborhood. It's feeling important. It's just as important as any other music. It's just as important as the civil rights movement. I think they are comfortable being at home. They are going to always be good at home. They've got to step out. They've got to make songs and videos and make them go viral. My favorite band: Junkyard Band, but they took cues from Trouble Funk, and I could never forget Chuck Brown, the Godfather.

Ryan Galich, Musician

Go-Go to me is a lifestyle. I went to one show as a fan and immediately went to the gig life. Working in NE at the age of 15, right next door to the Ice Box. Seeing all the Globe posters on the telephone poles and buying PA tapes. It was just something I wanted to be a part of. Since I knew Bubba and he was the first person I met in Go-Go, it's always and forever BYB4Life. The Bad Boys of GO-GO era was very special, and I'll never forget it.

John Gates, Fan, and Music Collector

Go-Go to me is enjoyable music—raw and hard beats that will make you move. I have two favorite bands, and I can't pick one: Rare Essence and Ayre Rayde.

Moe Gentry, Sound Engineer, Manager

Go-Go is simply non-stop music. Favorite band: Rare Essence

Rob Graham Sr., Musician

It started as an event—in other words, a date dance party where people would come to meet and mingle, and bands would play: Brute, 91 Congress, Young Senators, Los Latinos, and others in the mid-to-late '60s. My memory is it was the Soul Searchers first. Because many don't know Chuck was a minister and they added gospel before highlighting Chuck Brown and the Soul Searchers.

Kenny "Kwick" Gross, Musician

Go-Go to me is an outlet from everything bad that could be happening around me at any given time. Something about "THAT POCKET" is an instant mood changer. #SIP Sit in the Pocket. I am a BYB baby 4 life.

David Green, Musician (original member of Rare Essence)

Go-Go is a percussion-laced rhythm that does not stop. It's full of forceful drive. My favorite is Chuck Brown or my group RE. I love Trouble Funk as well.

James "Slim Jim" Harrington, Percussionist, Clothing Designer
Go-Go is the percussive drive that continues between songs with other rhythmic instruments that create a song. If that percussion is not there, it's funk or R&B. My favorite band was EU, mostly because of the inspiration driven into me by Shorty Tim.

Thomas "Go-Go Wheels" Harvey, Musician
Well, for me, I live, sleep, and breathe Go-Go—period. Go-Go is my culture, the fabric of our lives. I can speak on that because I have been there from the beginning when all the bands had their own style of music. The legendary groups that are still out have their own. Nowadays, you hear these bands and the first thing you say is, "Who is that?" Go-Go is a feeling you have to experience. Yes, it sounds good on CD, tape, or record, but it doesn't replace being there, feeling the beat, actually being in the audience, being a part of the show, the call-and-response, getting your name called—it's the best feeling in the world. To me, it's like a leaf falling from a tree and trying to catch it—that's how beautiful it is to me. My favorite bands are Chuck Brown, rest his soul, Rare Essence, and Junkyard Band.

Benjamin "Scotty" Haskell, Musician
Music from the soul of at-risk young folks wanting a better life using their gifts to do so. My favorite band: Chuck Brown, is the real deal, then, of course, RE, then EU for me.

Derrick Holmes, Musician (DCVybe)
Go-Go is a DMV swing with Latin percussion under musical rhythms. My favorite bands throughout my life: JYB and Chuck Brown.

Tawna House, Vocalist
Music that unifies people, unlike any other genre. Favorite band: EU.

Kevin Hughes, Fan
Go-Go is the fabric of a musical culture that has always been misunderstood!!! Yes, we all know that it was built on CALL-and-RESPONSE, but when you are on that dance floor, off GO-GO, your body starts communicating with itself or others. Your body begins to EXPRESS. It's like going to church and getting the Holy Spirit in you!!! My Quote to you: "Go-Go Is My Roots." My MOTHER birthed ME, but GO-GO raised ME. [Favorite band]: TROUBLE BAND & SHOW, aka

TROUBLE FUNK.

Malachai Johns, Musician, Manager, Booking Agent (Allive Entertainment)
The undisputed, indigenous sound of the DMV. Characterized by dominant, driving percussion underlying a melting pot of genres focusing mostly on funk, hip-hop, and R&B with a layer of rock and pop. In other words, "It's the beat." Which band is my favorite? Mambo Sauce, but I'm biased. Or Northeast Groovers, but I'm also biased, lol!

Curtis Johnson, Musician (Chuck Brown and the Soul Searchers, Eternity Band)
In short, it's a style that was created and followed by many. I am a Go-Go-ologist, a creator of the genre, along with Chuck. My favorite band: #1 Chuck Brown and the Soul Searchers, #2 Curtis Johnson and the band Eternity.

Darrell Johnson, Fan
Rare Essence, Little Benny, enough said.

Jacques Johnson, Musician
To me, Go-Go is a way of life for me. RE is my favorite group.

Marcus Johnson, Recording Artist
Go-Go to me is D.C.'s Afrocentric expression and contribution to the African diaspora. Although Chuck Brown created the sound based on wanting to keep the people dancing like a DJ versus taking a break in between songs, the second generation, Rare Essence, EU, early Junkyard, began with the hypnotic mixtures of percussive funk, African beats, and this thing that has grown into the D.C. swing! It has transcended Go-Go, and many of our musicians are hired by mainstream, jazz, and other genres because of it! I also think it was built out of the lack of access to expensive synthesizers in the early '80s, yet we had access to create rhythms on a lunchroom table, a schoolroom desk, or really anything! I find myself rocking a Go-Go beat when I wake up, in the shower, when I'm feeling good, etc., and it has definitely transcended my music. I was in Europe one time and a couple came up to me crying. I thought that they were upset at our sound.

On the contrary, they asked what was in our music that made them feel so good! It was truly a spiritual experience for them! That's why Shorty

[Corleone] and I have gotten together for Crank + FLO. But from the old school, I can never forget how I felt when I heard Rare Essence with Go-Go Mickey, Funk, Little Benny, and the rest of the crew. My sister and I would always sneak downstairs to listen to the PA tapes!

Sharon Johnson, Fan
Chuck Brown, baby.

Sharon McDonald Johnson, Fan
Go-Go is a style of funk music that has a heavy percussion beat. Go-Go is synonymous with D.C. My favorite band is Trouble Funk.

Terry "TLaRock" Keaton, Classic Hip Hop MC
Go-Go, AKA Funk Music. Favorite is CHUCK BROWN.

Khalid Keene, Performer, Producer
Like we said in our Pretty Boy$ song, "Chillin' at The Go-Go:" "Hop out the shower, dress, hop into my ride, throw in da bumpin' tape, my head moves side to side. Fire up my engine, turn my headlights on, my tires squeak when I leave, I won't be back 'til dawn. Cuz I'm going to the Go-Go, the place to be, to check out EU, BENNY, CHUCK, JUNKYARD, and RE!" For my youngins that may not know what da hell I'm talkin' bout, Experience Unlimited, Lil Benny, Chuck Brown, Junkyard Band, Rare Essence, and can't forget TROUBLE FUNK. Hahaha.

Patrick Kesteven, Fan
When I think of Go-Go, I always think of Chuck Brown.

William Lansdown, Fan
Percussions, urban sound. Favorite band: JYB

Mark "Godfather" Lawson, Musician
You don't see it in its original format anymore with the dancing and stuff on the stage. You might catch it. Go-Go was like the steps and crowd participation. You included the crowd in there when you performed. You would break it down and have the percussion lead you into the next song. The percussion will lead you into the chant that's going on. A lot of chants – "Where y'all from?" "Who's number 1?" Roll Call. You have fun together. You include the audience in what's going on, and you get the dancers up on stage, and they do their little thing. It's a call-and-response thing—my favorite Band: Godfather and Friends.

Laurie Fridovich Lee, Fan

Go-Go is uniquely D.C., and that beat always makes me feel at home. Chuck Brown is like the granddaddy of Go-Go to me—and I always turn it up when they play him on The Groove on SiriusXM. But I will always have a place in my heart for EU since Sugar Bear was such an ambassador for the music and so kind to the fans.

John "Cabalou" Locust, Vocalist

Go-Go to me, it's a sound- I like the jazzier style like Chuck Brown, Rare Essence, and Ayre Rayde. All you did was brought the beat in for so many bars, hype the crowd- that's when you break it down, rapping in it and talking to a few people and hyping them up with the beat, then ease the groove back in and play with it for a little while and then take it to the top or the bridge. Like Chuck said, "Gimmie the bridge y'all, gimmie the bridge y'all now." My favorite group is Rare Essence, hands down.

Thomas Lytle, Record Executive, DJ

Chuck Brown and Rare Essence top my list. I really fell in love with Go-Go when I attended an RE show at IBEX! The one thing I do know is this… don't judge this genre of African American music until you've been to a Go-Go. Guaranteed, you'll get hooked!

Ignatius Mason, Musician, Manager

My explanation has always been R&B had a child called "rock." R&B had another child called "Go-Go." If you're asking what's my favorite band in Go-Go, it would have to be Optimystic Tribe.

Victoria Cookie Mayo, Door Manager

TO ME, Go-Go is a collaboration of rhythm and percussion with the flair of strings and horns graced by the interactive communication of the band and its audience.
It's hard to choose "one" favorite group.....
I absolutely loved E.U. during the "EU Freeze" "Ooh La La La" era…
Trouble Funk during the "Drop Da Bomb," "E Flat Boogie" era…
Rare Essence 80-86
Chuck Brown 83-88
Suttle Thoughts 2002-2005
Familiar Faces 2004-2008
Go-Go is a complex musical relationship for me.

33

Demetrius Mcghee, Musician
GO-GO IS A WAY OF LIFE FOR PEOPLE FROM THE DIRT. MY FAVORITE BAND IS TROUBLE FUNK AND CHUCK BROWN.

Lawrence "Ghost" McRae, Drummer, Podcast Host
Go-Go is music that feeds the mind and soul. Our ancestors move through the beat; you must feel Go-Go, not only hear it. My favorite band is whoever is cranking that pocket, but if I had to pick one, it would be Rare Essence, without a doubt.

Jeno Meyers, Musician
Go-Go is a steady pocket beat that keeps going from song to song nonstop. Rare Essence has always been my favorite. They always brought excitement to the shows they did in my area growing up.

Cherie Mitchell-Agurs, Musician
Go-Go music is the sound of D.C. It is rhythmic, funky, hypnotic, and spiritual. It soothes the soul. I don't have a favorite band. I love and miss Chuck Brown, though. I love EU, Rare Essence, Backyard Band, and of course, Be'la Dona. Each band is different, and I get a different type of nourishment from each one of them. Now that I think about it, Chuck Brown was my favorite. I studied and learned all of his music growing up. Once I played in his band, I already knew the songs. I just had to learn his live arrangements.

Montu Mitchell, Love DC Go-Go Brand
Go-Go is something that is very communal. It's community. It's the voice of Washingtonians and the nearby area.

Tony Mobley, Photographer
Growing up, my favorite band was probably a cross between EU and RE, but I was also a big JYB fan. Go-Go for me was life, the blood of my youth growing up in D.C. It was homegrown, and we were proud as youngins to represent the genre and the city. There's no greater feeling than meeting people in my travels, and once you tell them you're from D.C., they automatically speak on an experience they had either at a Go-Go or how they were introduced to the music.

Kennith "DJ K Rock" Moorer, DJ (MC Lyte)
It's the tribal music of the indigenous aboriginal Washingtonians. Favorite Band: Backyard Band.

Dewayne Morris, Host
Go-Go is everything. My life, the beat, the energy, and the sound of those congas and the drummer's beat. There's no sound like Go-Go in my eyes. Favorite Band: Backyard Band BYB4LIFE

Tony Morrison, Fan
Go-Go to me is like a movement through all cultures of music and beats. Favorite band: Sirius Company

Michael Muse, Vocalist
Go-Go is our primal energy. My favorite Go-Go band of all time is Mass Extinction.

Eric Neal, Fan
The beat and the sound of it live is nothing but a unicorn—no other music like it on the planet. All time fav band is JYB, JYB4life. But currently, I would say MCB gets most of my attention now.

Seán Patrick Nichols, Fan
Go-Go is a musical and rhythmic gumbo that is also ear candy! My favorite, without hesitation, is Chuck!

Derek "DP" Paige Jr., Musician
Go-Go seems a little deeper than just the music for me. I was literally raised off of Go-Go, but not just the music, the people involved. All the way up until I started playing and becoming involved. It's the feeling when you walk through the door to set up. The bass vibration or a certain beat. Almost liberating. Emancipating. For me there's no feeling freer than closing your eyes and hearing that beat. Favorite band: Honestly, every band that has ever played what's considered Go-Go is my favorite.

Tony Parks, Fan
Go-Go to me is 1979-1984 Essence, Chuck, EU, Trouble, Redds & the Boys, Petworth, Peacemakers, Mass Extinction, Ayre Rayde, Class Band, and School Boys. My favorite is Essence 1979-1984 and 1985 Chuck.

Demont "Peekaso" Pinder, Artist
Go-Go to me is the heartbeat of the District of Columbia, created by The Godfather Chuck Brown. The sound is very unique, driven by percussions and cowbells. It's a special culture to experience the music—it jumps in

your bones and forces you to adapt to the rhythm.

As a big fan and lover of the genre, it's hard to say who my favorite band is only because they're all special to the Pinder story in their own way. I've worked with and developed many beautiful relationships and became family with a lot of them.

Vernell "Winko" Powell, Musician (Junkyard Band)
To me, GO-GO is the world! My everything! A culture, a movement, a lifesaver. It's poetry for a lot. It's Black.

Kamilah Martin Proctor, Fan
Backyard band - #Ibex

Brandon "Boski Da Toastman" Pugh, Producer
Go-Go is a hybrid genre of music with percussive roots from Latin and African music. It has a unique swing to it, adding flavor to typical measure counts. Funky melodies, jazzy and gospel chords mixed with familiar lyricism. Being led by a "lead talker," "the one" who conducts the band, controls the crowd by way of call-and-response, and hitting the right grooves at the right time. Go-Go has essentially evolved over the years, adapting new sounds such as "crank" and "bounce," diversifying the Go-Go sound. Go-Go itself can merely be broken down into subgenres. Still keeping the Godfather, Chuck Brown's, legacy alive one gig at a time. Backyard is my favorite band. #byb4life

Jon Quinton, Musician and Manager (Raw Deal Band 954)
To say Go-Go is a percussive, beat-driven music genre with a heavy focus on repeating lyrics and call-and-response from an MC-style host would be the typical right answer. To just say it's a regional music that originated from the DMV AREA, which is known for remaking cover songs using heavy percussion, would be accurate but not all-inclusive of what Go-Go truly represents.

GO-GO IS all the aforementioned, but for me, Go-Go is a lifestyle. It's a feeling that is really captured in its true essence at a live performance.

It's addictive and transformative. It definitely gets in your soul and makes you want to dance. It's a CULTURE all in itself.

My favorite band (of course) is RAW DEAL BAND 954.

I also like DC VYBE as a close second.

Chester Reis, Producer

Go-Go is a musical and cultural experience that originated in Washington, D.C. The ethos of the music and culture stems from the continent of Africa, its people, and its reliance on drum/conga cadences. The applications of the drums were varied, from sending messages to villages to announce harvests, hunts, and warnings of dangerous events. The rhythms were also utilized to celebrate, praise, and worship communally. It's said that Go-Go in D.C. was created by Chuck Brown, who used Afro-Latin rhythms to tie songs together seamlessly. The goal was to keep the live music going in order to maintain the energy of the partygoers and encourage participants to dance and spend money on drinks lol.

Go-Go morphed into a transplanted cultural cathartic experience. A place where people would meet, be seen, and see others. A place where the beats called to our innate memories, where somehow, we were transported back to our point of origin. A place where we could escape the conditions and circumstances we had from living in lower social/economic locations and escape from the pressures of the jobs we worked, Monday through Friday, to survive. The Go-Go was our weekend vacation where we related and released with others. As a musician, it challenges you to multitask, to listen carefully in order to play. I've played and produced the music for decades, and some of the best musicians in other genres have an inability to play Go-Go. It's a swing that you must hear in collaborators and feel before you play a lick, beat, drum, or press a key. Go-Go is our mothers' milk. Some of us know why; others answer the call because it's who we are. I will always love Go-Go music. I AM, You ARE...Go-Go Music.

I can't name one [favorite band], but Rare Essence with Lil Benny and Junkyard with Buggs and Winko—I can't have one without the other for me.

Harland Ricks, Fan

Go-Go, to me, is a lot of things. Mainly, it's a soundtrack to my life coming up in D.C. It's spiritual music, meaning it boosts my mood in times that are trying for me. It's a genre of music that, being from the city, I can call mine. Go-Go is what I say, "RUNS THROUGH MY BLOOD." Go-Go is a music that I don't think I could live without. My favorite band, I have to go with 2 bands and one person because, over the span of 47 years, I have seen and heard a lot. So, my first band is EU. Growing up on Wheeler

Road and Southern Avenue, right up the street from Valley Green, Southeast, Home of SUGAR BEAR, those free shows they would play every summer for his birthday is part of what drew me to the band, along with their up-tempo style of playing. My second band would be L!SSEN. They came along and blended R&B, hip-hop, jazz, and Go-Go together PERFECTLY, along with having a catalog of ORIGINAL MUSIC, ENOUGH SAID. And my favorite person right now is Steve Roy. Steve is a TRIPLE THREAT on the stage and one of the top performers in every aspect: singing, rapping, and lead mic. The energy that he brings to the stage – not just his stage, but any stage he is invited on – keeps the party rocking, and I appreciate a great showman.

Antonio Robinson, Musician (Mass Extinction, Proper Utensils)
Go-Go is a hard-driving percussion beat layered with instrumental grooves with a front man or rapper to hype the party. My favorite groups- sorry, I have more than one, but in this order: None other than Chuck Brown and the Soul Searchers, Mass Extinction, Lil Benny and the Masters, Experience Unlimited, Trouble Funk, Peacemakers, Rare Essence, Junkyard, Petworth. I'm just old school, but the grooves back then were originals with not too many cover tunes, and each band could be recognized by the songs that they played.

Kelly Rodman, Fan
Go-Go is a conversation. It's the call-and-response between souls connected rhythmically. Go-Go is the heartbeat of a region of people who hustle and grind and take pride in being from the Nation's Capital and the area around the 495 Beltway. Go-Go is a wave of joy and love pulsating that leaves a trail of harmony behind. EU and Rare Essence were a huge part of the soundtrack of my formative years. But thanks to Chuck Brown, my exposure to jazz and blues grew. His incorporation of using standards in his music allowed me to appreciate the expansiveness of live instrumentation through Go-Go music. He is the Godfather—we must give him respect and homage.

John "DJ Big John" Royster
For me, Go-Go is a culture, community, and a way of life. My favorite band, hands down, is JunkYard. In fact, my top three bands, in no particular order, are JunkYard, JYB, and the Good Junk.

Jeanette Russell, Fan
I love the beat. Favorite Band: Junkyard

Ian Salmon, Comedian

My favorite band is Pump Blenders because I was in the band. Go-Go, to me, is a musical movement that gave D.C. an identity that was unique to anywhere else in the world. It is a simple form of music that made us proud as a music community. Go-Go made me proud to say I was from D.C.!

Bo Sampson, Record Executive

Go-Go is the sound that started in the Nation's Capital, Washington, D.C.! And it is the official sound of Washington, D.C.! Heavy percussion! Call-and-response from the crowd! Favorite band: Trouble Funk, EU, Backyard, Be'la Dona, Rare Essence: it is a tie!

Malik Savage, Manager (Let It Flow band)

Go-Go is a subgenre of funk music with an emphasis on specific rhythmic patterns and live audience call-and-response. Go-Go was originated by African American musicians in the Washington, D.C. area during the mid-60s to late-70s—my favorite band: Chuck Brown, The Old Rare Essence, JYB, EU.

Mia Scott, Vocalist

Go-Go is A Movement!! A part of our culture of music that does something indescribable to the soul!!! Go-Go is a feel!! I have 3 [favorite bands]: Northeast Groovers, Junkyard Band, and BackYard Band. Chuck Brown is my favorite Go-Go artist because he represented LOVE and Integrity!!

Rico Scott, DJ

Go-Go is an African rhythmic sound of percussion, energy-driven music that strives to touch the feeling of your heart, no matter if you're Black or White. The sound takes you to a place where you let all that out when playing in the band or watching as a fan. It's our music in Washington, D.C. AKA The DMV. My favorite is hard to say, for I love Junkyard, Backyard, NEG, DC Vybe, Trouble, What Band, Faycez U Know, Sirius Company, TCB, TOB, and more. Rare Essence is my favorite, as my first connection to Go-Go, because I would go listen to them practice on Xenia and then be at Cheiry's or the Eastside, maybe even run up to the Ibex or the Black Hole. It didn't matter where they were. I was gonna be there. Then, I started moving equipment for them and then went over to helping Lil Benny, but Rare Essence is the one for me.

Garrett "Starchild Jr." Shider, Musician (Parliament-Funkadelic)
Go-Go is a D.C. staple!!! It's D.C. culture! It's the hangout in D.C., it's tribal, provocative, and intense!
My favorite band is the Backyard Band. They have always been funky as hell to me!! They are rock stars!

Bones Simmons, Videographer
Go-Go Is Kool to listen to... Lots of users and will never go beyond the DMV... Favorite Band: REDDS & THE BOYS

Brandy Louis Simms, Fan
Growing up in the DMV, I listened to Go-Go on the radio and always liked the beat. Go-Go has a distinct sound that separates it from other forms of music. I was a huge fan of EU featuring Sugar Bear because I enjoyed listening to their songs. I was a high school student at Newport Prep when "Da Butt" was released and me and my friends would have fun dancing to that song whenever it was played. Of course, the Godfather of Go-Go, Chuck Brown, is legendary. His music has been featured in movies and is still played on the radio today. Chuck Brown's legacy will live on forever!

David Smith, Musician
Go-Go is a genre of music created by Chuck Brown. The term Go-Go was formed when Chuck would play music, and instead of stopping between songs, the music would just go and go and go, and subsequently, the term Go-Go was applied to it.
My favorite band would have to be Rare Essence. They were the gold standard to which all bands were measured. Back then, each Go-Go band had their own individual sound. Within 15 seconds, you could tell the difference between Chuck Brown, Trouble Funk, Rare Essence, EU, Junkyard, and Ayre Rayde. They all had their own unique style. Today's bands all sound the same.

Michelle Smith, Hostess
Go-Go is a genre of soulful music that consists of African, R&B, jazz and funk that forms a unique percussion-driven sound in which your body will react to. My favorite band is Familiar Faces featuring Donnell Floyd.

Jay Solis, Fan
GO-GO is what can be. Favorite Band: AYRE RAYDE

Eric Solomon, Fan

Well, I will say this, I love all Go-Go, and I'm telling my age, but my favorite all-time band is Class Band with Tidy, RE (Rare Essence) with Funk and Benny, and JY (Junkyard Band).

Kim "Tweet" Sullivan, Musician

When I was just a fan among my peers watching Trouble Funk for the first time, it was a sound that was very raw with a lot of energy. The drums were in syncopation with the congas and cowbells, a sound that happens one time when the group is in their element. The sound was in stereo back then. The horns and keyboards were powerful. Once I became a musician myself, my description didn't apply anymore on account of the change in how the sound is projected. A true Go-Go musician who understands the root of how the sound should be harnessed, they are truly the real musicians from that era who can transform it in this day and time. The new bands project a new sound of Go-Go which is pretty damn good but could never be the sound I grew up on.

My favorite band would have to be Chuck Brown, even though he no longer exists. The bands I have admired no longer exist, meaning EU, Rare Essence, Redds & the Boys, Ayre Rayde, Junk Yard, and Trouble Funk. Even though some of these groups are still among us, they do not have that same sound they projected in the early years. If I had to go with today's band, in my opinion, I would say Wisdom Speaks! Whop is one of the originals back in the day, who harnesses the sound which the originators structured for bands to follow.

Harry Thomas Jr., Former D.C. City Councilmember and Fan

Go-Go is the heart and soul of D.C., and it is the often unheard and unseen voice of our communities that are often voiceless, highlighted by neighborhood shout-outs in the lyrics. My favorite band: Chuck Brown and the Soul Searchers.

William Tucker Jr., Fan

In my opinion, Go-Go is less a genre than a presentation or environment, a lo-fi continuous jam session. I've always been partial to Trouble Funk and Rare Essence.

Derrick Ward, Vocalist

What is Go-Go? To me, Go-Go is the magnetic soundtrack to the ebb and flow of the DMV. Within every quadrant and its suburbs, the homegrown genre permeates the air to bring the familiar and unfamiliar together, through call-and-response, as one people.

Pam Ward-Goldbold, Vocalist
Go-Go (to me) is an infectious groove that makes your body move!! It is beats, rhythm, crowd, and artist interaction... it's always a party! JYB is my favorite band! I have been a Junkyard fan since I was a little girl growing up in UPTOWN D.C. I have always loved and admired the sound and stage performances. They captured me with their totality in performance!!!

Arvelle Watts, Musician
Technically, Go-Go is percussive-driven music in a swing format where there are no breaks between songs, and the lead vocalist involves the audience through call-and-response cadences. Organically, it's a feeling that you will not understand until you are at a live performance. Favorite band: Backyard Band

Warren "Black Pooh" Weems, Musician (Junkyard Band)
Go-Go to me is an expression of our inner feelings through the music and culture, trying to escape what's going on in our Hood, and finding a space for happiness to release stress. My favorite band, of course, is jyb4life.

Randi Weinstein, Fan
I love Go-Go music! Favorite band: JUNKYARD BAND

Geoffrey West, Musician (James Brown, Mass Extinction, WestMob)
Go-Go is the heartbeat of our culture that expands past music and the band to the gathering of friends, old and new, to celebrate life and love of each other. Of course, my favorite band will always be the one I created. Mass Extinction was a neighborhood band started by myself and my best friend at the time. Eventually, I taught my siblings how to play and that's when Mass started to get noticed. That was in 1977 and we are still carrying the torch as the WestMob.

Bobbie Westmoreland, Writer/ Activist
Go-Go is the soundtrack to D.C. A sub-genre of funk music that is heavy on percussion and often includes call-and-response between the artists and the audience. Best served live. Favorite Band: Junkyard

Logan Westbrooks, Founder of Source Records
Chuck Brown and the Soul Searchers is Go-Go. My favorite band is Chuck

Brown and the Soul Searchers.

Marlon Williams, Musician
That conga beat. Favorite band: 80/81: E.U. 82: RE. 84: Ayre Rayde.

Raenell Williams, Manager
IMO, Go-Go is a CULTURE, and our music is tribal. Junkyard Band (JYB) is and has always been my favorite band! I've always loved their ruggedness. Not to mention, they give the best performances.

Salih "Bootsy Vegas" Williams, Vocalist, Radio Personality
Go-Go is a percussion-driven base form of music behind R&B and hip-hop rhythms with hooks and shout-outs to the crowd. They're all my favorites, but if I had to choose one, stuck on an island for life, I would choose Rare Essence.

Melissa A. Weber, Radio Programmer, Music Professor
To me, Go-Go is the indigenous music of Washington D.C., born from the decade of classic funk – the 1970s; and forever not only representing that original funky groove sound, with the integral ingredient of conga drums and other hand percussion instruments but also the concept and importance of "big bands" (five members or greater in quantity) and neighborhood-based live music bands, performing regionally indigenous sounds, in the Black community. D.C. and New Orleans are the last two cities left in the U.S. where this is happening and regularly supported by their respective communities.

I can't pick one favorite band, but there are four that have sentimental value to me. I first heard Go-Go on the "urban contemporary" radio station WAIL FM 105 in New Orleans when I was a kid. This was in the mid-1980s and, as I learned later, during a period when there was an attempt to distribute and popularize Go-Go nationally, outside of the metro D.C. and surrounding area. This didn't work in most places, but in New Orleans, it worked. I recorded a song off that station onto my cassette player and jammed it for years. I had no idea who it was or what they were talking about. Many years later, I learned it was "Meet Me at the Go-Go" by Hot Cold Sweat, originally released in 1982. The one band that most New Orleanians who are my age recall, if they were asked about Go-Go, would be Trouble Funk. TF records were played all over the place on WAIL FM, nightclubs, and block parties. To this day, it is not unusual to hear one of the complete sides from the Trouble Funk Live album from 1981 (with

"Drop the Bomb" on it) played in the middle of the day on a local, commercial Black radio station. We love our Trouble Funk.

I became aware of a 1980s BBC documentary titled after a song by Class Band, "Welcome to the Go-Go." The band performed that song live in the film, and I must have watched that single performance from the film 100 times. I was so mesmerized. Watching them perform turned my love of Go-Go from being a passive fan to an active one. It was the spark that made me buy a plane ticket to visit D.C. for the first time, specifically to go to the Go-Go and finally experience this music live and in person. And then, once I was there for the first time, the first live Go-Go I attended was Rare Essence at Club U on U Street.

I'm from the home of funk, and the birthplace of jazz, so live music scenes are nothing new to me. But when I walked into those doors, the power of the sound and energy of RE was nothing I'd ever experienced before. I also have to mention Chuck Brown and the Soul Searchers, who performed at Essence Festival in New Orleans in 2003, a few years before I visited D.C. That was the first Go-Go set I ever saw live, albeit not in D.C. I'll never forget it as long as I live. The band played in one of the small super lounges, and the headlining lounge groups would do two sets. Brown turned his two sets into one long set, and that space was packed from wall to wall with D.C. folks partying, dancing, and doing the call-and-response. All I could do was take it in 'cause it was my first Go-Go show. I knew from then on that Go-Go had to be a part of my life forever.

Antonio "Tony Sharp" Williams, Vocalist
Go-Go is a feel. I don't have a favorite band right now.

Kim Moody Williams, Fan
Go-Go is HOME! ITS D.C. It's a combination of love, jazz, and drums all put together like gumbo. My favorite band—wooo, THAT'S HARD!!! WOOOOOOOOOO, ummmmm, EU.

Theodore Williams, Musician
To me, as an "old head," it's the sound of the percussionists with that beat that takes hold of you when hearing it or playing it.

Vee Williams, Fan
Go-Go for me is our heritage- Percussion, the rhythms, the vibe—all Motherland. Crank is some shit you feel in your soul. My favorite? Them

big bad NE GROOVERS!!!! HANDS DOWN. Chuck will always be on nobody's list for me because he had a lane of his own.

Tony Wood, Producer

Go-Go is Chuck Brown, and the fact he was our culture. When you think of Go-Go, Chuck Brown is the first thing that comes to mind, he is the foundation for the sound. And I'm a big fan of Sugar Bear and what he has meant to Go-Go—another legend of the D.C. sound. So, EU is my favorite because of that.

Tony Woods, Comedian

Go-Go is the light that brought me out of the darkness of my awkward teenage years! The first Go-Go I went to was the Pump Blenders at Takoma Park Junior High (I wasn't even gonna go in, I just gave some of my friends a ride; it wasn't a junior high school dance, it was a 16 and up affair!). Then I went to see EU at NW Gardens, and I was hooked! And then, I went to the Howard Theatre and saw James Funk and RAR-EE-SSEN-CE. I joined the US NAVY straight outta high school, and the only Go-Go I could take with me was a cassette tape of Trouble Funk's "Drop the Bomb!" I used to play it for my Navy buddies from across the country, and it was mind-blowing to all of them! I LOVE GO-GO! GOD BLESS ALL WHO MAKE AND LOVE GO-GO.

Woody Woods, UM Wear Pocket Beats

Go-Go was the place where we went... RE is my best band.

Chapter 3: The Inception of a New Sound

Washington, D.C., has always been a musical city, from Pearl Bailey to Duke Ellington, Marvin Gaye, and then the creation of its own musical genre, Go-Go. D.C. even had ties to Motown in the mid-1960s, when Raynoma Gordy Singleton, co-founder of Motown and ex-wife of Berry Gordy, and her second husband, Eddie Singleton, founded Shrine Records in Logan Circle. From shows on the Wilson Boat Line to cabarets to the birth of Go-Go, music has always been a part of the fabric of the city.

Go-Go has been around, formally, for more than 50 years, and the community is vast, with plenty of newer bands playing alongside some of the pioneers who have been around since the beginning days of the genre.

The changes are probably the most striking to the people involved in Go-Go since its beginnings. Three pioneers of the genre: Timothy "Teebone" David, former percussionist with Trouble Funk; Gregory "Sugar Bear" Elliott of EU; and John "Big Horn" Jones, co-founder of Rare Essence and others, shared with me their unique perspectives on Go-Go's past, present, and future. Below are excerpts from interviews with each of them, talking about the genre they love in their own words.

Interviews were edited for length and clarity.

Timothy "Teebone" David, Trouble Funk
Timothy "Teebone" David, the legendary percussionist for the group Trouble Funk, was perfecting his craft in the 60s and 70s. His style and sound contributed heavily to Trouble Funk's success as the first Go-Go band to travel overseas from the D.C. area. David has been involved in Go-Go since its inception when Chuck Brown dubbed this style of music "Go-Go." Below he shares some memories about Trouble and Go-Go's earliest days.

Back in 1969, before Rare Essence, Experience Unlimited, Trouble Funk, and all of the bands that came onto the music scene later during the development of the Go-Go genre, there were groups like Triple Threat, Mousetrap, 100 Years Time, 95th Congress, 2000 BC, Aggression, Black

Heat, the Young Senators, Spectrum LTD, of course, The Soul Searchers, and many more groups. These groups played all over D.C. and Prince George's County in rooms like The Ebony Inn, the Candlelight Room, The Burgundy Room, the Maverick Room, the Squad Room, the Masonic Temple, and the LaGamma Ballroom.

Even though everyone was playing Top 40 music, D.C. had its sound, and it was still different from any other city because it always had that brassy and percussive sound. There was always a conga beat in every song, and there were always horns in every song even though the songs, the Top 40 songs that they were playing, didn't have those ingredients. The groups here would add these elements to make it a D.C. sound, which worked.

David, who comes from a musical family, watched his father enjoy success as a member of the Four Echoes, who broadcasted every Sunday from radio station WUST, now the current site of the 9:30 Club.

The first time David heard Chuck Brown was at the Squad Room. He was amazed by the sound because the group was clear and precise.

When we started playing with Chuck at Club LeBaron when Go-Go was actually dubbed Go-Go, I thought it was kind of interesting the way they were using the percussion breakdown between each song and vamping on the best part of the song.

[Our] band was [called] Trouble Band and Show until we started playing at the Club LeBaron opening for Chuck Brown. This was when Chuck was playing Go-Go, and we were still playing the Top 40 sound. We would play a song, and then we would stop and talk to the audience and then play another song. We were still doing the cabaret-style thing and would play for 2 or 3 hours before Chuck arrived. This was when Club LeBaron was doing shows from midnight to 6 in the morning, and Chuck would always play last. Before Chuck got there, we would play and play all night, but the kids would not dance. The group was sounding good too. Trouble Band and Show was a great group that played great music, but we weren't playing what the kids wanted to hear! It just didn't have that beat that moved them.

Once the decision to explore original music was made, along with some trial and error, the band's direction and popularity changed.

One day we just started working original material into the frame of what the groups were doing, like Rare Essence, another group playing with us. Rare Essence had this long roll that David Green always played on the roto toms. He used to do this long roll on the roto toms over to the timbales, and we took that roll and started "Roll With It." We took that beat, made "Roll With It," and created our own music with it and our own style.

That would become the style that Trouble was known for.

It was like a funk sound, but it was also very percussive, and once we played that song, the kids would come out on the dance floor and start dancing because that was the right beat they liked. We would play that song to get them up and then stay in that groove until we got everybody in the club up there dancing. Then we started doing the rest of our show, going out of that song and into another song, picking up the style that Chuck had introduced us to, not stopping, just going from one song to another. When we would go into the Top 40 songs, we would go into the beat we were doing, and the kids would sit right down. We had to go back and change it and go right back to that original song, and they would come right back onto the floor, so basically, what we were doing was playing that one song all night. We stayed with that beat, went out of it, and just started singing the "Roll With It" hook lines and adding different stuff. The kids eventually started liking the songs we were doing and started chanting all the time. "Everybody talkin' bout this and that, but that Trouble Funk is where it's at," and that's when we changed the band's name from Trouble Band and Show to Trouble Funk.

There wasn't a lot of original music except for the top groups at the time. When I started playing, Leadhead, Young Senators, Chuck Brown and the Soul Searchers, and Aggression were the top groups, and they were doing everything. Any of the big festivals that happened in D.C., those groups were always on the show. We used to have this big outdoor festival here every summer, given by this guy named Brut. I'm not sure if it was on the monument grounds or in some big park, but those groups were always there. That was the place that everyone would go to. It was the big summer show of the year. All of these groups had the same style. They were playing Top 40 music, but each one of those groups had an original song played on the radio every day, and they were all known for it. The Young Senators went on to be Eddie Kendricks' backup band. All the other groups, I really don't know what happened to them except for Chuck Brown and the Soul Searchers.

48

Trouble Funk toured extensively throughout the United States, including the legendary Apollo Theatre. They also teamed up to tour with several punk bands, including Minor Threat and Big Boys. Trouble Funk was also the band that made their mark, being the first Go-Go band to tour overseas.

Trouble had a record, "Straight Up Funk Go-Go Style," our first live LP, and our phone number was on it. The guys that join the army would go overseas and take a little bit of home with them. One guy from Palmer Park, Maryland, was stationed in Frankfort, Germany, and took all of his Go-Go records so he would have home with him. He was in a nightclub one night, and I guess the DJ was playing something he really didn't like, and he gave the DJ the record and said, 'Put this on, Man. I guarantee you everybody in here will like it!' He put on Straight Up Funk Go-Go Style, and the club manager heard it and immediately set the club off. The manager asked how he could get in touch with these guys, and the guy told him that the phone number was on the record and to 'just call them,' and that's what happened. They called us and set up a tour.

Once Trouble landed overseas, the momentum and popularity snowballed.

We went over to Germany, and we did a couple of shows. The word spread, and while we were there, we picked up a couple more shows, and then the word spread. People were saying, 'There's this group from D.C. called Trouble Funk, and it's nothing you've ever heard like this before,' and that's how it all started. Trouble Funk was the first band to go overseas. We went over the first time in 1982 or 83. We did a brief tour, including Germany, Amsterdam, and a couple of other spots, and then returned to D.C. We went over again. While we were there, the DJs had started picking up records from here because they heard tunes like "Sardines" and "E.U. Freeze." They were being played over there in the clubs, and the people took to it. Overseas, they like music, period. And if you come over there with an energetic group like Trouble, you don't have to stop when you start playing. We played for hours straight- 2 hours, 3 hours. We would never stop, and if we did stop, it was briefly for applause or just to let everybody in the club cool down, and then we would go right back into it and play another 15, 20, or 30 minutes. People had never heard anything like that.

Over there, it was more lucrative, and you got a better response. Overseas, when we finished playing, people showed that they enjoyed themselves by applauding 10 or 15 minutes after you were off stage. It happened at every venue that we went to. At one club in particular, we were in the dressing room 10 minutes after we had stopped playing and were starting to take our stage stuff off and get dressed. The guy came down and said, 'The people upstairs are tearing up my club, and y'all gotta go on and do another song!' We were already ready to go, and he said, 'Please do another song.' We went and did one more song and then had to change our whole show. If we had to do an hour, we would play for 45 minutes, and then we would come back on and do a 15-minute encore and make it part of the show because once we left the stage, the people would be applauding and it was even bigger when we left the next time. So, we just incorporated that encore into our show.

It helped to do shows overseas. Overseas you got paid. And it was never a problem. I would imagine that whatever we asked for, we got. Every venue that we played in over there was sold out. I never knew what they were charging at the door, but I don't ever recall us getting to a place and somebody saying, 'We didn't sell any tickets, so we can't do the show.' It was organized, and people came out. And it wasn't just for Trouble Funk. It was the fact that people over there like live music. They love American musicians. I saw Bo Diddly in Germany, and it was sold out.

As one of the pioneers of Go-Go, David shared what he thinks would take this generation of bands to tour overseas today and hopefully have the same, if not more considerable, success that Trouble Funk enjoyed during their extensive touring overseas.

I think the only way the groups playing the bounce beat can go overseas now is to have original material. You can't go overseas playing someone else's music. It just wouldn't work. People overseas wouldn't want to see a group come over there that didn't have original music that was already on the radio worldwide. It would have to be something that they've already heard you do. They would never come to see you just because you are from D.C. And, if they were to come see you and you had a tour going, the word would get out, 'Don't see that group because they played all the stuff that I heard on the radio- a regular R&B song. They didn't play any original music so I'm not going to see them again.' What would have to happen would be that the groups would have to start playing some original material to get past the Beltway to go anywhere- across the country or overseas. You have to commercialize yourself and do your own commercial- which would be an original record. Make your mark.

On July 19, 1986, Trouble Funk played at the Montreux Jazz Festival in Montreux, Switzerland. Their set list was:

A Groove
Pump Me Up
Still Smokin'
Let's Get Small
Drop the Bomb
In the Mix (Don't Touch That Stereo)
Good to Go

Gregory "Sugar Bear" Elliott, EU

Gregory "Sugar Bear" Elliott was heavily influenced by the guitar sounds of the legendary Jimi Hendrix, although he never saw him play live. He knew that he wanted to have a rock band, something different coming out of Southeast D.C. in the 70s. Sugar Bear, who has used that nickname since his babysitter, Ethel Knight, started calling him that over 60 years ago, took his love of rock music, and developed his own instantly identifiable sound within the Go-Go genre. In the beginning, there was no mistaking that you heard Experience Unlimited with hard-edged songs such as "EU Freeze" with its heavy guitar riffs and rock sound. Below he shares thoughts on the band's beginnings and what made them stand out in the music world.

EU got started in 1973. When I heard Chuck Brown and the Soul Searchers, I was in the 10th grade in 1970 at Ballou High School. They played at all of our homecomings.

Rock. That was our thing, rock. We were coming out as a black rock group. In 1973, we won a talent show at Ballou, and the winner got to open for Chuck Brown at the Panorama Room. That was in the summertime, and by September, we were opening for Chuck Brown at the Panorama Room.

My favorite era of EU was the "Ooh La La La" era and Future Funk. It was Sugarfoot Ricky, me, Too Tall Steve, Eric Handon, Ooh La Tony, Tino, Lowell on keyboards, CJ on horns, Go-Go Mike: That was the band! This was before Ju Ju joined.

Although EU has always been a well-known band in D.C., they received national and international attention for "Da Butt," a song recorded for Spike Lee's "School Daze."

Charles Stephenson was our manager at the time. Spike Lee was coming off of his movie "She's Gotta Have It," and he wanted to go by and see the band. We were at the 9:30 Club. The original one was on F Street, 930 F Street, and he came in, and it was packed. It was 80% white and a few blacks, and they were partying, so Spike was right there. It was love at first sight. We just clicked. He asked if we'd like to be in a movie. I said, "Yeah," and I didn't know who he was from Adam and Eve, and then one thing led to another. It was a Friday, and by Thursday, I was in New York recording "DaButt." That's why it's good to be ready all the time. The band members who recorded the song were Me, Ju Ju, and Kent Wood. That's it.

In addition to his pioneering work with EU, Sugar Bear was one of the cornerstones of the Grown and Sexy era of Go-Go, along with Maiesha and the Hiphuggers. This smooth, R&B-heavy sound allowed a generation of Washingtonians to grow along with the sound and continue to see shows rather than outgrow it.

Go-Go wasn't doing anything when we came out with Maiesha and the Hip Huggers, featuring myself. We came out and brought that fresh element in with this so-called Grown and Sexy, and that's when all the other bands said, "Wow! They are packing them in 7 nights a week. We have to transition to this." We kind of like started this stuff. It's a blessing for the artist but a curse because everybody lost their originality. We had to start playing cover songs from EU on down to Essence. All of us have got our own songs. Some of us have hits, and some don't, but we have relevant songs that people like. So, we got away from that, and that's, to me, ever since then, nothing has changed. Nothing.

Bounce is Go-Go. It is now because it's just a different style of Go-Go, the bounce beat, and they play a lot of cover songs as well with the bounce beat. It's definitely a complimentary style because it's like a fresh injection of fresh air, but that has also run its course.

Bear says that of the 50 years of Go-Go that he has lived through and played through, the music of the '80s remains his favorite, but he wishes that the international attention the genre received during that time continued during the '90s, '00s, and beyond.

Because of "Da Butt," I was able to see the world. And ["Shake Your Thang"] the collaboration with Salt N Pepa. It allowed us to stretch our Go-Go elements around the country and the world. A lot of people have never seen bands before, period. They've seen a lot of rap groups, so with EU, they saw us play instruments and they got a treat. It was a double treat. And we played our own songs, and they knew all the words to our songs. And that was a blessing. That was my best time.

Hip-hop was way more prominent and is still bigger today because of the lack of unity in our Go-Go community. We don't support each other. Everybody's out for themselves. [Salt N Pepa] taught me a lot, and I taught them a lot. The chemistry worked perfectly when we made "Shake Your Thang" years ago. Even before that, with Kurtis Blow's "Party Time," it worked. With [Grace Jones'] "Slave to the Rhythm," it worked clearly, but nobody knew how to market it. Jill Scott came out with "It's Love."

Go-Go all up in there, but she never mentions Go-Go one time. But everybody likes it because of the beat. That's been our biggest problem. We've never had the spotlight on us, and the only time we had it was like maybe when Chuck had "Bustin' Loose" or [Rare Essence's] "Body Moves," but "Body Moves" didn't get enough airplay to me there wasn't enough airplay up and down the East Coast. Trouble Funk with "Drop the Bomb" and EU with "Da Butt," so we put a mark on it. And the sad part about it, when we had "Da Butt" out, I was on *Soul Train* telling people about RE, Chuck Brown, Junkyard, etc., right? But nothing came behind it. Nothing. And I know that people were itching for it.

They liked what they saw. They liked our show. They liked the drums, the congas, the stage, the energy, the stage presence—all of that, but nothing came behind that. 25 years later. Nothing's come behind that. Nothing. 30 years later. Nothing.

I'm not saying that no one has written [a hit], but I haven't heard one. And I'm not hatin' on nobody. A hit makes the world go round for you and others. Trust me. It does. That's real talk.

Do you know, we did one show. I'll never forget it. EU, Chuck Brown, Essence, and Biz Markie were at the Apollo Theater in New York—the headquarters for hip-hop. EU was the hottest thing, and Essence played before us and Chuck Brown. I tried right there. That was going to be a movement. It was going to be a Go-Go tour with Biz Markie. It sold out

53

at the Apollo. Sold it out. But after that, there was so much animosity and hate. They were calling us sellouts. I told them all, yes, I am a sell-out. I sell out arenas around the country every week. What are you selling out?

It's kinda crazy, but even at the Go-Go Live I, it was a big show for our Go-Go culture, but everybody was talking about EU and Essence. Chuck Brown was cool. He was doing his thing, but the talk of the town was EU and Essence. Even from that show, nothing transpired because everybody was trippin'.' I have no answer for it. EU and Essence carried Go-Go through the 90s and into the millennium. The sounds changed, but the names were still relevant. Who is the hottest band in the city? It doesn't matter because even a band playing in a hotel lobby with cover tunes, and people will think it's crankin'.' They'll love it.

John "Big Horn" Jones

John "Big Horn" Jones is one of the founding members of Rare Essence. He is most notable for playing the trombone and his "stepping" skills. Rare Essence has always had a tight front line with choreography, one of the things that set the group apart. Jones lends some of his memories to the creation and background of Rare Essence.

I am one of the original members of the group that we started back in… well, a lot of people think it was 1976 when we started, but we actually started before then. We just began using the name Rare Essence a few years after we started. We were at St. Thomas More Catholic School in Southeast D.C. I think I was in the 7th grade and Footz was in the 8th grade, and Whiteboy and Ned, we were all in the same class, and we just got together one day and said, 'Hey, let's form a band,' and so from there, things just started coming together.

In the beginning, I was playing the trumpet, not the trombone. So, we had a trumpet player, which was me. We had Ned, who's playing bass. Actually, a lot of people don't remember- maybe he doesn't remember that his guitar, he used to play bass on a lead guitar until he got an actual bass guitar. And Andre played the guitar. He had this cherry red guitar. I remember that, and I remember the group Wild Cherry used to be out there, and 'Play that Funky Music White Boy' was out. He got the name, whether he remembers it or not, 'Whiteboy' because he happened to have just been the lightest member in the group at the time, so we called him Whiteboy. The nickname they gave me was 'Big Horn' because I played the biggest horn in the band, and everybody seemed to have a nickname.

Big Horn says the group's early days were marked by creative energy.

There was a lot of creativity in the group. We used to play a lot of Top 40s, and then we were creating our own songs. It just seemed like they were coming from out of the blue. Somebody would hit a chord or hit a drum beat and then next thing you know we started putting songs together. The creativity was just there, and it was just growing and growing, and we were young and ambitious, so we wanted to do the music thing. It just seemed to blossom every time we did something. Something new would come up besides what we were playing."

Body Moves was Rare Essence's first bonafide hit.

"When we went into the studio to do our first record, which was 'Body Moves,' actually, that wasn't going to be the first record that we were going to record. The first record we had put together, a song with lyrics and music, was called 'Shake It, Don't Break It.' 'Body Moves' came out of nowhere. Godfather hit a chord one day, and the next thing you know, Footz hit a beat, Jungle Boogie came in, Funky Ned with the bass, Whiteboy with the guitar, and the horns came in, and the words just came together. I was like, 'Wow'! A lot of people don't know that we recorded enough material, actually, for a whole album. Some of that was put on the Greatest Hits CD, but there is still some in the studio that hasn't been released."

Chapter 4: And Then There Were Four...

3 significant groups emerged after Chuck Brown and the Soul Searchers established the sound of Go-Go: Rare Essence, Trouble Funk, and Experience Unlimited. Along with Chuck Brown, they make up Go-Go's "main four." Some may classify The Young Senators as one of the initial groups as well—they had a hit with the track "The Jungle" and then went on to become the band for Eddie Kendrick, a former member of the Temptations. Still, most agree that Essence, Trouble, EU, and Chuck are the "core four."

Each of these groups had their own style and sound and dedicated fan followings. For example, Rare Essence fans would wear RE's traditional colors, red and white, to stand out and let people know they were representing their favorite band at the show. There was a rival between the bands because they all had the potential to be the BEST. These pioneering bands had a distinct sound and catalogs of original music. Even if it wasn't "original," as in the case with some of Chuck Brown's songs, such as "Moody's Mood," "Run Joe," "Day-O," and some others, Chuck created them in his own style. In my opinion, legions of fans learned about jazz music and jazz artists through Chuck's interpretations.

Experience Unlimited, later shortened to EU, was a Go-Go band with a rock edge as their sound was much more rock leaning than Chuck, Trouble Funk, or Rare Essence. Tino Jackson would be front and center on that electric guitar like he was possessed. That set Experience Unlimited apart from the rest of the groups. They had a very large following.

Trouble Funk was the band that traveled the world representing Go-Go and even played at the Montreux Jazz Festival in Switzerland. In my opinion, they were the Ambassadors. Young people from Washington, D.C., would join the military, go overseas to these military bases and bring a piece of home with them--their favorite Go-Go cassettes or records. This would expose others to the music.

The story of Trouble Funk is that one of these military young men stationed in Germany brought a Trouble Funk album to the club for the DJ to play, and the crowd went wild. Back in the day, these albums had the phone number on the back, and a promoter called and invited Trouble Funk to play in Germany. They picked up some other shows while in Europe. Trouble Funk's music also could crossover into the HarDCore arena, D.C.'s thriving '80s-era punk rock scene. Trouble Funk ended up on tours with The Red Hot Chili Peppers and even played on some punk rock shows. Trouble was the first Go-Go band to tour outside of the United States. Trouble Funk still has relationships with bands outside of the genre and, a few years ago, played in D.C. for the 4th of July with rock icons Heart, Joan Jett, the Foo Fighters, and others. Trouble Funk was also featured in an episode of the Foo Fighter's Sonic Highways series that aired on HBO.

Last, but certainly not least is Rare Essence: The Inner City Groovers or The Wickedest Band Alive, depending on which era you grew up in. Rare Essence seemed to be the most popular for the longest amount of time. They really held rank. There was a time when they easily played 5 or 6 nights a week and packed the venue each and every night. Rare Essence also brought the "show" in "band and show." It was more than just their music; the actual show was well worth the price of admission- sometimes $5 and a canned good. Their choreography was unmatched, and their use of props and uniforms was extremely creative and helped Rare Essence solidify their spot as the top band in D.C. for decades.

Here are some thoughts from band members that belonged to these pioneering groups that defined the Golden Age of Go-Go.

Chuck Brown and the Soul Searchers
"After speaking with both Ricky [Wellman] and Chuck [Brown] individually, they both told me a very similar story. A while after Ricky joined the band, Chuck persuaded Ricky to primarily play one consistent beat and tempo throughout the night. That particular beat is based on the drumbeat used in Grover Washington Jr.'s recording 'Mr. Magic.' Chuck often mentioned that the beat reminded him of his youth in the church with his mom. Ricky's unique interpretation of that beat is the genesis of Go-Go music. Ricky, reluctant to try it at the time, was urged by Chuck to try it and watch the folks respond on the dance floor. The rest is history. In summary, it was Chuck's idea and Ricky's implementation of the idea."- "Too Tall" Steve Wellman, EU, Chuck Brown, and Redds & the Boys

"I was with The Soul Searchers, and we were out of town at a jazz club.

We were jazz-oriented. Roland Kirk was there. Roland was famous for playing 3 saxophones at the same time. He was also blind. He had on his African dashiki. He played his one sax, and then he had all three. One he invented himself. And he was in harmony. It was blowing my mind. Then he had the piccolos, and he would play with his nose. The guy blew my mind. So, when we got back, I was living on 13th Street at the time. I had 4 horns, so I picked up 2 at home and tried it. I had 2 sounds coming out. I had to figure out how to do this. It would be a trip if I could play 2 trumpets simultaneously. I just practiced with that and figured out how to make it work. It's within. But over the years, no one ever knew I would do it. It blew people's minds. I practiced and practiced. It still fascinates people."- Donald Tillery, trumpet and vocals for Chuck Brown and the Soul Searchers.

"I remember one time, Chuck D. from Public Enemy after we had done a show at the Capital Centre, asked me, 'Who is this old man who is rockin' this arena?' He was talking about Chuck Brown. I remember Chuck D. when he first saw Chuck Brown. Remember, Go-Go was so powerful that you could not sell out the Capital Centre without having a Go-Go band on the show."- Tarek Stevens, Whistle

"I was with them [The Soul Searchers] with the Soul Train thing. Bustin' Loose was the main thing, but we were just getting into that Go-Go thing. I don't think they really knew it was Go-Go. I just think they loved the Bustin' Loose sound."- Donald Tillery

"Chuck always told me to "be yourself." When it comes to your playing, always give people your best. I learned that from being on the stage with him. Once he got on the stage, he became a different Chuck Brown. He would smile! You could tell he loved the people when he got on that stage. He would give his best. And it seemed like the people were his family."- Donald Tillery

"As a member of the Soul Searchers, I was an active participant in the creation of the D.C. Go-Go style of music. Originally, we typically played the 'cabaret' style where the band played top 40 R&B or funk tunes, and the crowd would get up from their tables complete with setups and dance. At the end of each tune, the dancers would return to their seats and rest up for the next song."- John "JB" Buchanan, Chuck Brown & The Soul Searchers, Rare Essence, Proper Utensils

"I remember one cabaret gig at the Burgundy Room. Chuck Brown was a bit hesitant in starting a new tune we just learned, so we jammed and improvised in a jazz style over the chords of that song, along with an Afro-Cuban beat with congas and cowbell until Chuck got comfortable enough to start singing the tune. The crowd went wild! They never knew what hit them. 'What was the new song you guys played before the last song?' they asked. Eventually, we expanded that concept to segue between all the tunes we performed in a continuous pattern that did not stop until we played a slow song or ballad. Sometimes that set could go on for over an hour and a half."- John "JB" Buchanan

Rare Essence
In the 70s, when Rare Essence was starting out, Ms. Mack, Ms. Neal, and Ms. Sis, the Momagers, wanted to protect the group and their investments and treated Rare Essence as a business rather than a hobby. They strategically built from the ground up.

"In the early stages of Rare Essence, a lot of the guys didn't understand everything that was in process. We were young ourselves. We would do a gig, get paid, and then put the balance in an account. We were trying to set the business up in the beginning. We had been renting equipment and knew that we needed to own our own stuff. We started buying our equipment. We needed new mics, a sound system, and a truck. What we did was invest in ourselves. It was like that for a few years. Now, we ended up with enough sound equipment to set up two full stages. All of that costs money, and don't forget the upkeep. After a few years, we were able to get paid more money." – Andre "Whiteboy" Johnson, founding member of Rare Essence.

As a business entity, Rare Essence was the first Go-Go band to form a corporation and have checks issued from a business account with taxes deducted. Some of the band members liked this method, while others did not. Ms. Mack also expected the band members to wear uniforms for the shows so that everyone would be in sync.

"We liked fashion, and we had to wear uniforms. We had designers who would make stuff for us. You could see what we were wearing when you saw the Go-Go Live (at the Capital Center). It was funny gear. Now they just wear what we used to call 'play clothes'- blue jeans and raggedy shoes."- Mark "Godfather" Lawson, keyboardist Rare Essence, Little Benny and the Masters, Godfather and Friends.

Rare Essence changed the face of music and the music business in D.C. Ms. Annie Mack, the mother of Quentin "Footz" Davidson and James "Funk" Thomas, was a pioneer for women in the D.C. music scene as one of the first female managers, and she demanded and earned respect.

"Ms. Mack wanted it to be professional. We would have legal meetings with professional attorneys to learn about the business. Footz's grandmother, Ms. Sis, saw that Ms. Mack was trying to help us, so they bought our first P.A. system and our first truck. Before you knew it, we were on our way. All of us had very important parts in making sure that the organization ran the way it was supposed to."- Mark "Godfather" Lawson

Rare Essence was not only a fan favorite, but also a favorite of musicians of other bands as well. It would be commonplace to see musicians from various bands checking out Rare Essence.

"In my mind, Rare Essence was the standard of Go-Go back in the day. I liked all of the bands back in the day. I liked EU- they all had their own style. I liked Trouble Funk. I liked Chuck Brown. But I loved Rare Essence. Every band member from Rare Essence should be in the Go-Go Hall of Fame, separate from the band. I think every individual member of Rare Essence influenced Go-Go more than anybody else has done. Individually they've influenced people. I'm not talking about the new band. I'm talking about the original guys.

I can point to every last one of them and say why. You talk about DC, the cowbell, the smoothness of his sax, his stepping, and Big Horn. He was playing that trombone back in the day. He influenced a lot of trombone players. And Funky Ned, again, who will go down as the most influential bass player to play Go-Go. Whiteboy influenced all of these guitar players. All of them. He had that clean sound that everybody wanted to emulate because his sound was so nice and crisp and clean. And you can go down the entire list. We were all playing R&B until Chuck started doing Go-Go, and then we all switched over to that, so I am old enough to have been here when Go-Go started, and they were clearly the Go-Go standard of bands." – Terry Lambert, drums, bass, Little Benny and the Masters, Total Experience, Godfather and Friends.

"I liked Benny. When he was with Rare Essence, I thought he was a heck of an entertainer. I volunteered to show Benny how to do the two trumpets.

I looked at this young guy and knew he had potential. He could perform! He could rap! I had a thing that if the man upstairs took me, I even told my daughter I said to leave my horns to Benny. That's what I wanted, my horn to go to him. And then I found out that he had passed. What takes these young musicians is living the fast life. That nightlife- it can burn you out. Between Chuck and Benny doing 5 or 6 nights and, Benny was working too! (He was an electrician). He was working, and then he was doing Rare Essence back then. Chuck got sick, and his energy level was gone, and then Chuck asked Benny to come, and then Benny had to come in there. It's not easy when you're working 6 or 7 nights."- Donald Tillery, trumpet and vocals, Chuck Brown and the Soul Searchers.

"We went to Disney World, and we had a ball. We had a heck of a time. We were the type of band that would play cover tunes and put them in our own form. We would put a dance rhythm to the song and put in a step that we did. We used to make adaptations of other people's music, and then we'd take it and change it and put a heavy percussion on the music they already created. If you listen to the music of 'Take Me Out to the Go-Go,' we're using the Cracker Jack commercial, Mary Had a Little Lamb, Do You See what I See- it's all incorporated into the song."- Mark "Godfather" Lawson, keyboardist, Rare Essence, Little Benny and the Masters, Godfather and Friends.

"My favorite band in the world, bar none, is Rare Essence, the Inner City Groovers. Anybody would tell you, I've followed them from the beginning when I was a young kid when they were playing for a quarter and a can of beans. They just spoke to my soul. Lawrence (Maniac) was in the band. I'll never forget and Whiteboy, Footz, Scotty, Godfather, Jungle Boogie, and Benny. Funk wasn't even talking at the time. DC, Big Horn. Nobody did it better. What disappointed me was when they started opening up the high hat. Every band back then, I don't care who you were, had their own sound. You could drive in the car, you didn't even have to hear the lead talker, and you knew who it was because they had their own style and sound. Essence was the serious inner-city sound of soul. They had soul. They had it on lock. They were like Earth, Wind and Fire. Trouble was really funk. They were like Parliament. They were a funk band. And they hit their percussion so hard with TeeBone playing with the drumsticks, and they had the percussion set up like nobody else and Tony plucking that bass.

He really used that bass guitar with Trouble, like the rhythmic section that it was supposed to be with the drum. And then, EU was a rock band, and it was crazy because Bear played the bass and Tony played the bass, but they played two different styles. They had that lick. Bear played like Flea from the Red Hot Chili Peppers when he played it. Bear played it hard. He would thump that bass. EU's style was rockish, and they played much faster than anyone else. And everything fell underneath it. Chuck was still the R&B Soul artist that founded it. He was still really playing more R&B style. Although Chuck created Go-Go music, these young dudes were responsible for elevating because we weren't checking for Chuck back then. He took his spot back because, let's be clear, in 1985, he became a juggernaut. Chuck Brown, in 1985, shut down every Go-Go band in the city. He was the icon. He became the king."- Tarek Stevens, Whistle

"Mike Muse was like a superstar in D.C. When he joined Essence, he was the first Go-Go vocalist. He was like the Marvin Gaye of Go-Go. Being very good-looking, handsome, and a vocalist, he became like a local celebrity. During the 80s, Go-Go became like- Go-Go is iconic right now, but these cats were like Superstars. They were local, legendary stars."- Tarek Stevens, Whistle

"I was a singer at first, but when I saw Jungle Boogie, it changed my life. I wanted to do that. From there, the rest is history, and I told Jungle Boogie, "I want to be like you." What's so ironic about it, when I became Heartbeat, I was about 17 or 18, and Big Al Winkler, one of the top sound men out here, was with Ayre Rayde at the time. Al said that he was going to pick up Jungle Boogie, and I told Al that I wanted to go with him. I put some congas in his trunk. So, I was with Boogie, taking him home, and we were going to see Junkyard that night, and Al asked, 'Boogie, do you want to see Junkyard with us tonight?' And he said he did. So, on the way in, we're talking, and we were on our way to the 9:30 Club listening to music, and Boogie says, 'This youngin is sharp as shit!' It was the Wind Me Up Chuck tape with me on it. And when Al started laughing, Boogie pulled that tape out of his knapsack, and it was me. He said this is Heartbeat right here, so after the Junkyard show, we took him back to his house, and I opened the trunk and gave Boogie some congas. I said whenever you need to work out, I'm here. He said, "Shawty, that's you?" I told him that he was my inspiration."- Hosea "Heartbeat" Williams, Gerardo, Chuck Brown, Central Groove, Dog Eat Dog

"I failed a whole year of school. My parents left for work, and I left for school, and I had this big mirror and me and Rick's bedroom, and I would just create moves. That's why I'm the head of CPU because they do my moves to this day. Then one night, I was playing with Ayre Rayde, and Rick was with Hot Cold Sweat, and we were down at the Metro Club, and I created this move called Over and Under. They used to say, "Heyyy, Go-Go Mickeyyy," but the thing about it was when Rick and I were at High Point High School, Mick and I were boys, and Mick came to my high school and picked me up in Beltsville, MD. Keep in mind that he lives all the way in NE, and he came and picked me up to work out. I showed him that move, and every conga player today does it. We were at the Metro Club one night, and they let me get on with Rare Essence, and Whiteboy was late, and Rick went up there and ran the one with Mickey... They did the "Hey Go-Go Mickey thing," and then Mickey started doing that move like I taught him, and after the show, everybody was like, "Hey, where'd you get that from?" And Mickey's so humble, he was like, "No, that's not my shit, it's his!"

And today, every conga player in Go-Go emulates that move that I showed Mick on all of their moves. If there were a copyright on that, I'd be a millionaire. That's one thing I give to Mick, man. I created a lot of stuff that dudes do now that I don't get credit for. I don't care about that, like over and under that I do, and Bouncy does it too- the elbows. Like Tidy always says, Elbows and Assess. That's one thing people say about me is that I invented many moves in Go-Go. Mickey is the G.O.A.T., for him to tell everybody, "No, I didn't create that move. That was him." That's why I say CPU is so courageous and powerful because they know now because when the GOAT tells you, 'No, that wasn't me. That was him.' They look at me like, Damn, are you sure? Mickey was like Yeah. That came from missing a whole year of school."- Hosea "Heartbeat" Williams, Chuck Brown, Central Groove, Gerardo and Dog Eat Dog.

"Until I joined Rare Essence in 1986, I had only heard the music of Rare Essence from a distance since we ended up on the same circuit playing the same style of music. I quite often felt like a fish out of water just coming into this group that had already had 14 years of history. I was the only keyboard player then and learned the new material by word of mouth. In some instances, it was difficult, if not impossible, to approach the legacy of musical nuances that the former keyboard players had left behind. By that time, Go-Go had become the standard in the young club scene in D.C. The almost rabid following of Rare Essence knew that music better than I did, and eventually, we started to create new music."- John "JB" Buchanan

"My favorite period is the "mid to late 80s because that is when Go-Go was more about showmanship. When we were doing those shows at the Coliseum, we had to gear up for that. We had to do these great big rehearsals. We would pull out these big props, and everybody was wearing the tuxedos and all of that there, so it was really about showmanship at that point. The fans even got excited because we would have them wear red and white at the Coliseum, so we knew who in the audience was there for us. We knew who was there for EU, and who was there for Trouble Funk."- Andre "Whiteboy" Johnson, guitarist and founding member of Rare Essence.

Trouble Funk
Trouble Funk is synonymous with the emergence of the non-stop, percussion-driven, best-seen live, experience the party, audience participatory call, and response, grassroots, homegrown music called Go-Go.

In 1978, Trouble Funk burst onto the music scene with their booming vocals, infectious percussion, and tight horn section. In its infancy, the group consisted of the writing team of band leader, bassist, and vocalist "Big" Tony Fisher, keyboardists Robert "Syke Dyke" Reed and James Avery, and trumpet player Taylor Reed. The group was rounded out with the musical prowess of drummer Emmett "Rick" Nixon, percussionists Mack Carey and Timothy "Teebone" David, guitarist Chester Davis, trombonist Gerald Reed, and saxophonist David Rudd.

The musical landscape of the 1980s was peppered with anthems "Drop the Bomb," "Pump Me Up," "Let's Get Small," "So Early in the Morning," "Saturday Night Live from Washington, D.C. Parts 1 & 2," "Say What?" and two R&B/ Hip Hop Billboard charting tracks, "Still Smokin'" and "Good to Go."

"I think it was our originality and the fact that we recorded so much material early on [that set us apart from the other groups], explains Emmett "Rick" Nixon, Trouble Funk's original drummer citing Chuck Brown as their biggest competitor on the scene.
"Drop the Bomb" was the first Go-Go record released outside Washington, D.C., and was released on the pioneering label Sugar Hill Records.

Trouble Funk differed from the other three groups due to their raw, party-driven style. They captured the attention of various genres, catapulting themselves onto the national and international music scene. They would frequently tour with notable punk rock acts Minor Threat and the Big Boys while still gracing the stages of major music festivals with legendary artists such as Curtis Mayfield, Parliament Funkadelic, Red Hot Chili Peppers, UB40, Def Leppard, and Fishbone, to name a few. Trouble Funk also recorded with Kurtis Blow and appeared in his video for "I'm Chillin.'"

In the mid-80s, while Trouble Funk was signed to Island Records, their live performances were captured on the big screen in the film "Good to Go," starring Art Garfunkel. The film, not what you would call a blockbuster by any stretch of the imagination, was produced by Island Pictures and showcased Go-Go music. Trouble Funk was on 5 of the 13 tracks on the soundtrack. The movie is now called "Short Fuse."

During Trouble Funk's obligation with Island Records, they worked with the legendary Bootsy Collins, who produced the Trouble Funk album "Trouble Over Here, Trouble Over There."

From 1986 to 1988, Trouble Funk toured extensively throughout the United States, playing legendary venues such as Madison Square Garden and Apollo Theatre and on worldwide stages with multiple stops in Brussels, Paris, Amsterdam, London, Spain, Nice, Denmark, Germany, and Japan. A stop in Switzerland included a performance at the highly regarded Montreux Jazz Festival. 1994 brought Trouble Funk back to Japan for an extended tour.

"We were the ambassadors of Go-Go music. Chuck Brown was glad that we were the first group to travel around the world introducing Go-Go to the world," explains Taylor Reed, one of the founding members of Trouble Funk.

The members of Trouble Funk have fostered relationships with musicians from back in the day. One such person is Dave Grohl, formerly of Nirvana, currently of The Foo Fighters. In 2014, Grohl sat down with "Big" Tony Fisher to discuss Go-Go for the HBO docuseries Foo Fighters: Sonic Highways. Grohl, Fisher, and Trouble Funk have played together during various events and festivals.

In 2023, Trouble Funk is still on the scene, and their music has been kept relevant through sampling. "Pump Me Up" is one of the most sampled tracks of all time, being sampled in over 70 different songs.

Experience Unlimited

"When Ju Ju and Shorty Tim (Glover) were on Grace Jones' 'Slave to the Rhythm,' that thing was mastered like a hit record. When EU did 'Party Time' with Kurtis Blow and Full Force, and by that time, let's be clear about one thing, Spike Lee came up with the whole concept of 'Da Butt.' Spike Lee came up with the concept in the apartment with Monty Ross, and then he brought in Marcus Miller, the famous bass player- he's a professional. He'd been working with Luther Vandross for years. So now you have guys that are used to recording in a certain way to give you that professional sound. It was 'foreign' music to other people with a 'foreign' sound, but anybody who went to a live Go-Go was captivated and would always tell you, 'Man, I went to this thing called Go-Go.' They wouldn't even know how to say it. They would call it **Go-Go**, not **a** **Go-Go**. "- Tarek Stevens, Whistle.

"It was in 1980-81 when I joined Experience Unlimited. Before joining the group, I was exposed to Go-Go in 76. I was in a different band at the time, and we were playing a whole different type of music. A good friend of mine named Sly, who was the light man for Chuck Brown, would say, 'Come on, Tino. Come with me to the Chuck Brown shows.' I went to a Chuck Brown show, and it was like a whole different animal seeing that type of club atmosphere and the people that were there, and it just so happens, one night, Chuck Brown's bass player, God Rest his soul, John Euell didn't show up so Sly put me on the spot. He said, 'My friend Tino plays bass," I'm a guitar player, you know, everybody knows. So, Chuck says, 'Son, go ahead and play the bass.' I got onstage and played bass and being that I used to go see Chuck from time to time, I was familiar with his songs, and I played it, and he was so elated that that's how Chuck and I began having a bond with each other and he never forgot that through the years."- Tino Jackson, guitarist EU

When I was in Junior High School in the 70s, Sugar Bear and the guys would come to school. They would play hooky, and they would find out what classroom I was in, and I would see them at the door like, "Come on, come on with us." And it just so happened EU had a store called The House of Peace on Morris Road in Southeast. A record store is what it was, and we would go into this record store. We would just jam, and their band manager, Charles Stephenson, got whiff of it and said that we couldn't do that anymore. So, Sugar Bear decided we'll do it at night when the store closes, trying to be sneaky, so we decided to do that at night, and the group that I was playing with at the time, the group, is called Taack.

We would play with various groups. We were playing at clubs and colleges. We were doing different things than what Sugar Bear and them were doing. We would play rock, and we would play cover tunes that were rock. And it just happened that the bass player looked like Shine- like his twin brother.

His name was Shine. His name was Robert Freeman. He became a minister and had a big ministry down in Waldorf through the years, so him, the drummer Ghost, and me, late at night, 11:30 at night, we would just go up to the House of Peace, and we would jam. There were other well-known musicians, and they would come, and the first night we were there, we started playing, and after we finished, 'Ok, now you guys come up and play.' They said, 'No, we don't want to play. We just want to watch you guys play. We don't want to play anymore.'

It was like, oh, this is a whole different thing. These guys can play." The way Ghost played, he's Rick Wellman's nephew, and Shine and Bear were good friends and looked so much alike. What transpired from there, Bear said, "Look, Man. I want you to play in the band, and there was a lot of turmoil in the group I was playing with at the time, so I said, "OK." And that's how things transpired between Bear, Butch, and I. Butch was the drummer for EU at the time. Bear always wanted to play rock. And from that day forth, everything took off. "Who is this guy Tino? Where did he come from?" Because I wasn't on the Go-Go scene. Some of the people that played music knew who I was. We would learn different grooves, and I'd say, "Play this groove, Bear, " which transpired into a song. And then it became a song that we would play every night. For instance, "EU Freeze." I said Bear, play this groove, and the congas played, and we would play that part. And then it evolved into something else. We're gonna call it EU Freeze! Because we were more in that time, musically evolving into our own, we had that creative instinct where we wanted to play this and that, and we would practice at the EU House. We had a house over there on M Street NW.

I lived there, Butch lived there, and Butch and I would go downstairs, Bear would come over, and then the horns would come over, and I would say, 'Play these parts for the horn parts.' And we had that creative gel at the time. And we would just create things, and then on stage, we would try things, and that's how "Ooh La La La" came along. It was just an instinct. Then we ended up hooking up with Shine. The bass player that used to play in my group. He started producing us. And we just wrote songs, and we collaborated with each other and came out with these different songs. And then Lowell Tucker, who played with Fate's Destiny, a group from around our area, started playing with EU along with Jerry, who lived in Waldorf, and we created Future Funk. That's how that evolved, and that song was the song that got a lot of attention as far as EU. Mind you, at the time, there were no keyboards. I still consider those guys in Trouble Funk good friends of mine. They would say, 'How in the world are they playing, and they don't have a keyboard player?' Then it hit them, 'OK, the guitar player is playing heavy chords to cover for the keyboards that weren't there.' Metro Man. He was there.

He had played with a group called Symba. We started playing, and people were like, "Oh! This is the new EU!" There was one club in particular that we played in. One club and it was Trouble Funk's rehearsal place called The Squad Room. The Squad Room changed its name to Club LeBaron in Palmer Park. Trouble Funk had this massive equipment, and we just came in with our stuff. Our soundman Ben. Ben Benjamin, who became a renowned doctor- he and Reo would always battle each other. We would come in there and play and do our thing- we had no keyboard player, just guitar and horns, and that was our style. Everybody liked us because we were so different. I would play these power chords, and nobody else was playing power chords. My style of playing and Bear's style of playing complimented each other. They would have to complement each other because there were no keyboards.

"During the early, early years, there was a cat that played horns, and he played the trumpet- Young Boy Lee. Then you had Vernon. And you had Hunter, who played the trombone. But our high point with the horns was Too Tall Steve, CJ, and Go-Go Mike, and you couldn't put anything between them. And at that time, Sugarfoot Ricky came aboard. He was the drummer for Chuck. We played at the Paragon II every Sunday, and people wouldn't want to play after us. That was the best group that I think we had. This was maybe 82-83. There were a lot of guys coming and going. We played for quite a period with that particular unit. Future Funk, there was one guy singing with us, Eric, Eric Handen. This guy nobody, could sing like this guy. He would sound just like the Stylistics and just like the guy from Earth, Wind and Fire. We had seasoned musicians at the time, and we really were into our craft. We complemented each other. Nobody could touch us with the cover tunes."

"EU Freeze was the first song I did with EU that got radio play. I was at

Southeast Gardens, and I was driving to the show, Tidy and I, and the record came on the radio and I was like, "That's us! That's us!" WOL was the first station that played it. Everybody was requesting it, so the other radio stations had to play it. Everyone was calling the stations to request that song! The phones were ringing off the hook. Eventually, it got in light and then medium rotation and it gave us recognition. To this day, people in the audience still request this song. Future Funk and EU Freeze. We had so many other songs, but it was these two. At this time, there were no keyboard players. It was just Butch, Bear, Me, Young Boy Lee and Vernon, Hunter and Smokey, our conga player."

"We all collaborated when putting our songs together. 'Ooh La La La.' We played at the Howard Theatre, Cheriy's, and it was like a test. We would do things on the spot. We would play a groove to see if it worked. We would go live and play it and look at the response from the people. Ooh La Tony would do the raps to songs like 'Grip it and Hold It.' We said, 'Oh La La La,' and Trouble Funk said, 'Let's Get Small,' but that was 'Oh La La La.' It was a crazy thing at the time between us and Trouble Funk. We would start other songs and other grooves. After we moved out of the house on M street, the band started losing their creative juices."

"A lot of Go-Go bands didn't play at the 9:30 Club because they didn't have that rock element. We met Spike Lee. We would play at the original 9:30 Club on F Street, and we would have a line outside. And these people were actually coming to see us! Whites, Blacks, and everybody just had a good time! It was new to us and new to them because they had a chance to go see a Go-Go without all of the chaos."

"Kurtis Blow was very nice to us. We did a song with him, "Party Time." That was prior to the Virgin Record thing. We started working with various people because they started noticing us. The New York scene. We were at the Black Hole one night, and Salt n Pepa came to town. They came onstage, and the stage was shaking, and they had the turn tables. The turntables and records jumping. The D.C. crowd is really harsh on people. They got onstage, the record is jumping and the crowd started Booing them. Sugar Bear came on stage and said, "That's not cool. Y'all shouldn't do that to them. They came all the way from New York. They came to perform for y'all. They're entertainers." So, what we did was played the song. Salt n Pepa came on stage, and they fell in love with us because we showed them love. 'My mic sounds nice.' That was the record they had out at the time. And from that day forth, when they went back to

New York, they told everybody, Those guys EU, cool guys. When we go on tour, we want them on our tour. Salt and Pepa were like, 'You are like our brothers. Come with us.' It was us, Salt n Pepa, Guy, and Keith Sweat. That tour lasted for 13 months. Every city sold out. That was 88-89. We were gone from the city for several years, at the peak of our tour in 89. Marvin Ennis and I did "Taste of Your Love." Marvin was with Starpoint at the time. 'Taste of Your Love' was done at Black Pond Studios in Rockville."

Chapter 5: The Next Generation

After the emergence of the "core four," many other groups started to pop up. The school systems were still teaching music, and the music stores had instruments for those who wanted to learn. Besides, being in a band would bring popularity and girls.

Bands were forming in all quadrants of the city, and the enthusiasm spilled over into Maryland and Virginia (close to D.C.), and there was no shortage of Go-Go. There were The Peacemakers, Hot Cold Sweat, Petworth, Reality, The Pump Blenders, Junkyard Band, Ovation, Shady Groove, AM/FM, Mass Extension, Physical Wunder, Redds & the Boys, Prophecy, Little Benny and the Masters, Publicity, Chance Band and so many more. Each of these bands created original material and gained legions of fans.

One such band, Ayre Rayde, hailed from District Heights and Capitol Heights of Prince Georges County, Maryland. They were well known as Maryland's first Go-Go band. The band was formed in 1979 and consisted of original members Lionel Perry, Adrian "Egg" Norton, Tim Evans, Donald "Doc" Spencer, "Shorty" Quinn Robinson, Kevin Wheeler, Melvin and Jay Taylor, and Tim Proctor, while Daryl Spencer served as manager. Ayre Rayde came to prominence with their 1985 hit "Sock it to Me," by which time, some of the original band members had moved on.

Mama Spencer, Ms. Lois Spencer-Tibbs, was very involved with her sons Donald and Daryl and their friends and allowed them to practice in her home. This kept them away from the negativity the streets offered, and she knew they were all safe.

Some notable members that were a part of Ayre Rayde at some point include the late Mega Producer Carl "Chucky" Thompson, former Prince Georges Councilman Derrick Leon Davis, also known back then as "China Boogie," Clarence "Boolah" Roper, John "Cabalou" Locust, Eddie Winslow, Jeff Wallace, Keith and Ron Exum, William "Boogie" Dews, Paul "Rootie" Baltimore, "Conga" Kermit Meredith, Andre James, "Go-Go Mike" Simmons, Arvell "Cloudy" McLeod and "Go-Go Mickey" Freeman to name a few.

One music collector and Ayre Rayde fan, Jay Solis, explains, "I was first introduced to Go-Go at the age of 11. I was instantly hooked. I started collecting tapes like a madman. Nothing could stop me. I was still young, so the thought of actually going to a Go-Go seemed out of the question. I started out listening to whoever I could. Mass (Extension), Peacemakers, Essence, and EU. It was so easy to follow the Go-Go movement back then because everyone was into it, or, at the very least, they knew of it. The movement was strong. There were classic Go-Go albums being released left and right. And every neighborhood had their own band."

"But then, one day, I heard a tape of a band I had never heard before. The band had this awesome intro. I asked the dude playing it who the band was. He told me that it was Ayre Rayde. They are from Maryland. I thought to myself, Maryland? I'm from Maryland! I began learning as much as possible about this band that referred to themselves as 'Maryland's own.' They immediately became my band of choice. The fact that there was a Go-Go band out there, making it a top priority that they were from Maryland, completely fascinated me. Their catalog of original Go-Go grooves was impressive. From 'What's the Word' to 'Welcome to the Go- Go' and my personal favorite, 'D- Sharp.' Their musicianship as a band was tight. Their innovation to take Zapp's 'Doo wa Ditty,' flip it Go-Go style, and give us 'Freak-a-Deak' was genius. They showed the ability to adapt to any situation. And were able to reinvent themselves multiple times throughout their history and somehow literally never missed a beat. Ayre Rayde was my favorite Go-Go band back then and remains my favorite to this day."

Marlon Williams, a percussionist, was also a huge Ayre Rayde fan. "Ayre Raye was a hometown band from Capitol Heights, and everybody in the neighborhood loved them! One of my favorite memories is at the Oakcrest Recreation Center in '84. They had the ambulance lights on the speakers, and they had the smoke machine going. They were cranking so hard that it was ridiculous! I was supposed to be jumping up and down with the rest of my Capitol Heights crew, but I was just standing there in awe. They were hitting Chaka Kahn's 'I Feel for You.' I will never forget it."

The Pump Blenders was another group that had a significant following. Pump Blenders percussionist Terry Stanton talks about his years in the group.

"I joined the Pump Blenders in 1980. We were really getting up there at that time because we played at the Howard Theatre on Friday nights with Rare Essence and Class Band. We moved up because we used to open, and then the next thing you know, we started playing just prior to Rare Essence. We were doing a lot of shows in the 80s. The Howard Theatre was one of my favorite places to play. I used to love the crowd. It used to be packed. Rare Essence was there, so it was a nice crowd, and the crowd just loved us there. It was really a fun time back then."

Stanton continues, "[Manager] Mr. Busey was a jokester, but he was also serious when it came time for being serious. He was just an old man with a young mind. He used to make us laugh, but when he was serious, he was serious about his band. If you didn't come to practice, you didn't play when you came to it. Whether you were one of the best players in the band or not, it didn't matter. He had everything situated, and he was really adamant about it. He used to introduce us every show, whether it was at the Howard Theatre or if we played outside. He used to come up there and give us an introduction. He used to get up there and try to boost us up by dancing on the side of the stage where we could see him with a big ol smile on his face. He was really a great manager."

Redds & the Boys was another early iconic Go-Go band hailing from the Arthur Caper Housing Projects. Randy "Hollywood" Kilpatrick, an early group member, talks about the originality in sound the groups prided themselves on.

"Having an opportunity to play in the Go-Go band Redds & the Boys was definitely an essential highlight in establishing myself as a bassist in the DMV. I was privileged to be a part of the early stages of Go-Go music— the days when original music and distinguished styles separated every band. I had the opportunity to travel to many venues on the east coast to perform this great genre of music that consists of strong percussive syncopation, along with the smooth introduction of grooves and melodies that led to the full arrangement of our songs, right back to the tightly locked in percussive patterns driven by drums, congas, cowbells, tambourine, and bass slides. I was fortunate to do a few recordings with the band. The first album was titled "Love Boat."

It was followed up a few years later by the single and music video titled 'Movin' and Groovin', which eventually ascended the Billboard Music Charts. The band also had the great fortune to work in the studio on another recording project with a few members of one of the greatest bands in the land- Earth Wind and Fire, led by Verdine and Fred White. The band was featured in many magazine publications, including Rolling

Stone, Spin, Right On, and many others. A super shout out to Anthony "Redds" Williams, Carl "CJ" Jones, Reginald "Lil Beats" Daughtry, "Too Tall" Steve Coleman, Ivan Goff, Derrick "Doc" Pearson, Reggie "Shake-n-Bake" Baker, Nick Halsey, Chris "Geronimoe" Allen, Eddie "Steady Eddie" Hill, Wayne "Funkyfoot" Mickles, Milton "Go-Go Mickey" Freeman and Lee "Young Boy Lee" Tabron. Thanks for sharing the stage for many years of musical bliss, and a special thanks to Maxx Kidd for every opportunity he presented us with."

The roster of the group Physical Wunder reads as a Who's Who of those who gained prominence in the genre, and many are still playing with various bands to this day.

Kenny "Doc" Hughes describes his time with Physical Wunder.
"In 1984, the group was formed. There were 5 young kids, kind of like New Edition, and the backing band that was put together by drummer Wayne Mickle who later became the drummer for Redds & the Boys. The band was called Flight Band. I can't remember all of the five guys' names. I know that Mighty Moe [Hagans from EU] was one of them before he started playing congas. After failed attempts to satisfy all the parties involved, like parents, etc., Moe Ziegler [Manager and owner of Cheiry's nightclub] decided to ditch the five-boy act, and we kept playing as just the band, so Moe said we were going to keep the band as Physical Wunder. We became the house band at Cheiry's. I tried many rappers to be the frontman, but none took it seriously, so I started doing it, and that's how I kinda took over the band and started moving out the dead weight and got guys that wanted to play."

Some of these noted names who played with Physical Wunder are Elgin "Ginuwine" Baylor (Yes, THAT Ginuwine), Kevin "Bigfoot" Smith, Kevin Prince, Rick Froe, Reggie Sharpe, Larae "Ras Lidj" Daye, Darrell "Blue Eye" Arrington, Bruce Bailey, Derrick Doyle, Troy "Boy Troy" Williams, Craig Clipper, Bo Hughes, Tyrone Frazier, Derrick Hillard, Terrance T Smooth, Leroy Butts, Malik Savage, Tony Sharpe, and Mighty Moe Hagans.

"These guys played over a span from 1986 to 2000. I disbanded the group in 2000 after having a good run. We had several recordings- Get Physical (1977), Hey Good Lookin (1988), Hype with the Go-Go (1990), It's a Physical Thang (1992) and Return of the Phyz (1996)," Hughes proudly shares.

Spotlight: Charles Stephenson on the History of Go-Go

Charles Stephenson is a New York transplant who moved to D.C. during the earliest days of Go-Go and became the manager of the band Experience Unlimited during their first years. Charles has written several books on Go-Go, including "The Beat" with Kip Lornell, which is often referred to as The Bible of Go-Go. He has always had his finger on the pulse of the D.C. music scene and is also a historian of all things Go-Go. He shared with me some important history about the genre, including details on how it got its name.
***

Go-Go is now a Washington, D.C., culture that began in the late 60s in dance halls across the city. Deriving its name from Smokey Robinson's "Going to a Go-Go," it was an expression to identify the physical elements of the dance hall. So, instead of saying we are going to a dance, locals would say we are going to a Go-Go.

Various local bands who played at the Go-Go were usually playing top 40 tunes, which was what the audience wanted. Washington, D.C., was a bit unique because there was a multitude of bands who performed at these Go-Go's. Just to name a few, and I will get in trouble, but here goes: The Young Senators, Black Heat, The Soul Searchers, 95th Congress, Aggression, Brute, and 100 Years Time. These groups were very popular at dance halls. All expressed a unique musical quality.

However, in the early 1970s, music began to change. With the advent of disco music, DJs began to get a piece of the entertainment market, which started to threaten business for local bands. At that point, Chuck Brown started to develop a beat, a pocket that would keep people on the dance floor. Simultaneously, he was also experimenting with the use of other elements to engage the audience. He then borrowed from traditional African, Latin, blues, gospel, and R&B performers by adding call-and-response, thus making the music more personal. Go-Go music at its core is dance music, which incorporates a heavy pulsating beat, surrounded by the sound of congas, cowbells, and other percussion instruments, with a slice of horns. The lead talker acts as the griot and maestro of the band, conducting the music. Chuck perfected the sound, his audience grew, and other bands, such as Experience Unlimited, Rare Essence, and eventually Trouble, began to copy his musical recipe.

75

Spotlight: Darryll Brooks on "Go-Go Live"

Darryll Brooks (along with his partners, Carol Kirkendall and Gerald Scott) is synonymous with the phrase "promoters extraordinaire." Their history with events at Anacostia Park, Human Kindness Day on the Monument Grounds, and countless concerts has always been about doing something positive. It only makes sense that this would be the group that brought us the iconic "Go-Go Live at the Capital Centre" and "Go-Go Live II." Go-Go Live was a sold-out concert performance on October 9, 1987, with an exclusively Go-Go lineup. The show involved Chuck Brown and the Soul Searchers, Rare Essence, Experience Unlimited, Little Benny & The Masters, Junkyard Band, Hot Cold Sweat, Go-Go Lorenzo, and D.C. Scorpio being backed up by Chuck Brown and the Soul Searchers. Darryll Brooks explains his involvement with Go-Go and how "Go-Go Live" came about.
***

It just so happens that at that time, Tiger Flower or G Street Express was our name then. We had just finished doing a tour with Run DMC, the Raising Hell Tour, and we came home, and I'd heard a lot of buzz about this "Good to Go" movie. I was excited to see the guys I kinda worked with, my homeboys, in a movie. I had been on the road, and I'd seen a whole lot of other things, with a lot of other groups, hip hop groups, and self-contained groups in major markets, but now I saw something that was happening major in my city, D.C. So, I was excited. They were filming at the Pension building downtown. When I caught up with them, I walked in, and I talked to several of the guys I ran into in the middle of a break, and they were disgruntled.

They were upset about the content of the movie and their representation, our city's representation- how our city was being represented in the movie- drugs, killings, shootings, etc., etc., so I talked to Chuck, and he said the same thing. I talked to Sugar Bear. I talked to Ju Ju, and each one of them gave me their own thing- "This is garbage. This is not how we need to be represented."

I remember Sugar Bear said, "We're trying to stay away from that. We don't represent no drugs. We don't do that. We're trying to keep that out of our community." So, I said, "Well, F*ck that! We'll do our own movie. We don't need them to do a movie on us. Let's do our own movie. What do you think about that?" They said, "Yeah. That'd be interesting." I said, "I'll tell you what. Meet me at my office on Tuesday or Wednesday. (I forgot which day it was) and we can sit down and chop it up." So that day, I talked to my crew- Carol and Gerald and Gregory and I said, "Hey. What do you think about this idea?" And they said, "Ok. We can definitely do it, but it needs to be a cooperative venture where those guys in different bands be a part of it." And that makes it special, and initially, it was called "A Tribute to Go-Go" and the original flyer, and we tapped into people we had met along the way, like the Capital Center.

We had to talk them into having an all-Go-Go show because they had been frowning about bringing Go-Go to the Capital Center, and we told them that it's under control and it'll be a great event and you're not going to have any problems. We talked to the production crew there that ran the cameras because the Capital Center at the time was one of the few buildings that had a telescreen in the venue. So, they had a very experienced camera crew, and we discussed it with them as well. This is what we plan on doing. What do we need? What do you think? ... and they got on board. We also got involved with a sound company in Baltimore that does excellent sound, so we tied into them, but the main thing we did was each one of the groups Chuck Brown and the Soul Searchers, Rare Essence, Experience Unlimited, Little Benny, all of them had a vested stake into the project. One of our things was what your fee would have been, you're not going to charge us. It will be a part of the project itself, so we minimize our cost and all of the cost, the money, instead of paying you guys, will pay for the production, and we will share in the revenue that we make if we pull this off.

Back then, it was only VHS. They didn't have CDs then, and they didn't have DVDs then. So, each one had a share of it. They had a piece of it. And we brought on some of the younger groups that were very good with us; Hot Cold Sweat, Junkyard Band was one of them, so we filmed it. After we filmed it, we then had to edit it and turn it into a film. It was a 3-hour show, and back then, VHS's only taped 100 minutes or 99 minutes. So, we had to edit it down to fit and also chop it up to make it look like a show. And to be honest, the first two edits were horrible. Horrible! It was like amateur night. Then we had a guy who was working with us who was familiar with film and knew a little bit about it, and he brought in some graphics. We sat down in the studio in Baltimore, and to be honest, Carol, Gerald, and this guy named Pat Clark sat in that place in Baltimore daily, editing that video.

The order of the show is not how the show was on the video. As you know, Chuck Brown was the band for Scorpio, but Chuck Brown did not open the show, so that segment had to be edited. So, the sequence had a different flow to it. We were able to accomplish that. And the show did very well. We partnered with two radio stations- WOOK and WKYS- that were hot and somewhat involved in the Go-Go sound. We had local DJs emcee, and Gregory Hines, who was also one of our partners at the time, voiced over the show. Chris Thomas, we managed Chris Thomas at the time, so Chris Thomas, the Mayor of Rap City, was also a part of the project, and you can hear his voice in the intro of the video. It was like a mutual admiration society of arts, musicians, technicians, and families. Miss Mack and Annie Mack with Rare Essence. They were very instrumental in making sure that things ran smoothly, and collectively, we put it together.

And then we cut a deal with Douglas Records at the time because we'd heard all of the ghost stories of distribution and people not paying you, getting paid over 30 days or 60 days or 90 days. Our office was down at 11th and F Street over top of a shoe store. Douglas Records was right across the street, so we had a meeting with a guy named Lou Rosenfeld at Douglas. I said, this is what we'll do. We're going to press our own VHS, and we made some cassettes as well. And once you sell them, then you can get some more. We were exclusive with them. So, we went and got them pressed. We went out of town to get them pressed and came back with a truckload, and we delivered them. So, one day, Carol and I and I forgot who was with us. We were walking down F Street to get something to eat and saw a whole bunch of people in front of Douglas on the sidewalk and in the street.

I said, "I wonder what's going on." Douglas had Lou Rosenfeld put a big screen console TV in front of their window, and they ran the video on a loop so the video played over and over and over again. And videos were blowing out the door. We busted out laughing, walked down the street, got something to eat, and returned. We ended up selling a lot of videos. One of my biggest jokes was I got a call from Cathy Hughes, who had WOL at the time, and her joke to me was, "Darryll, the dope boys are looking for you." I said, "For what?" "Because you took all their money off the street. All the street money is buying that video!" That just made me laugh. I said, "Just don't tell them my address." And it did very well. That's the Go-Go Live story.

***Go-Go Live at the Capital Center was such a success in 1987 that Brooks
and company were approached to do Go-Go Live II.***
We got calls to do another one. Some of the people that we missed the
first time, we got the second time. We didn't really go after it as hard as
we did with the first one. We never packaged it. We never sold it. You
could only see it on television if you paid a couple of dollars. And that
was it. We ended up making a couple of other records with different
groups because everybody that had an idea to make a record was knocking
on our door. We spent a lot of money. We didn't know what we were
doing. And then, to be honest, I personally got fed up with different people
coming to my office, and I wasn't getting anything done, so I told my crew,
"Yo! I'm gonna find another tour to do.

Y'all can play this record stuff, but I'm gone." And I got another tour.
Everybody said, "Let's go!" and we jumped on another tour across the
country and didn't come back for several years. We just kept touring. And
what's really interesting is that I don't think I really grasped the impact of
Go-Go Live until maybe 10- 15 years – 20 years later. Number 1, I wasn't
socializing that much when I came back home when I came off the road.
Number 2, some of the guys who were adults that I helped with- their sons,
brothers, and sisters, I didn't know were glued to their televisions,
watching that video every day, watching the video over and over and over
and over again. I never really grasped that because I wasn't around.

So, I ended up being on one of those podcasts that Heartbeat did-
Heartbeat's Conga Hour because I was promoting [the annual R&B
concert] Summer Spirit Festival. And there was a room full of guys, and
Heartbeat started off the program. He said, "Unk, you don't know the
impact you made." And I said, "What are you talking about, Man?" This
particular time, he was at a car dealership. And there was a bunch of guys
sitting around the room, and each one of them kind of acknowledged my
being there. I said, "Hey, Hey. How are y'all doing?" And they said,
"You don't understand…"

Each one gave a story about how their brothers, cousins, the bands they
started, why some of them started the bands and why some of them played
congas, why some of them are guitar players, they took music in school
because their older brothers and sisters went to the concert. They heard so
much about it and saw it on tape. They wanted to emulate what their
brothers and sisters were doing or witnessing because they were live at the

event. And that started them to want to be in, to do music. [E]verybody told their story, and it was still astonishing to me the impact because when you are on your own trajectory, you don't get a chance to look from side to side or behind you to see what's going on because you're busy doing what you're doing. You're plowing the field that you're plowing. And you find out later, oh by the way, there's some ... those sprouts are growing up to be real trees, and they're bearing new fruit, and I had the opportunity to witness some of the people talking about what that had done in their lives. There were a lot of people bootlegging it. There were a lot of people when videos came out, and the different platforms came out, and PA Palace was printing them up like crazy. Sometimes we tried to stop it, and on the other side, we didn't care because it did nothing but embrace something that was positive that was manifested out of D.C., so if D.C. wanted it, let D.C. have it. It would be different if nobody cared about it. So, the whole one or two generations that grew up with that as their milepost.

I was never around. My crew in Tiger Flower, in G Street Express, and CD Enterprises managed Salt n Pepa for six or seven years. And Kid n Play. I was out in California with them doing movies. I wasn't home. You know what I mean? We had an office in Manhattan. When I was on the road with Heavy D. or Public Enemy. We did 3 Public Enemy tours. We did the Dope Jam tour. We did the Def Jam tour. We did the Def Comedy tour. We did the Shower of Stars. We were always gone. We took the Bar-Kays across the country.

We were in Australia and Japan with Salt n Pepa. I was managing Wayne Wonder. I wasn't here. And nobody was saying, "Hey, Darryll, this is what's going on here." I was a bachelor at that time. My family was gone. My daughter was in college, and then she graduated. My son was in Florida. None of my immediate family- my two kids- weren't around. My sister was running the ... she was Lieutenant Colonel at the Prince Georges County Detention Center- she ran the jail over there in Upper Marlboro. We weren't talking about concerts or what that tape meant. Carol was in Virginia or on the road with me. How would I have known? We didn't have social media like that. The D.C. Library, the Martin Luther King Library, has it. People have done movies with it. The three Go-Go movies that I've seen documentaries on Go-Go that I've seen all have got a piece of it and put it in their movies. It's like the highlights or pinnacles of the documentaries that they've done. I've been in a few of them.
I'm very proud of those things. That's why I ended up starting I Hear Ya

Entertainment. I reactivated the label, and we're doing a release of Junkyard's first single on October 20th (2022). I've got records on Sugar Bear. I've got records on Sirius Company. I've got records on We Are One Experience. So those are the things I'm doing now. It's all new music. We did videos. I did two Christmas videos. There's one Christmas video with We Are One and another with Sirius Company. I've got videos on Junkyard that are going to be released on the 20th. And videos on We Are One. They've got a Christmas video and also a regular video for "Feeling that You're Feeling." It's different doing it online. When we were doing records, we were going to New Jersey or Philly to get them pressed and sell them. Now you just… it comes online, and you might not get money for 100 years.

Chapter 6: Who Sampled Who?

A listing of some of the most sampled songs in go-go
In May 2012, just as the Beastie Boys were both celebrating their induction into the Rock and Roll Hall of Fame and mourning the death of Beastie Boy Adam "MCA" Yauch, the group was hit with a lawsuit filed by TufAmerica Inc./Tuff City. At the time, the company administered the rights to the music catalog of Trouble Funk.

"That's my publishing company, and that's their job to go after the money," Tony Fisher, the leader of Trouble Funk, explained at the time.

The suit alleged that Trouble Funk's "Drop the Bomb," released in 1982, was sampled in three Beastie Boys songs: "Hold it Now, Hit It," "The New Style," and "Shadrach." The filing also claimed that Trouble's "Say What?," also released in 1982, was sampled on Beastie Boys' "Car Thief."

Tuff City has bought rights to old songs and then filed suit against artists who have sampled these songs without permission. They have successfully enforced their copyrights for years.
Fisher shared, "We toured with Beastie Boys, and I really admired them. They opened for us. It was them, Red Hot Chili Peppers and Fishbone. When you sample other people's music, you have to pay for it. It's business."

At the time, Trouble Funk was also in litigation with State Property, a Philadelphia rap group led by Beanie Sigel and signed to Roc-A-Fella Records.

According to the website "WhoSampledWho?" many Go-Go bands have been sampled. The Soul Searchers' "Ashley's Roachclip," released in 1974, makes it into the Top 20 samples, coming in at number 11, according to WhoSampled.com. The song has been sampled 473 times—277 drum samples alone.
Go-Go fans know the influence that it has had on artists from all genres, but many people outside of D.C. may not realize that some of their favorite songs borrow from the music.

Below is a listing of some of the most-sampled songs in Go-Go.
Trouble Funk's "Pump Me Up" has been sampled 154 times. Here are

some of those 154 songs:

Song	Artist
Pump Up the Volume	M|A|R|R|S
If I Ruled the World	Kurtis Blow
What I'm After	Lords of the Underground
Pump Me Up	Will Smith
Teddy's Jam	Guy
The Boogie That Be	Black Eyed Peas
Jazzy Sensation	Afrika Bambaataa and the Jazzy 5
Pump Me Up	Grandmaster Melle Mel & the Furious Five
Too Funky	George Michael
Mega Mix III	2 Live Crew
Funky Piano	EPMD
Scratch Monopoly	T La Rock
Dance to My Ministry	Brand Nubian
Play That Funky Music	Vanilla Ice
Leave It Up to the Cut Professor	Doug E. Fresh & the Get Fresh Crew
In My House	Jeff Redd
Not Just Another Groove	Run DMC
Drop the Bomb	2 Live Crew
Why Should I Dog U Out?	George Clinton
I'm the Master	UTFO
Back to Basix	Kid 'N Play
The Music Ain't Loud Enough	DJ Kool
What the Hell You Come in Here For	DJ Kool

Trouble Funk's "Drop the Bomb" has been sampled 37 times.

Song	Artist
The New Style	Beastie Boys
Car Thief	Beastie Boys
Hold It Now, Hit It	Beastie Boys
Drop the Bomb	Brand Nubian
Da Bomb (Remix- The Explosive Mix)	Kriss Kross featuring Da Brat
Pump Me Up	Grand Master Melle Mel & the Furious Five

Power to the People	Public Enemy
Hittin' Switches	Erick Sermon
Don't Cry Big Girls	MC Lyte
4 Ever My Best	Stetsasonic
Back on Wax	Kid 'N Play
What the Hell You Come in Here For	DJ Kool
So Let the Fun Begin (TSAL Mix)	Stetsasonic

Trouble Funk's "Let's Get Small" has been sampled 31 times. A few are:

Song	Artist
Bitches Ain't Shit	Dr. Dre and Snoop Dogg feat. Daz Dillinger, Kurupt & Jewell
Criminal Minded	Boogie Down Productions
Party's Getting Rough	Beastie Boys
Hold It Now, Hit It	Beastie Boys
We Be Ballin' (Street Mix)	Ice Cube feat. Michael Jackson and Shaquille O'Neal
Beastie Groove	Beastie Boys

Trouble Funk's "So Early In the Morning" has been sampled 14 times. Here are a few:

Song	Artist
Ain't Nothin To It	K9 Posse
Arkade Funk	Tilt
Get Down	LL Cool J
OPP (Charming Radio Remix)	Naughty By Nature
What the Hell You Come in Here For	DJ Kool
It Takes Two (Remix by the Mixbusters)	Rob Base and DJ E-Z Rock

Trouble Funk's "Saturday Night Live From Washington, D.C. Part 2" was sampled 7 times. A few notable songs:

Song	Artist
Rock the Bells	LL Cool J
Rollin With Kid 'N Play	Kid 'N Play
I'll Take Your Man	Salt N Pepa

The Soul Searchers "Ashley's Roachclip" has been sampled 473 times. A few notable songs:

Song	Artist
Paid In Full	Eric B. & Rakim
Hey Young World	Slick Rick
Set Adrift on Memory Bliss	PM Dawn
Run's House	Run DMC
Girl You Know It's True	Milli Vanilli
Jack the Ripper	LL Cool J
Unbelievable	EMF
Come Undone	Duran Duran
Step Off	Grandmaster Melle Mel & the Furious Five
Baby Don't Forget My Number	Milli Vanilli
Jackin For Beats	Ice Cube
Nuff Respect	Big Daddy Kane
Sweet Thing	Mick Jagger
I Know You Got Soul (Richie Rich Mega Mix)	Eric B. & Rakim
Breakdown	T La Rock
The Power	Power Jam feat. Chill Rob G

Chuck Brown and the Soul Searchers' "Bustin' Loose" has been sampled 39 times.

Song	Artist
Hot In Herre	Nelly
Eric B. Made My Day	Eric B. & Rakim
I Ain't Mad at All	Public Enemy
Hit Squad Heist	EMPD
Who You Funkin With	Afrika Bambaataa & Soulsonic Force
Dangerous	LL Cool J

Chuck Brown and the Soul Searchers' "We Need Some Money" has been sampled 13 times.

Song	Artist
Rollin With Kid 'N Play	Kid 'N Play
Paid In Full (Derek B.'s Urban Respray)	Eric B. & Rakim
Dana Dane is Coming To Town	Dana Dane
I Need Money	Wreckx-N-Effect

The Soul Searchers' "Blow Your Whistle" was sampled 10 times.

Song	Artist
Tambourine	Eve feat. Swizz Beats
Who Stole the Soul	Public Enemy
Droppin Rhymes on Drums	Def Jef feat. Etta James

Junkyard Band's "Sardines" has been sampled 8 times.

Song	Artist
Clock Strikes (Remix)	Timbaland and Magoo feat. Mad Skillz
Invisbl Skratch Piklz vs. Da Klamz Uv Deth	Invisibl Skratch Piklz
The Maestro (Live)	Beastie Boys
God Made Me Funky	Def Jef
We're the Band	Stetsasonic
King Kumoniwanalei	Cut Chemist and Short Kut
The Jam	MC Zappa
When I Battle Part 2	Smoov Lyn

Rare Essence's "Overnight Scenario" has been sampled 2 times.

Song	Artist
Do It Again (Put Ya Hands Up)	Jay Z feat. Beanie Sigel and Amil
Scenario	Logic

Rare Essence's "Body Moves" has been sampled 1 time.

Song	Artist
Turntable Mix (Flash Got More Bounce)	Grandmaster Flash

Rare Essence's "Take Me Out to the Go-Go" has been sampled 1 time.

Song	Artist
Aww Skeet Skeet	Lil Jon and the East Side Boyz

Spotlight: Junkyard Band

Gone are the plastic 5-gallon buckets, the Quaker State oil cans, the hubcap rims, the plastic toy horns, and the red Toys R' Us keyboard with the 14 keys, but these items will never be forgotten by the talented group of young men that started about 40 years ago using this "junk" to make music.

After all, that junk is what, in 1980, gave these young men from the Barry Farms Housing Project in Southeast Washington, D.C., their name and their start as the Junkyard Band.

Reflecting on how it all started, lead talker Steven "Buggs" Herrion reveals, "[drummer] Heavy One (Willie Gaston) and I had a battle of the bands. Heavy One had his own band, and I had my own band, and we battled down in Barry Farms, and that's how we started. Heavy One's band out-cranked us, and that's when I got in my feelings, and then we came together and said that we should go on and combine both bands and make it Junkyard. I started Junkyard when I was 14 years old."

Over the years, Herrion and the others have enjoyed more success than most from their humble beginnings as basically street performers, ranging in age from 8-14, playing homemade instruments on the streets of D.C. to being signed to a record deal with Russell Simmons and Rick Rubin's Def Jam label while LL Cool J was on the label. Junkyard's biggest hits, "Sardines" and "The Word," were released on Def Jam in 1986. *Rolling Stone* magazine, at one time, had cited "Sardines" as the most popular Go-Go song of all time.

"To be signed at a young age, we were just young and having fun," Herrion says. We left all the business to [managers] Moe [Shorter] and Derrick [McCrae]. We were just out there having fun but being signed with Def Jam was big for us, and to be signed to them with LL Cool J was a big thing for us!"

Vernell "Winko" Powell states, "During Def Jam, it was Me [congas], Buggs [lead talker], Pratt [vocals], Little Pop, Chung Young [keyboards] and Baker [keyboards], Heavy One [drums] and Footloose [buckets]. Chung Young played the keyboards with Bake. That's where the synthesizer came from. It came from Chung. He was from Thailand. His family was from Thailand."

Junkyard appeared in the movie "D.C. Cab" in 1983 and then, in 1988, they were on-screen alongside rap pioneers Run DMC in the movie "Tougher Than Leather." Locally, they appeared in a 1984 television commercial for the then-popular men's clothing store Cavalier.

Only two original members remain with the group today- Steven "Buggs" Herrion and Vernell "Winko" Powell. Tragically, of the original members, 3 are no longer with us- Willie "Heavy One" Gaston, Shelton "Shorty Pop" Watkins, and Derrick "Lil Derrick" Ingram.

As for the longevity of the band's success, which is still clearly a fan favorite, Herrion believes that the departed members would have loved it. "Heavy One would love it for advancing our music and fulfilling our dream. Derrick would have loved it because he was a bounce-beat king. He used to do the pop for us down at 19th and M (Streets), so I know he would love it now. Pop would have loved it too."

Jason Lane, who played keyboards, elaborates, "We had a brotherhood and a bond, and even though those three guys are gone, they're still a part of us. Regardless of if we live 70 years and we are still doing this in 20 more years, they will still be a part of us."
Every band member credits manager Moe Shorter as the glue that has held it together throughout the years. Shorter had stepped away from managing the day-to-day operations for a time but always made himself available to the band.

Lane reiterates, "Thanks to Moe Shorter and Big Derrick because here were a bunch of young men who could have gone the wrong way, and we're talking all these years later, and we're still here. And we've lost a lot of young people along the way, so big thanks to them because they didn't have to take their time."

And the specific lessons learned and instilled in these men at such a young age still resonates with the band members as some have gone on to play with other bands, and some have stepped away from music altogether. Darrell "Blue Eye" Arrington shares, "Because of Moe, I know what I know. That's why I don't take any mess. He made us business savvy."

The band has splintered over the years to form several new incarnations of the band, such as Art of Junk, JY Band, and J-Mob.
The band has played at the legendary Apollo Theatre and the Kennedy Center and has continued to perform for fans for decades, but the group members still have fond members of JYB's earliest days.

Daniel Muhammed, formerly Daniel Baker, shares, "It was a fun time. It was real fun and I still think about it now a lot of times. What I liked about it is that we would go out here every weekend and have something to do. We weren't around the neighborhood and bored like we used to be. We had something to do. We would go to 19th and M or Georgetown, put the bucket out, and make some money. We'd go to Marshall's and get our own school clothes. We might get $100 apiece from making it on 19th and M or Georgetown. 19th and M was like our money maker. We'd do that to do Christmas shopping stuff like that. It wasn't a heavy load on our parents- our clothes and stuff. We'd have our own money to buy it, which was cool. Now that you think about it, it was real cool.

Being signed to Def Jam was a cool thing for us. We used to go to New York maybe twice a month to play at the Pyramid Club, Palladium Club, or Danceteria—one of those 3 clubs. And then Def Jam put out 'The Word' and 'Sardines.' We recorded down here, and they took the recordings up to New York and finished it there. That was Rick Rubin that did the mix. It was fun. We felt like we were going to start getting rich. Go-Go itself didn't push a lot out there. Of course, back in those times, it was more original. Now these times it's more listening to the radio and playing more radio music and stuff like that.

I left Junkyard in 2008. I wanted to do something different. I wanted to do more studio work and maybe some tours. Now, I work at the Smithsonian. I don't even know if I have the energy to do it (music) anymore.

Chapter 7: Family Affair

The Go-Go community is a close-knit community; sometimes, it is a literal family business. Several families have been involved in the genre for generations. Some of these family "dynasties" got their start during the pioneering days of Go-Go and have family members playing in bands to this day. These families include:

- The Wellman/ Coleman family, who have been involved in the creation of Go-Go with Chuck Brown and the Soul Searchers;
- The Mack/Thomas/Davidson family, which was firmly rooted in Rare Essence,
- The Busey family, of the Busey Brothers and Pump Blenders fame;
- The Freeman family, who go back three generations in their contributions to music in Washington, D.C.; and
- The West family turned a family band, Mass Extension, into the touring band for none other than James Brown, the King of Soul.

Each family has a unique story about their entry into the music business, their love for Go-Go, and how they successfully mixed business and family affairs over the years.

The Wellman/Coleman Family (as told by "Too Tall" Steve Coleman) ***

In the early 1960s, **Frank Wellman** learned to play the drums. In 1966, he partnered with his friend and neighbor Chuck Brown (guitar) and John Euell (bass) to form the Soul Searchers. After adding a fourth member, Lloyd Pinchback (flute), the band began playing locally, benefitting from the tremendous live support of Frank's nine sisters, five brothers, parents, and close family friends.

Frank's parents, James and Mamie Wellman, lived in Fairmont Heights, MD, and Frank stored a set of his drums on their front porch. Many family members learned to play drums on that drum set on the Wellman front porch.

After honing their percussive skills on grandma's front porch, many

90

Wellman family members joined or formed bands in their youth, following in the footsteps of the family idol, **Ricky "Tricky Sugarfoot" Wellman,** who at 13 years old joined his first band, The Jaguars, in the late 60s.

After The Jaguars, Ricky went on to play with a who's who of notable artists, including Miles Davis, Carlos Santana, Chuck Brown and the Soul Searchers, Peaches and Herb and EU, to name a few.

Other family members lent their skills to several Go-Go bands, while others opted for the more traditional bands. Family members who contributed to the Go-Go culture include **Maurice "Ghost" Wellman,** who played with several bands, Go-Go and non-Go-Go, including Groovemakers, TAACK, **EU,** and Raw. **Steve "Too Tall" Coleman** played the trumpet with Young Sound, Fate's Destiny, and the Go-Go bands **EU, Redds and the Boys, and Chuck Brown and the Soul Searchers. Syeed Mahdi** continues to play with Prophecy. **Dwayne "Kiggo" Wellman** played with **Guess Band, Pump City Groovers, EU, Little Benny and the Masters, and Chuck Brown. Wali "Gogo Wali" McJunkins** played with **Guess Band, Physical Wunder, Pure Elegance, and Pump City Groovers,** and **Tynetta Mahdi** played congas with **Royalty Band.**

Several members of the family did not play for Go-Go bands, including **Barry "Bootleg" Wellman,** who played with Stratocasters, Lil 'Rock, System 6, Expression, New Perspective, C Barnes Project, Monte Tillman Project, and Diversified Motown Group.

Vincent Coleman played percussion with System 6 and Expression, while **Glen "Prescott" Ellison**, who grew up in Chicago, played with Arrested Development, Mi Phi Mi, Brian McKnight, Stevie Wonder, Earth, Wind & Fire, and Justin Timberlake. **Darnell Wellman** and **Mustapha Mahdi** also honed their skills on Grandma's front porch.

In the mid-70s, Steve's group Fate's Destiny held band practice in the garage at the Wellman compound, where other budding local musicians would often visit and hang out to fellowship. During one of those rehearsals, a young local drummer, Raymond Calhoun, sat in with Fate's Destiny. Unexpectantly, Ricky just happened to stop by Grandma's (as we all did in those days), joining us in the garage. It was a day to remember as Ricky and Raymond took turns on the drums, both playing their hearts out. Needless to say, Raymond never came back to the garage but went to join the Gap Band and penned their colossal hit "Outstanding."

The Mack/Thomas/Davidson Family, as told by Devin Davidson (Quentin "Footz" Davidson's son)
***

Rare Essence was conceived by Quentin "Footz" Davidson Sr. and a group of his childhood friends: Michael "Funky Ned" Neal, Andre "Whiteboy" Johnson, and John "Big Horn" Jones. As a child prodigy, Davidson spent hours playing the drums in his urban home in Washington Highlands, in Southeast Washington, D.C. His mother, Annie Lee Mack-Thomas, tried to enroll him in drumming lessons but soon found out that there was nothing more for him to learn about the instrument. Influenced by the sounds of Parliament and Chuck Brown, of course, the group of middle schoolers of St. Thomas Moore named themselves "Connection Unlimited" and began playing at local events and talent shows. During early management, they switched the name to "The Young Dynamos" before deciding upon the name "Rare Essence," which Davidson named after seeing a magazine ad for a perfume called "Essence Rare."

Quentin Davidson's older brother, James "Funk" Thomas, was already involved in the local music scene as Chuck Brown's DJ, known back then as a street jockey. Thomas studied Brown's music and showmanship. At shows, Brown would challenge Thomas to engage with the crowd between sets- talking to them and getting them hyped. This is where Thomas began to craft his own style as a performer. In the early years of Rare Essence's formation, he used his music industry knowledge to assist them with management.

As the buzz of the neighborhood band grew, members began to audition and flock in. Notable names include Jungle Boogie, Little Benny, Michael Muse, Rory "DC" Felton, and Davidson's cousin, David Green. With this came more responsibility in overseeing the band's business. Rare Essence built in-house representation with Davidson's and Thomas' mother, Annie Lee Mack-Thomas, better known as Ms. Mack, their grandmother, Mattie Lee Mack, better known as Miss Sis, and Margarine Neal, Michael Neal's mother. Together, these women oversaw the business operations and dedicated time, money, and resources to get their sons' visions off the ground.

Mattie Thomas, known as "Miss Sis," was the band's treasurer. With an 8th-grade education and being the daughter of slaves, she worked as an elevator operator at the post office. She saved up money to buy a house in Washington Highlands, becoming the first black family to do so. She believed so deeply in her family that she dedicated money to aid them in buying equipment, instruments, uniforms, and eventually a second home that they would use as an office and rehearsal space right next door. Soon 851 and 853 Xenia Street SE became a sound of its own.

Sis' daughter Annie Lee Mack-Thomas, Ms. Mack, and Mrs. Neal served as the band's managers. Since the start of their shows, Ms. Mack would stand front and center at the front door overseeing everyone that came out to see their band perform. She was a no-nonsense woman who viewed the band as an extension of her family. As a passionate mother, she held her sons and bandmates to a very high standard and viewed them the musical conglomerate they are today, even back then. Together Ms. Mack, Sis, and Mrs. Neal nurtured the band's musical aspirations. Whether it was ensuring that promoters adequately compensated the band or fending off the evils of the D.C. streets during the crack epidemic, they were loving women who became the face of the brand and the music.

Footz would dedicate his brain power to push the brand of Rare Essence. His aspirations were for Go-Go to become worldwide. He owned an arcade on Florida Avenue called "Mack Attack Arcade," where he played Go-Go music outside to attract the youth. He branded the band so that each member was a star on their own, whether it be Go-Go Mickey or Donnell Floyd. He even gave money to a young Anwan "Big G' Glover so that he could start his own band, which would later be called "Backyard Band."

The Busey Family, as recounted by Keith "Showtime" Busey
***
Clifton, George, Herman, and Anna Busey were siblings born in the 1930s in Washington, D.C. George, Herman, and Anna were all involved in music. George Busey played the organ and was a vocalist and used these talents to play with several bands as they were booked up and down the East Coast. He also had a group called Busey's Soul Blenders, and they released "Soul Power." This hit record paved the way for family name recognition and opened many doors for the family.

Herman Busey played the guitar, bass, and keyboard and was also a vocalist. He sat in with the group The Orioles from his mid-20s to his 30s. Herman also formed a gospel group and was in a group with "Sir" Joe

93

Quarterman called The Scholars. Quarterman went on to have a hit song, "(I Got) So Much Trouble in My Mind," with Sir Joe Quarterman and Free Soul in 1973.

Anna Busey also played the organ in church and was a gospel singer. Although George and Herman never played in a band together due to differing musical tastes, Anna and Herman and two of Anna's daughters had a gospel group and toured throughout the East Coast.

Herman Busey had two sons, Keith, and Clifton, AKA "Boo," that were very interested in music. That may have come from watching their father performing on stage when they were young.

Keith shares, "My father and mother took us to a James Brown concert at the Howard Theater when we were young, and the line was wrapped around the block. That's when Clifton and I both knew what we wanted to do. It was in either 1967 or 68. Around that time, when we were between 6 and 8 years old, my father bought Clifton a drum set and a bass and amp for me. We practiced every day. We wanted to make Dad proud."

Since Herman played the guitar, Clifton played drums, and Keith bass, they would be the entertainment at family functions. Keith says the first song he ever learned on the bass was Stevie Wonder's "I Was Made to Love Her."

George Busey had two sons following in their father's footsteps – Andre and George Jr., also called Georgie. Andre was considerably older than George and, unbeknownst to Keith and Clifton, he was teaching George.

Keith recalls, "Andre was an incredible keyboard player. He would walk about 20 blocks to play over at our house since all of the instruments were there. Andre played a big part in all of it. He was the oldest male cousin, about 5 years older. Clifton was 2 years younger than me, and then George was a couple of years younger than Clifton.

In 1971-72 the Busey Brothers 4 was formed and named after the Jackson 5, their idols, and James Brown. The band consisted of Keith Busey on bass, Clifton John "Boo" Busey on drums, George Busey on keyboards/organ, and Kevin Ricardo Wilson as the lead vocalist. Kevin was the grandson of Anna Busey. Kevin later took the name of Cassanova Kev, the Prince of Go-Go. The group played R&B hits but also original material.

"Our first show was on television. It was during the Clothes-A-Thon where they would give away clothes to people in need. Uncle George got them to let us play on the show. We were like phenoms. The house I grew up in at 609 Sheridan Street, NW, became the practice house. Mobs of girls would be at the window watching us practice. We were spoiled as kids with all these girls that liked us," Keith describes.

Between 1974 and 1979, there were always block parties on Sheridan Street with the Busey Brothers 4 as headliners, Mass Extension, the Mighty Peacemakers, and Petworth.

Due to George Sr.'s connections, as kids, the Busey Brothers 4 were able to play in clubs where they were too young to play, much less get into. George Sr. saw to it that they could play by putting on kiddie cabarets. At the time, 1974-75, they were the youngest band on the scene. They opened for many bands, including their "big brother band" Black Heat. The bass player, Chip, for Black Heat was also a vocalist and became Keith's mentor. George was about 8 years old, and Andre was responsible for showing him his parts.

These kiddie cabarets were the vehicle that got their name famous. According to Keith, "George Sr. and Herman decided to take the Busey 4 and go into the studio to record some original songs. They felt so good about what they had recorded that George and Herman got in the car, drove all the way from D.C. to Detroit, straight to Motown, and met with some executives there. They loved it. The feedback was that they needed to work on the vocals and then come back. This was exciting news to them!"

Kevin's father was a tailor and made all their outfits. They had eight different outfits and practiced in front of the mirror. They were also taught to always look at the Exit sign in the back of the room and smile at the Exit sign so that the crowd thinks you are smiling at them. If people see that you enjoy it, they will also enjoy it.

During this time, the popularity of the Busey Brothers 4 was growing. One of their biggest shows (pre-Go-Go) was doing 4 songs at Anacostia Park with the big groups of the time- Father's Children, Leadhead, and 100 Years Time. They were slated to play right in the middle of the show.

They played all originals, and when they were finished, they had to run to George Sr.'s van because they were mobbed.

The next school year, due to George Sr.'s connections, the Busey Brothers 4 were able to play at the 9:00 am high school assemblies at Eastern, McKinley Tech, and Coolidge.

Between 1975 and 1976, Andre Busey eventually joined the group. The sound became more mature, and they could play more challenging music. This was when the group's name changed to The Busey Brothers. They played more clubs and cabarets. Up to now, the group never had a guitar player and hadn't planned on having one until they saw and heard James Bell, and he was so good that he was the first non-family member to join the group.

In this period, Keith was 16, Clifton was 14, Kevin was 14, and George was 11 or 12. Again, due to George Sr.'s connections, just as they were entering high school, they became Little Royal's band touring with him up and down the East Coast. Little Royal was supposedly James Brown's half-brother.

Keith reminisces, "In high school and junior high, we played in the D.C. parks under Mayor Marian Barry. We earned $187 every 2 weeks. We saw all the other guys in the other bands in line on payday, also picking up their checks. Keep in mind that we are from uptown. Rare Essence is from Southeast. They had a gig playing on the [show] mobile in Emery Heights for Georgia Avenue Day. We had never seen them before. They came onstage, and I was ready to quit when I saw them. They were that good. They had a full band. There were only 4 or 5 of us. That's how good and polished Ms. Mack had them. We thought we were polished!"

Around 1977-78, Keith and Clifton's parents saw that this affected their sons' grades and held them out until their grades picked up.
"It was sort of like a family rivalry. Kevin and George went on to become the Pump Blenders and Clifton and I were still the Busey Brothers. Andre stayed with the Busey Brothers. Our parents were very strict, so Clifton and I were very disciplined and put a lot into it."

In 1978-79 when Keith was in high school, Go-Go was really starting to take shape. In 1977, groups like the Commodores with their live version of "Brick House" and "Holy Ghost" by the Bar-Kays, allowed for more percussion. Music itself was changing.

"It was great to drive around throughout the city and see your name on a poster. Imagine being in high school and seeing that!"

When Keith was in high school, they played every Thursday night at 4th and Rhode Island Avenue at the Maverick Room (which was also Disco Tres Chic) with Experience Unlimited (E.U.). They were like the little brother group to them. This was in 1978-79, when E.U.'s members included Gregory "Sugar Bear" Elliott, Vernon McDonald, Hunter, and Young Boy Lee. This was even before the song "E.U. Freeze." Frog used to sing "Knock Em Out Sugar Ray."

Keith remembers getting a call from Ms. Mack, who wanted the Busey Brothers to open for Rare Essence down at Northwest Gardens. They were already booked, but 2 weeks later, they played with Rare Essence and E.U. at Sugar Ray's gym. The show went so well that they played at Club LeBaron with Rare Essence and E.U.

During this same time, the Pump Blenders started to gain traction. There would soon be a change in direction for the Busey Brothers. The interest in continuing with the Busey Brothers had faded, so Keith and Clifton entered the service from 1981 to 1984. The Pump Blenders and Go-Go were in full effect by then. In 1984, the Pump Blenders recorded an album with Reo Edwards called "Work That Body."

Once Keith and Clifton returned home, at the urging of friends and fans, they resurrected The Busey Brothers, and their first show was with Reality Band, which was popular then. It was early 1985.
"During this time, Cassanova Kevin quit the Pump Blenders. He got into drugs and played with the Busey Brothers for a few shows. His last show was in May 1986."

They were very good friends with Gregory "Googie" Burton of Reality, a fantastic bassist and sound engineer. He ran sound for the Busey Brothers that night at their show at Coolidge. It was a great show. The resurrection of the Busey Brothers was short-lived as the interest again fizzled out. Their last show was at the Silver Spring Armory in 1986.

The Pump Blenders were still going strong as one of the popular bands of the time, and George Sr. called for Keith to join the group. Clifton, however, did not join. Most of the time, as fans will remember, George Sr. always brought the Pump Blenders on stage. As time went on, Clifton would share those duties with George Sr.

Keith became a full-fledged member of the Pump Blenders by 1987. In 1988, they went into Rockville, Maryland's Omega Studio, to record their next album, "I Want You Back."

"Uncle George was the manager, and band members came and went. Kevin was with us when we recorded in 1988, but the addiction took his career after that. At this time, Rare Essence was eating up all of the spots in D.C., so George took the Pump Blenders out of D.C. and played exclusively in Maryland. Many groups had to go through Uncle George to get on shows with the Pump Blenders in Montgomery County, Frederick, and Hagerstown, Maryland."

In the early 90s, Kevin was able to straighten out his life. He was working, got married, and had 2 children. This kept him focused on family life, and he was a dedicated husband and father. Sadly, he passed away from leukemia at 35 in 1977.

In the mid-90s, Keith left the Pump Blenders. Soon after, George also left the group. There have been several incarnations of the Pump Blenders since that time. With no Busey's in the group, drummer Gerald Brooks has kept it all together over the decades.

For a time, Keith stopped playing music altogether and decided to change direction. He started meeting people like entertainers Captain Fly and Greg Cooper and decided to return to his roots, focusing more on the R&B side of music. He became a musical director and played with groups such as HALO in 1997, opening for major acts like some of the old 70s soul superstars. Other acts had an interest in Keith playing bass.

Keith created the Unit Band in 1997. They were gaining notoriety as a great, steady backup band for the groups coming through D.C. They were also working with D.C. legends Al Johnson and Jean Carne.

By 2000, Keith Wilder, one of the founders of the group Heatwave, came to see Keith play and hired the Unit Band to become Heatwave. They went on the road with Heatwave. In 2002, Keith got a call from the legendary Stylistics, and he continues to tour with them on and off. In 2006, he became the musical director for the 70s Soul Jam with groups like Ray, Goodman, and Brown, Blue Magic, the Emotions, Jean Carne,

Carl Carlton, and the Jones Girls. As of 2023, he continues to work with the Stylistics and is still the musical director for the 70s Soul Jam.

In March of 2003, George "Uncle George" Busey passed away. Andre Busey passed away at the age of 56 in 2012. Clifton "Boo" Busey died from a freak accident at 49 in 2012.

The Freeman/Scott Family, as told by Milton "Go-Go Mickey" Freeman, Brion "BJ" Scott, and "Lil Mickey" Freeman
***

The Freeman/ Scott Family is another legacy family in the D.C. Music Business. Milton "Go-Go Mickey" Freeman has been playing music for the past 50+ years, starting when he was just 2 years old in 1969 playing the drums. His father was a bit of a legend with his bands, Mickey and the Blazers and Dipped in Funk. Two of Go-Go Mickey's sons, Brion "BJ" Scott and "Lil Mickey" Freeman have also made names for themselves on the Go-Go scene as notable percussionists like their father.

Big Mickey spent the latter part of the 60s and early 70s playing in clubs around D.C. A few clubs were The Part 3 in Northwest, a club on Kennedy Street Northwest called Jackie Lee's Lounge, and The Manhole in Southeast. Both Dipped in Funk, and Mickey and the Blazers were 4-piece groups, with the core being a lead guitar, bass guitar, drums, and a saxophone player with different female vocalists. Mickey did most of the singing, and he also played guitar. They played every night and drew a crowd wherever they performed, playing whatever was popular in the 60s and 70s. It's been said that Lil Mickey looks just like his grandfather. Big Mickey may have been a bit "thicker," but they share a face.

"My father started playing at age 15 in 1962. My father passed away when I was 11, so he was playing until his passing in 1978," clarifies Go-Go Mickey. "My father started me on the drums even though he was a guitar player. Some of my favorite memories are going to different kiddie cabarets with him and having the girls chasing me around the club at the kiddie cabarets. My father played with James Brown for a minute. He couldn't read music, so that was a short gig for him. He also played with the Four Clovers. Chuck Brown and Bobby Parker played with my Pops. My mother played piano in Church, where I was every Sunday. She made me fall in love with James Brown."

99

Mickey shares, "My sons Brion, Lil Mickey, and Malik play music. They all play timbales. Brion and Lil Mickey play congas, and Brion also plays bass. Lil Mickey knows the business and his way around the studio and production. I play just what you've seen on stage. I tried guitar after my father died, but it was too much for me."

His grandmother got him his first set of congas from Chuck Levin's. As the story goes, told by both Mickey and Gregory "Googie" Burton, founder of Reality Band, in 1980, Mickey was just a kid, outside playing and throwing rocks. He heard music, knocked on Googie's door, and asked to come in. There was a set of congas, and Mickey asked if he could play. Googie gave him something to play, and Mickey played it and added his own twist to it. Googie told Mickey that he could join the band if he had his own set of congas. Mickey went home and told his grandmother, who called Googie on the phone. She asked if he had said Mickey could join the band if he had his congas. Googie said this was true, so Mickey's grandmother took him to Chuck Levin's that day and bought him his first set of congas. Reality Band had their new conga player.

This paid off as Go-Go Mickey has had an amazing career and is revered by his peers as one of the best. He has played with Rare Essence, Ayre Rayde, Redds and the Boys, Reality Band, Team Familiar, and Still Familiar, and is currently with Push Play and District Kings. It was 1984 when Mickey joined Rare Essence, which was like his dream come true. Some of his very best moments were with Rare Essence, but also some not so good.

He remarks, "My best moments would be with Rare Essence and some bad. We used to travel playing with all the rappers. I mean all the heavy hitters. Then comes the dark clouds of losing band members. Footz was the main reason that I got into RE. It was a huge loss."

Like his father, Lil Mickey started very young as well. It was sometime between 1991 and 1992 when he was just 3 or 4.

"I got interested just being around music, hearing pops play all the old PA tapes and it being in me, honestly," explains Lil Mickey.
BJ recalls that in 2002-2003, he officially started playing in concert band in middle school. However, he got his unofficial musical start in 1998 when he got his first drum set from his dad. He was about 9 years old.

Both BJ and Lil Mickey say that their father was the person who interested them in music, although BJ also cites Michael Jackson as a significant influence on him at a young age. He was also musically influenced by Mavin Gaye and Stevie Wonder as well.

Lil Mickey, on the other hand, although being influenced by his father like BJ, credits his influences as "Trouble Funk, a lot of the 70s/80s/90s music as well including Quincy Jones, Bobby Hutcherson, Frank Sinatra, Louis Armstrong, Jimi Hendrix, Dennis Chambers, Sheila E., Tito Puente, The Neptunes, Pharrell, Timbaland, and Swizz Beats.

BJ shares that the first band he ever played with was a school band called Expanding Horizons, and he was 14 years old. Little Mickey played the trumpet in the elementary school band at 10 and played in his first Go-Go band, Mad Collision Band, at 13. Besides being a member of Mad Collision Band, Lil Mickey has been a member of EU, Team Familiar, and Suttle.

BJ has been a member of PAB, MCB, Fatal Attraction, Faze2, Rare Essence, L.O.U.D., QLICK, Top5, Round of Applause, UCB, Trouble Funk, and Sirius Company. He has filled in with Backyard Band, TCB, L!SSEN, Northeast Groovers, The Chuck Brown Band, EU, and WHAT Band.

While BJ shares that his favorite band to play with is Rare Essence, Lil Mickey has enjoyed playing with all the bands he has played with and states that they were all good for different reasons. Onstage, BJ plays congas and timbales/ Roto toms, but off stage, he can play the 5-string bass, piano, and drums. Lil Mickey plays drums, all percussion, and trumpet, although he says he is a little rusty on the trumpet.

When people compare BJ to his father or brother, he shares that people do it all the time, but he takes it in stride and gets used to it. Lil Mickey reveals that it's annoying when people try to compare them with each other. The three have sometimes played together on the same stage, but neither Mickey, BJ, nor Lil Mickey feels they are competing. BJ says that the thought has never crossed his mind, while Lil Mickey explains that "outside of friendly competition, I'm focused on something different."

Go-Go Mickey shares this sentiment about his sons, "BJ and Lil Mick are both smart. They know what they want, and they know their worth. At their ages, they know more than I did. I just wanted to play. They know how to deal with certain situations. I always taught them that you can't get on stage for free. They used to. I know I did."

Besides playing music, Lil Mickey has a passion for photography. He shares, "I enjoy music and photography because it's all art. Art is how we decorate space. Music is how we decorate time. The camera is just another instrument. Musical rhythm. Visual rhythm. Timing in music and recording of the time. Paint a picture. Tell a story. It's all a canvas."

If BJ were to give any advice to his father, I would tell him to "always be open-minded musically." Lil Mickey adds, "The only musical advice that I would give Pops is that Anything is possible. Even when you think it can't be done, it can. There's a way around it. Dig into the business side of things deeper. Adapt to the new sound- revamp and re-innovate. Try something different."

As for advice for BJ, Lil Mickey shares, "Get more into the production side of things and be more creative. Spend an hour a day creating. Mix both live instruments and digital together. Learn the music business as much as you can."

For Lil Mickey, BJ advises that "it's ok to be yourself but study the ones before you." BJ and Lil Mickey have some "best memories" with their father. BJ's favorite memory with his father is hanging out with him every day in his 6th-grade year, while Lil Mickey loved going to the recording studio with him when he was a kid.

Lil Mickey figured out that his father was a "big deal" when they would go places, and everyone would have a story to tell. BJ, on the other hand, was very young when he first saw his father on stage, and it was then that he knew that his father was a "big deal."
Big Mickey left a legacy through his son and grandsons, and the Freeman/ Scott family continues performing onstage and captivating crowds. Hopefully, the next generations will continue entertaining crowds for years.

The West Family, shared by Gerald West
Another prominent musical family hailing from D.C., 13th Street in NW to be exact, would be the West Family. In 1978, brothers Geoffrey "Boogie" West and Sheldon West formed a neighborhood band with Geoffrey's best

friend, Michael Lynch.

By 1979, the band was now a full-fledged Go-Go band called Mass Extinction, and some of the members had been replaced with West family members. Geoffrey "Boogie" West was on keyboards, Sheldon on vocals, Thomas West on percussion, Darrell West on bass guitar, Gerald West on lead guitar, Victoria West on vocals, and Gary West on percussion.

The family released several popular songs, "Have Some Fun," "48 Boogie," and the wildly popular song and dance craze "Happy Feet."
The band was later renamed Mass Extension due to some legalities. They were the first group signed to Island Records.

"We released our Go-Go classic 'Happy Feet' in 1985. 'Happy Feet' was one of the major reasons that attracted Island Records to the Go-Go scene and sparked the movie Good to Go. 'Happy Feet' was a dance phenomenon that went clear across the country. It was a national, and international hit that charted in the UK." states Gerald West.

He continues, "In 1986, we were hired to perform at Princeton University for Brooke Shields."

Gerald West explains, "In 1991, we performed at The Rayburn building in Washington, D.C., and James Brown would receive the key to the city on this particular day. We were so honored to perform and introduce our music to the Godfather of Soul. When we finished performing that day, James Brown invited us to South Carolina for an audition, and he signed us on the spot, and we became the New JBs, his backup band as well as backing us as a separate entity."

The majority of the family left to tour. Darrell, Sheldon, and Victoria were vocalists, Gary was on drums, Gerald played lead guitar, and Geoffrey was on the keyboards. They brought along two additional family members, Brian West on bass guitar and Greg West, who joined "Boogie" on the keyboards.

"In 1992, we appeared on Bet Video Soul with James Brown and Donnie Simpson."

After the death of James Brown, the family came home, and several members of the family- Geoffrey and Gerald decided to form the group,

The West Mob, which has a powerful fan following and continues to play.

Spotlight: Khari Pratt on Northeast Groovers

Northeast Groovers was another important group that changed the landscape of Go-Go music in the mid-late 80s. The group not only released nationally known hits "The Water," "Booty Call," and "Van Damme" but also developed several of the top musicians still playing in this genre today in and out of the Washington, D.C., area. Khari Pratt, founder of Northeast Groovers, discusses the group's humble beginnings, how they all learned to maneuver through a business that did not have a blueprint and still come out on top, and how they still command crowds decades later.
***

We started in about 1987. A lot of the people that were in the group that most people saw were already gone. Many of the originals were already gone by the time we hit. A bunch of my friends from the neighborhood were original members. They weren't real musicians, so eventually, we had to move forward and get some new people in here, and that's when we took off.

We all learned together. I came to my mother because I started the group with Tom (Tommy Guns). I came to her, and I had this idea that I wanted to be in a Go-Go band. I wanted to have a band, and she said, "Ok, sure, ok, whatever." And then, eventually, we started to sound pretty good, and she said, "Ok, if you are serious about it, I'll manage you." She didn't have any manager experience or anything like that. Of course, she had a job and dealt with people, but we grew together in a lot of everything Northeast did, and she did as a manager. The whole band, the management, security, we all just grew together. It just went from there, and it took off. My mother didn't have any musical background, but my father did. He plays bass guitar, lead guitar, and my brother plays drums. One year for Christmas, he bought my brother some drums and he put a guitar in my hand and that was it.

I think each band member had a particular group they liked. Tom and I were real Junkyard fans. A couple of the other guys really liked Chuck Brown, and then you had a couple of RE fans, so initially, when we first started, it was like this big mash-up of all the bands we liked. I kind of idolized Funky Ned, who played with Rare Essence, so it's what my style is more like. Initially, it was this big mash up and then we started to come into our own. As we got different members in, we had better musicians from other areas; that's why we initially called ourselves Northeast Groovers because all of us were from Northeast. Then you know Hug was from Southeast, and Chris and Kurt, the first rapper, was from Bladensburg and Seat Pleasant, so we started to come into our own, and it just fell together.

One of our first shows was over in Northeast at a rec center. We played outside, and I remember Backyard being there. I didn't know who they were at the time. It wasn't until we started performing together at WUST that I began to know who those guys were, but initially, I remember these two real tall guys on the front line, and yeah, they came out, if not the same year, maybe shortly after. It wasn't much longer. We kinda all just grew up together.

For a few years, it was us (NEG and BYB being new on the scene). Backyard started to hit real good, then you had Pleasure, Hot Cold Sweat was still going good, Huck a Bucks came out a few years later, Precise. Back then, there were a lot of good bands. We were pulling, Backyard was pulling, and Junkyard was pulling (crowds). It just seemed like it was really good for Go-Go. You could put one of those shows together, and it is just us and Junkyard, one of those Wilmer's Park shows with us, Junkyard, Rare Essence, EU, and it was just like this sea of people. It just doesn't seem like it's like that anymore.

I love the stage. I love the stage and I love the reaction that we get from the people other than the fighting part. The music seems like it's an instant dance. I mean, as soon as you hear the beat, you can't help but dance to it. I think that's the part I miss the most—the crowds. I love to be onstage. Mambo Sauce gave me that because we had a very large following. Unfortunately, it's not in our hometown, but we have a large following.

In the 90s, Northeast Groovers added two sexy on-stage dancers, Sunshine and Juicy, who not only became a staple of the band's shows but created a lot of controversy in the genre.

All of that was Pearl (Ms. Pratt). We did a show at a school off Route 1 or 301and Sunshine and Juicy attended that school and we saw them dancing in the crowd. We had that thing where we would let people onstage, and I guess she saw something when they got up onstage. She said, "We can use this." They started coming, and then the next thing you know, they started coming all the time, and then it was like they're here all the time and they look nice, so we started to buy them... like my mother would buy them bathing suits and different outfits to put them in. I think it got real carried away because the women in the crowd wanted to compete with them, so those were the ones that were just completely going naked, and it's like, ok, these girls are getting all this attention. These girls had on a bathing suit, and the next thing was to take it all off.

At the time, there was a lot of things going on in Go-Go that would be considered degrading. Everybody tried to put that drumstick thing on us and that wasn't us. (The Rare Essence Pool Party event) We put the girls up there, but they weren't up there to just take their clothes off, their outfits. When you look at the videos, they did the same dances that the band did. I can't say we stood in the mirror and choreographed it, but everybody was on the same accord. A lot of the girls in the crowd got up there and wanted to get naked and get on the floor and take it somewhere else, but initially, when we had the dancers, it was, everything was, we had the same little steps we did the Van Damme dance together and things like that so it was kind of the girls were just something for the guys to look at as we (the band) were something for the girls to look at also.

As I said, many females took it elsewhere and wanted to compete, so they took their clothes off. Sunshine and Juicy always had outfits on. Initially, some of them may have been bathing suits. We were getting their hair done and everything so initially, before it became this thing where people were like Oh, this is a problem. We looked at it like it was no different from a female walking down the beach in a bathing suit. Nobody touched them. My mother made sure that people weren't just up there reaching and touching. If you tried to touch them, we had security for that. It wasn't like a strip club. Initially, it was just female dancers, and it was just added to our whole show. When we came to perform, we were putting on a show. We wanted to give people their money's worth.

We had way more females at our show than males. And then a lot of other groups, I remember G came to our show. He said, "One thing I can say about you is that you always got the ladies," so I don't know if it was us, the guys in the band, bringing all the women or if it was the fact that we had these female dancers up there and it was underlying competition where they were like "Oh they've got these dancers, and we look better than these dancers, and we can do more than these dancers so I don't know, but we always had a lot of females.

On the popularity of all the band's members

The crazy thing with that is that when you talk about Northeast Groovers, unlike a lot of the other bands that were coming up, you may have known the drummer, or everyone knew the front line. Well, Northeast Groovers is the whole band is popular and I think that was due to Chris (Rapper) like the way he directed the show. He was like a Puffy up there, like a guy in the studio who would sit back and produce this masterpiece. So, he was always calling on us. He was calling on Khari, and he was calling on Smoke, unlike a lot of the other bands where you only knew maybe, like in RE, you know Mickey, but you don't really know who the keyboard players were. You didn't know Funky Ned until he started rapping. So, the way we did ours was everybody just was a big part of the band so it really wasn't just one person that ok let me take him out of the equation, and it's still successful. That's why, like we've done little semi-reunions, people won't accept it unless everybody's there.

On the band's most significant years

The biggest years for us I would probably say were between 92 to 96. We had the core. The core in the music section was me on the bass, and you had Maestro on keyboards, 88 on keyboards, and Joe Dye on the guitar. Then you had the posse, which was percussion which was Smoke (Samuel Dews). For a minute, it was Smoke and Jammin Jeff (Jeff Warren), then Smoke and Stomp Dogg (Larry Atwater) and Dig Dug. He's been there from Day one. And then, on the front line, you had Hugg (Leonard Huggins), 32 (David Ellis), and Rappa/ Chris [Black]. That was the core band. Over the years, we swapped. When 32 left, we had [Gene] Pratt, and Bruce [Bailey] even played with us for a minute, and we had the fill-ins like Rocket Rob on the congas. He was a part of the band. He didn't play all the time, but he was there. The guitar was the interchangeable piece that always switched after Joe Dye. We had Joe Dye, a guy named Picks, and another guy named Reds (Malachai Johns) on the guitar. That was the one position that constantly changed. But the rest pretty much stayed the same.

The Water, Van Damme, and Booty Call seemed to be big hits. They are still playing that to this day. I even hear it in Atlanta sometimes. Those were the studio songs. When the radio was playing the live music, a lot of people liked Off the Muscle, and we had a lot of hits. When I think back on it, it's like 5 albums, about 5 or 6 albums.

107

It's funny, early on, I might have been playing the drums, and somebody else might have been playing congas, and then the bass player, and we'd say, oh, that sounds good, and then we would switch back to our regular instruments and make it work. Our concept was that if we didn't look around my mother's basement and see the majority of the band kinda bobbing their heads, it didn't leave the basement. So, everybody was responsible for their own position, so it wasn't like a person came in there and was like, I got this song in my head, this is all the parts to it, I did my part, Chris did his part, and it just came together. Later, a lot of the hits, the "Van Damme" and hits like that, just came onstage. It would be something that maybe we did the night before at a party, a house party for fun, or we saw a movie. Everybody would come with their part, and the next thing you know, once we did it onstage, we took it back home and practiced on it, and there was a song.

Other than the people who knew about my house, when I was growing up, I think one of the craziest things was that my basement would flood about 7 inches of water, and it wouldn't stop. We had our chords lying in the water, and we would stand on bricks, whatever we could stand on, to practice. I didn't have a speaker, so I was plugging my guitar into a radio—one of those big radios you used to walk around with on your shoulder. I'd plug my guitar into that, and that's what I'd practice through. My basement wasn't a finished basement. You could still see the dirt down there. It was just a hole down there, but we would go down there with water, bugs, and all and practice.

On the band's most considerable success and eventual break-up
There are so many, but I think the highlight for me is because I was a young guy, and (at the height of their success, they may have been 20 or 21. Khari was one of the younger ones until Smoke came. He was younger than me.) I think for me, I wanted to be at the Cap Center and then to actually get there. That was a big highlight for me.

The biggest failure was as a group, not knowing how to deal with the success. For some people, success went to their heads. We had a lot of egos in the band. I think I speak for probably every fan in the Maryland and D.C. area was the breakup.

I am not even sure anybody can really answer the question of why we broke up because all I could see was egos. The money wasn't coming in like it used to because the crowd started to fall off. It's because we changed. Instead of sticking to what we'd been doing, that's why I said not knowing how to deal with success, which is a lot of people. You get to a certain point, and people don't know how difficult it is to stay there. So, when the next new thing comes out, and it seems to be working, you try to switch to that, and that's not you. So, we had some bands, like Backyard, that were closing on us. And we saw this working for them, and we lost ourselves. We started to lose members, and it just fell apart. I remember a conversation sitting in my house, and Suttle Thoughts had just come out, and we were hearing that they were making all this money with this grown and sexy thing.

The name Northeast Groovers had been tarnished so we couldn't get into a lot of those Grown and Sexy clubs, so we came up with the idea that we were going to switch- we were going to go into these clubs under a different name, and eventually, that ended up with the split of the band. That's where SOULO came from, and then the other half of the band went to WHAT? Band. Basically, WHAT? Band initially, I don't remember everybody that was in that band. It was Chris. He started WHAT? Band. He used a guy named Joel, who was Northeast's last drummer. So basically, he took Joel and Michelle Blackwell. She was with Northeast after Suttle Thoughts and Rocket Rob, so the 4 of them went to WHAT? Stomp Dogg, me, Dig Dug, Maestro, and everybody else in the band went to SOULO.

WHAT? Band was playing Northeast Groover's stuff. We were playing some of it, but we had some originals, which, I guess, just like most bands that split up, you have 2 bands playing the same thing. Eventually, the management side, cause my mother was the owner of SOULO, but she wasn't and didn't want to manage SOULO. We had some other guys managing the band, and it got out there. It got out there pretty good, and we put out a CD and did a couple of shows in Philly, and then it just fell apart.

I just stopped playing altogether. I had a family. I stopped playing and was just working. And then Reds (Malachai Johns), the guitar player [who played with Northeast Groovers], came to me, and he had an idea where he wanted to put a group together that's going to play original music, and we were going to do it like the big guys do it. Initially, I didn't want to be a part of it. He hand-picked each person for that band and he pushed it, and it worked. And that was that. I left the band before, though. At one time, I was engaged to be married, and I couldn't do everything I was trying to do, and then he let me hear this song a month afterward, and I was like, "Oh, Man! I really like this song! This is totally different!" See, the Go-Go thing had just really burned me out, so when I heard one of the songs he did with Mambo Sauce, I was like, "Yeah. I'm in. I'll make it work."

We wanted to make sure that we did business completely differently from the Go-Go industry because we thought that was one of the reasons that Go-Go was in the state it was in. We decided we wouldn't play week in and week out 4-5 days a week. It makes it hard to sell your music. It's like you're pimping yourself. It makes it hard to sell your music because people hear it day in and day out so why would they buy it?

Pratt was intrigued and soon joined Mambo Sauce.
With Mambo Sauce, we were only doing big venues. Until we went on tour. We went on a 30-city tour. I think it was about 28 cities. We recorded music, worked on an album, and only took worthwhile shows—not weekly spots in a club. The business was just run differently. When I thought about it, we got about $3,000 to perform "Welcome to D.C." Not a 45-minute set. Not a whole show. Just that song. It's all in how you present it. A lot of people took to Mambo Sauce. On the CD there were some uplifting songs.

I can't say which I liked better- Northeast Groovers or Mambo Sauce because they were completely different. I just like performing. I just love to be on stage, so I'm happy whenever I have my guitar in my hand.

Chapter 8: Behind the Beat

Behind the Beat was a series I started while writing for Examiner.com. I wanted to dissect certain popular songs to make the reader feel like they were watching the creation and the recording happen. I started with some of my personal favorites that also happened to be culturally iconic songs and PA tapes of the genre that people would instantly feel connected to.

In this chapter, you will be right there along with Chuck Brown, Ricky Wellman, Donald Tillery, and John Buchanan as they talk about recording "Bustin' Loose." You'll also have the opportunity to "hang out" with Andre "Whiteboy" Johnson, Mark "Godfather" Lawson, and Rory "DC" Felton of Rare Essence as they discuss the making of "Take Me Out to the Go-Go." Iconic Radio Personality Albie D., Vernell "Wink" Powell, and David "32" Ellis talk about Junkyard Band's hit "Sardines." D.C. Scorpio lets us into the ins and outs of "Stone Cold Hustler." "$55 Motel" is broken down by Vinnie D. as he brings us with him into the studio with Michael "Funky Ned" Neal and Byron "BJ" Jackson. Finally, sound engineer extraordinaire Moe Gentry brings us back to August 5, 1982, to Highland, where the most sought-after PA tape/CD, Rare Essence Highland, was recorded when the band had insufficient power. Did that stop them?

Behind the Beat: Bustin' Loose with Chuck Brown and the Soul Searchers

The song credited with creating the blueprint for an entire musical genre, "Bustin' Loose," was released by Chuck Brown and the Soul Searchers in the fall of 1978.

Even though this song is over 40 years old, it is still as infectious today as it was in 1978. Although the Soul Searchers released two prior albums, "Bustin' Loose," a single from the third album of the same name, brought Go-Go, this new musical creation from the nation's capital, Washington, D.C. into the spotlight of the masses.

The group, who had by then changed the name to Chuck Brown and the Soul Searchers, enjoyed nationwide success as "Bustin' Loose" stayed on the Billboard Hot R&B Singles chart at #1 from February 17, 1979, to March 10, 1979, when it was replaced at the number 1 spot by Instant Funk's "I Got My Mind Made Up (You Can Get It Girl)."

Chuck Brown knew that "Bustin' Loose" would be the breakout hit for the group. He says, "I just had that feeling. We had been playing the song for two years before we were ready to cut it in the studio. I had been searching for my own sound like James Brown had his own sound, and Go-Go was just catching on when we first started playing the song live at the Maverick Room."

John "JB" Buchanan and Donald Tillery, who both added their talents to the hit song with background vocals and Buchanan with the APR 2600 synthesizer and Tillery with trumpet and tambourine, concur that Brown came up with the actual concept for "Bustin' Loose."

Brown relays, "I came up with the concept for the song. I was feeling uptight at the time. I felt like I had to get a hit record, and things were really tough. I was booking the band for a while and I just felt like Bustin' Loose! That was the way I felt. 'Bustin' Loose' makes you feel fine, regardless of how you feel!"

The whole band co-wrote and arranged the song. The intro chords, in particular, were my creation," states Buchanan regarding his contributions.

"Everyone in the band at the time came up with parts of the song," Tillery agrees. "The groove itself started with an old Grover Washington, Jr. tune called 'Mr. Magic.' 'Mr. Magic' was one of the first songs that we did at our shows. The idea just came about from grooving to the 'Mr. Magic' instrumental and we just added our spin to it in a way. I give credit where credit is due, and I'll give credit to the late, great Grover Washington, Jr. for the instrumental."

He continues, "Basically, Chuck came up with the words and the title for it. Ricky Wellman, the drummer, came up with the beat. He was known as one of the best drummers around. We all kinda put in with the tambourine. Leroy (Fleming) added in that cowbell, Jerry Wilder came up with that funky rhythm cover for the bass, and the horn lines were something that Leroy, Buchanan, and I created. We knew each other's vibes, so if one person started with a horn line, we could pick it up. By us being friends on and off stage and also great musicians, it also helped us. Chuck added the raps to it because he could rap off the top of his head. Curtis Johnson came up with that rhythm. Again, we were close on stage and off the stage which helped us make it better."

Everyone was thrilled to record the song in Philadelphia at Sigma Sound at the request of producer James Purdie. This was where Teddy Pendergrass, Lou Rawls, Stephanie Mills, and many others recorded hits at the time.

One little-known fact about the recording session is that John Buchanan was not present the first day the group went to Philadelphia to record "Bustin' Loose." He explains, "I was a band director and science teacher at Kelly Miller Junior High School in D.C. then. I actually missed the first recording session due to D.C. Public Schools standardized testing that was scheduled at the same time. I was shocked to find out that Chuck went on without me, hence why Lincoln Ross was hired to play trombone. I came up the next day and overdubbed the background vocals."

Brown explains that there were previous incarnations of the Soul Searchers prior to the release of "Bustin' Loose," which included four original Soul Searchers- Frank Wellman, Lloyd Pinchback, John Euell, and Brown. The group that had been put together by 1978, then Chuck Brown and the Soul Searchers, comprised some legends in their own rights.

He recalls, "John Buchanan came out of Notre Dame. About a year after graduating from college, he got with us. Frank's son, Ricky Wellman, joined the band in '76. He started playing the beat I was trying to put together. Leroy (Fleming) came with us around '76. He was a great man, a great horn player, had so much soul and so much feel. When he came off the road with Eddie Kendricks, I asked him if he would come with us. He stayed with us for around 13 years. His solo fit that sound on 'Bustin' Loose.'

Nobody sounded like Leroy! Tillery was versatile. He could sing those high falsetto songs. He could sing background, and he could play two trumpets at the same time! Lincoln Ross played trombone on 'Bustin' Loose. Jerry Wilder was a great bass player at the time. This young man was awesome then. I knew he was going to be hot. He had a great sound. At that time, Jerry and Ronnie Hudson (who played with Isaac Hayes) were the best bass players in the area. Skip Fennell played keyboards on 'Bustin' Loose.' He was blind and a great keyboard player. He was doing the chops on that record. He had that church feel. He was a great jazz pianist, also. On congas, we had Gregory "Bright Moments" Gerran. We had Curtis Johnson on the organ. We hired him in '77, and he fit in very

113

good. He played that Hammond B3. He could handle it!"

Specifically, on "Bustin' Loose," Buchanan details that "Skip Fennell played the Fender Rhodes, Leroy Fleming played the tenor sax" and that Fennell, Curtis Johnson, Tillery, and Buchanan all contributed background vocals as well.

As far as stepping into his father Frank Wellman's shoes as the drummer for Chuck Brown and the Soul Searchers, Ricky Wellman smiles, "It was fantastic to step into my dad's footsteps knowing he was the original drummer for the Soul Searchers and he taught me everything I knew about drumming. I am especially appreciative for that, and it's truly a blessing from God."

Wellman and Brown recall what "Bustin' Loose" did for the group. Wellman emphatically states, "The record was the number one record nationally back in the day, and because of that, the group toured some in the United States, which gave the group national exposure. Also, the group appeared on Soul Train hosted by Don Cornelius to perform 'Bustin' Loose,' and anytime a record can reach number one, you have made a tremendous mark musically. Back in the day, to have a record become number one was not easy!"

Brown elaborates, "Our appearance on Soul Train was a highlight for me and touring all around the country... We shared the stage with so many great artists of the time: The Jacksons, Gladys Knight and the Pips, War, Tyrone Davis, Earth, Wind and Fire, Patti Labelle, Instant Funk...Oh, Man! We toured with all those people. There were so many of them. We were playing at the Coliseum, packing every place we played. It was an exciting time, something that you couldn't get used to. The energy was just there.

Every place we went to was a new experience, and the record was a hit everywhere we went. I liked opening for all those people, and it was a great experience watching all those other bands after we played. All the love we got on the road, we could never wait to get back to D.C. We played at the Howard Theatre when we got back from the road. It made us feel like we never wanted to leave D.C. again. We got such a great reception."

Regarding the tremendous reception that "Bustin' Loose" received from D.C., Tillery reveals, "It felt great to hear it on the radio and the people of

D.C. who bought the record, who called the stations to request the song- it was a beautiful thing. Also, people going to record stores to buy the album- if it weren't for the young folks who bought our record, the song wouldn't have been as successful."

"It was a real thrill to hear it for the first time on the radio. We had heard our tunes before, but this was the biggest sound we had ever produced," claims Buchanan.

Wellman reacted differently as he had experienced prior success at age 11 with the group The Famous Jaguars. He explains, "I was home and heard 'Bustin' Loose' playing on the radio, and yes, it was exciting, but not overwhelming. The reason was because I recorded my first 45 record when I was 11 years old, called 'Crazy Things' and 'Banana Fana' and the record received a tremendous amount of airplay.

Also, I recorded my first gospel album, 'Save Thyself,' when I was 14 years old with D.C.'s own gospel singer Myrna Summers. I had also been playing with Peaches and Herb during the weekends while I was still in high school. But, yes, it was still exciting."

Tillery has a fascinating take on just how socially relevant "Bustin' Loose" was at the time. He explains, "At the time, there were lots of young folks on drugs, drinking, and getting into trouble. It was rough for young kids. There were lots of shootings which was very bad in those years because lots of kids got into the drug game. I'm hoping in doing some of those Go-Go shows that these kids will be at our shows instead of being out in the streets. Lots of teens were having a lot of trouble and turned to drugs which took a lot of young people away from us."

Everyone in the group enjoyed success to various degrees. Wellman shares, "The entire musical experience, from playing live locally to traveling and performing for crowds and to see the crowd hyped with the group was overwhelming for me. It's like a high that no other drug can replace. All I can say is that it was a hell of a roller coaster ride, and 'Bustin' Loose' is a part of musical history in the fact that the record was in fact number one."

"Bustin' Loose," the Soul Searchers and Chuck Brown continue to make history. In early 2011, the D.C. Government issued a Recognition Resolution confirming the "Soul Searchers Band, along with Chuck

Brown, as the true originators of Go-Go." The Resolution was sponsored by Harry Thomas Jr. (D.C. City Council- Ward 5).

The Resolution recognized "the creative and genius talent of the band members who successfully wrote and performed great hits such as 'Bustin' Loose,' 'I Need Some Money and 'We the People' ... and Whereas the District of Columbia residents and City Council, the most appreciative and dedicated fans of Go-Go, recognize the Soul Searchers Band, along with Chuck Brown, as the true pioneers of Go-Go."

Tillery reflects, "Yes, it opened a couple of doors for me. People recognize me, and I am doing recordings with other bands. But, yes, it has also closed some doors. A lot of people wanted to see the Soul Searchers back together instead of seeing us as individuals as part of other bands. I would like for the Soul Searchers to come back, but I don't think it's going to happen any time soon, so time moves on."

As it stands, there was an attempt at putting the Soul Searchers back together in 2012 including Donald Tillery, John "JB" Buchanan, Curtis Johnson, Lloyd Pinchback, Lino Druitt, Rowland Smith, Wardell Howell, Ju Ju House, and Leron Young. Although rehearsals went on, the band did not materialize. There is another attempt presently with Donald Tillery leading the way.

Behind the Beat: Where You Wanna Go? Take Me Out to the Go-Go with Rare Essence

At the time that one of Rare Essence's all-time greatest hits, "Take Me Out to the Go-Go" was written and recorded. Rare Essence was a much different band than it is today. In light of the fact that Rare Essence has had a variety of incarnations over the years, one could be understandably confused as to who was actually on the recording of this song. When "Take Me Out to the Go-Go" was recorded, the band consisted of Quentin "Footz" Davidson on drums, David Green on roto toms and timbales, Tyrone "Jungle Boogie" Williams on congas, Michael "Funky Ned" Neal on bass, Andre "Whiteboy" Johnson on guitar, Benny "Little Benny" Harley on trumpet, Rory "DC" Felton on saxophone and cowbell, John "Big Horn" Jones on Trombone, Marky Owens and Mark "Godfather" Lawson on keyboards. The vocals were covered by Williams, Harley and Green.

According to Andre "Whiteboy" Johnson, the only original member remaining of the Rare Essence machine that cranked out original hits consistently, "although some of the early Rare Essence hits were recorded at Sigma Studios in Philadelphia, "Take Me Out to the Go-Go" was recorded at Bias Studios in Springfield, Virginia. It was recorded in the studio and mixed, but it was never mastered and therefore was never on any of the Rare Essence CDs. It can only be found on PA tapes. Mike Hughes produced the studio version of the song, and it has been one of the classic Rare Essence hits."

Johnson continues, "We just never released it. That song has been a mainstay on the Rare Essence playlist and catalog for over 40 years. When we play it at a club, regardless of the era that the crowd came up in, they know the song. Some may not have been born yet, but they know the song."

Mark "Godfather" Lawson recalls, "I came up with the music. Then Benny, Jungle Boogie, David Green, and I all sat down and started seeing what rhymed with what, and we came up with the words. The melodies came from songs from our childhood- nursery rhymes, TV commercials, and snippets. The part, 'What do you do when you're home doin' nothing' came from a Cracker Jack commercial. We didn't really get airplay on 'Take Me Out to the Go-Go,' but it was one of our favorite songs to play. This song had the percussion breakdowns in the middle of the song that the RE percussionists added themselves and put their signatures on. The song shows how you can use snippets, incorporate them into a song and have fun with it. This song was basically a medley of melodies, most coming from the playground. There was the 1950's rhyme, 'There's a soldier in the grass with a bullet in his ass,' a child's taunt, 'Cry baby, cry baby,' nursery rhymes 'Mary Had a Little Lamb' and 'London Bridge, and then the Christmas song, 'Do You Hear What I Hear?' the music from the circus, and, of course, 'Take Me Out to the Ballgame,' to name a few."

"The part of the song that asks, 'Where Ya Wanna Go? Where Ya Wanna Go?' was started by some guys from Uptown, 9th and Westminster- Gene Bean, Nevellon and Harvey Cooper. They used to come up to The Maverick Room, anywhere uptown. They just started the call and response, 'Where ya wanna go? Take me out to the Go-Go," Lawson adds.

"Mark (Lawson) started off every song that Rare Essence did back then, really," saxophonist Rory "DC" Felton confirms. "He wrote his own part. He never got credit for it. I don't know why. People don't know this, but

117

Mark plays horns too. Mark used to give us our parts- me, Benny, and Big Horn. We would go over to Ms. Lawson's house, and we would practice all night. The horns were tight! Mark was very creative. We made most of our songs right at the shows. Mark would start something, and maybe Funky Ned would come in with his part and then someone else. We would just ride with the crowd. The next day, we would go down in the basement and make it into a song. The people gave us our songs. We were really connected to the crowd."

Johnson agrees, "We have always been lucky with that. If it's something the crowd responds to, we keep going, but if not, we just move on to something else. We need to see what works." Felton explains at the time of the release of "Take Me Out to the Go-Go," his life was going against everything he had been taught as a country boy. "At that time, my interests were girls and the music. I'm from the country, so everything I was taught against was being thrown in my face- and I liked it! I came up here from rural Virginia when I was 16, and I went to Ballou. On the first day, Footz invited me to practice, and it took me four hours to get there. I was so lost! Practice was on Xenia Street SE, and I lived four blocks away on Homer Place SE. I just didn't know D.C. By the time I got there, practice was over. But, I'll tell you, looking out there and seeing people smiling and laughing- that was my happiness."

Over the years, "Take Me Out to the Go-Go" has spawned many different versions depending on who was in Rare Essence at the time. But, regardless of who was on vocals, the song still had the whimsical childlike essence to it.

The song also precipitated the very popular online platform TMOTGoGo, dedicated to urban music and culture in the D.C. Metropolitan area. Kevin "Kato" Hammond, owner and creator of TMOTTGoGo, explains, "When I first heard the song, I thought it was really catchy. Of course, I immediately recognized, 'Take Me Out to the Ballgame' but to hear it in the format that RE put it in, to me, was clever. It was such an excellent demonstration of the call-and-response activity that played such a prevalent part in Go-Go during that time. Benny would yell out to the crowd, 'Where ya wanna go? Where ya wanna go?' and the crowd would sing back, 'Take me out to the Go- Goooooo.'"

He continues, "As time went on, the song just grew and grew. Different parts an sections were added to it until, in my opinion, the song was eventually complete. It had become such an ingenious creation, like a wonderfully written novel. I mean, it had an intro that went straight into the rising action. By the time it got to the lyrics, 'Take me out to the Go-Go,' the song has reached its climax straight into the tip-top. But it wasn't over then. From there, it swiftly glided into its falling action and ended with the 'Take the time out' part. By the time it reached the end of the song, heck 20 minutes had gone by, yet not one boring or dead element in it! Without a doubt, it had become my favorite Go-Go song ever, actually, to the point that when I created TMOTTGoGo back in 1996, I named it after that song, with the frame of mind to gracefully build on it the same way that the song was built- one piece at a time."

Behind the Beat: Sardines with the Junkyard Band
Rewind to 1986, the year that Def Jam Records released "The Word" and, on the "B" side, "Sardines." "Sardines" is one of the few songs that propelled the Go-Go music genre into the national spotlight. In a poll, Rolling Stone magazine declared "Sardines" is the biggest Go-Go song of all time.

According to Vernell "Wink" Powell, Junkyard Band's conga player, when recording "Sardines" the group had not yet gained access to professional instruments. Powell recalls, "The only real instruments on that song [Sardines] were the small bongos, the cowbell, bass drum, snare, and cymbals. Everything else was buckets and cans!"

David "32" Ellis, Sr., a vocalist on the song, and Powell concur that at the time of the recording, the band was comprised of Steven "Buggs" Herrion as the lead vocalist and also contributing vocals were Mike Strong, Shelton "Shorty Pop" Watkins, and Ellis.

Daniel Baker and Krisinah "Chung Yung" Taylor can be heard on keyboards. As for the percussion, Powell played the "little bongos," Willie "Heavy One" Gaskins played drums, and Robert "Footloose" Smith played the buckets while Maurice Gray and "Lil Derrick" Ingram played the tin cans.

Although Junkyard made "Sardines" a hit, Powell reveals, "We knew 'Sardines' as a boy scout chant. We were boy scouts in Barry Farms before we were a band. We would be walking through the woods chanting the words." Time in the woods was a reality as Ellis adds, "Two or three times a week, we would have to go bucket hunting because the buckets would lose their tune and split down the middle."

Powell continues, "Moe Shorter and Derrick McCrae, our managers, figured out a way to put a beat behind it. We went into a studio on Connecticut Avenue near Dupont Circle and recorded the song. Rick Rubin from Def Jam produced it and mixed it. He put in added touches to make it sound more commercial. It was catchy."

"Sardines" opened doors for this group of youngsters who were in their teens when they recorded the song. "Being away from the neighborhood was the greatest gift the song gave me," states Powell. "Around this time, 1986, D.C. was off the chain. It was everything to me to get away from the neighborhood. The street that I lived on was the main street in Barry Farms and I never went out of my front door unless I was with my mom or dad because that was where most of the drug dealing was going on. I just always went out the back door."

Ellis remarks, "Sardines opened the doors to let people know that I'm an artist. People looked at us differently. It allowed people to hear our music. We were accepted with open arms by everyone. Back then, the radio stations were supporting the bands. Now, it's all about money. Back then, it was about the artist."

"Sardines" had a major impact on the music scene in the DMV.
Radio personality Bootsy Vegas shares, "The first time I heard 'Sardines,' I was at camp. It was just crankin,' and it felt like home. The funny story is that Bruce Bailey was my counselor at the camp, and he ended up playing with Junkyard." Albie Dee, formerly of WPGC 95.5, recalls, "I wasn't at WPGC when the song was released, but I remember it well when I heard it on Club 95. My first reaction was, 'What the hell is this?!' but when I saw the reaction at a club, I got IT!"

"When I first heard 'Sardines,' I saw it performed live," affirms Go-Go pioneer and former keyboard player for Rare Essence, Mark "Godfather" Lawson. "I remember the cheerleaders at the football game used to use that. Those kids [Junkyard Band] were able to adapt that into a song. They were able to do what we [Rare Essence] did with songs like 'Take Me Out to the Go-Go,' where we adapted rhymes from our childhood into songs."

Powell laughs, "We always play the song when we are out of town because they are more into the Old School stuff. And yes, I ate sardines, and I ate

120

pork and beans. I have eaten them together!"

Behind the Beat: Stone Cold Hustler with D.C. Rap Pioneer D.C. Scorpio

In the mid-80s, when Madness gear was all the rage and Go-Go fans repeatedly watched the Beta Max video tape of Go-Go Live at the Capital Center, the stage was set for the first wave of rap artists to burst onto the scene in Washington, D.C. Most notably, D.C. Scorpio. Before there was Wale, Garvey the Chosen One, Shy Glizzy, Logic and Lightshow, there was an entire movement of rap artists that paved the way for these artists that have gained more recent notoriety. No one can dispute that among this pioneering generation of the rap genre in the DMV, which included Fat Rodney, Vinnie D, Stinky

Dink and DJ Kool, the song most heard on a hot summer day, booming from the car stereo systems at Haines Point was "Stone Cold Hustler." Lanard "D.C. Scorpio" Thompson explains, "It was 1985 or 1986, and I was hustling on the block. I was chilling at my sister's house, and I was banging on the table, freestyling about my day. I knew Mike "Funky Ned" Neal from the band Rare Essence.

One night after a Go-Go, we hooked up and had a session in his studio in his mom's basement. The song was already formatted, so we put it together with members of Rare Essence. After that, we went to Omega Studios in Rockville, Maryland, and finished it up. We put it out on Kolossal Records, which was owned by Donnell Floyd and Quentin "Footz" Davidson of Rare Essence.

"When the song came out, I was 15 or 16. I was so excited! Just to have a record and everyone knew the song! And then, to be so young and be onstage at Go-Go Live at the Capital Center being backed by Chuck Brown in front of 30,000 people screaming for me and screaming the words to 'Stone Cold Hustler' was unreal."

Thompson also had the good fortune to be introduced to Darryll Brooks and Carol Kirkendall of G-Street Express/CD Enterprises. "Doug E. Fresh was having a rap contest at a club in D.C., Chapter III. After I won, I was approached by Darryll Brooks , and he was interested in taking 'Stone Cold Hustler' to the next level."

'Stone Cold Hustler" was undoubtedly a catalyst for introducing to the

121

world that Washington, D.C., was able to compete in the rap arena. Thompson states, "I consider myself the pioneer of rap music in D.C. I was the first rap artist to come out of D.C. with the impact to be taken seriously. This was the start of a wave of rap artists to come out of the D.C. area- Vinnie D., Fat Rodney, Stinky Dink, Romeo, Tony Blunt, Moet the Beast from SE, DJ Kool, Nonchalant, and others began to see my light for the city. Like the Darth Vader of D.C. Rappers from the area."

Thompson realizes that "Stone Cold Hustler" is a classic "like Coke. The music today is different because times have changed, and sounds have changed. People and ideas change, but original music stays the same. The song is always loved. Music needs change so it can grow and expand. I am so proud of my son, Wale. It's just another shot for the DMV to show that we got it!"

Behind the Beat: Rap Classic $55 Motel with Vinnie D
The setting is 1987 in the DMV. Guess Jeans, partying at Triples Night Club, fly hairdos and the many things that still make you smile to this day as you think back while scratching your head, trying to believe that it has been 35 years.

For a music lover, 1987 was also the year that a 20-year-old, Vincent "Vinnie D." Davis, unleashed one of the DMV's signature rap songs, "$55 Motel." And if you partied at Triples Night Club, then there is no doubt that you remember the Stagecoach Inn, which, according to Davis, was the muse for the hit. "The actual price was $54 and some change, "laughs Davis. The landscape has changed over the past 35 years, and the motel has been immortalized as the $55 motel has been knocked to the ground, as has Triples Night Club. The Stagecoach Inn was replaced by a CVS, and the spot where Triples once stood, where we danced inside until we were dripping with sweat, is now a 7-11.

Davis shares, "It's a true story that actually happened. I wrote that song in my bedroom at my Momma's house when I was about 17 or 18. That's about right because I was a Coolidge High graduate of the class of 1985. It's funny because I wasn't trying to be a rapper at all. That was the first rap that I ever wrote. I probably thought I could sing at the time and had been making songs since I was 14. It was also like a rebellion for me because my family was religious, so it was bittersweet to see your son winning through sinning. Momma was proud, though."

It was time for Davis to go into the studio. He worked closely with two members of Rare Essence, the hottest band in the city at the time. The Wickedest Band Alive, as the fans referred to them. Michael "Funky Ned" Neal and Byron "BJ" Jackson oversaw the recording. "I used Ned's equipment and a bigger sound than the demo. Byron is actually responsible for the hook on the song, and you can hear that pattern on many Essence tapes where the whistle was used. That beat was used through the 90s by every Go-Go band, and I smile when I hear it. The song is original. The bassline follows Anita Baker's "Been So Long" on the part where I am rapping her lyrics, and the final bridge of the song is the chord progression from Roberta Flack's "Killing Me Softly." I jacked chord progressions a bit, but creatively! I loved the way Junkyard played my song the most. They used to kill it. I always wanted to do it with them, but it just never happened for whatever reason. The pre-production was done in Ned's basement, and the actual song was recorded in a studio that was over the Discount Mart at Eastover Shopping Center in Oxon Hill, Maryland," Davis recalls.

Kolossal Records, a local record label in the mid to late 80s, released "$55 Motel." Again, the Rare Essence connection comes into play as Donnell Floyd and Quentin "Footz" Davidson, both members of Rare Essence, owned Kolossal Records. Davis makes it a point to misspell the "Kolossal" label. With a devilish grin, he explains, "It was Kolossal spelled wrong on purpose because they misspelled my name as 'Venny' when it is 'Vinnie'!"

Most artists can recall the "where" and the "when" of where they were the first time they ever heard their song being played on the radio. Davis has a different story. He quietly says, "I missed out on that joy. Believe it or not, they weren't really playing rap on FM radio like that back then. And the wild part is the song was considered vulgar , and they would spin the instrumental rather than the vocal version. I remember having problems initially, but AM radio played it, and it lights up a party with our generation to this day!"

Aside from not getting the airplay that "$55 Motel" deserved, Davis is happy with the outcome and credits what was going on in D.C. at the time of the song's release with its popularity and solid placement in the history of the music of D.C. "Those times were pure fun! Crystal Skate, Chuck E. Cheese, Go-Gos, high school Go-Gos, Georgetown University campus parties when the Hoyas were dominating, asymmetrical hair, and cool girls! You could get like 5 phone numbers after each party and the parties were live. There was none of this texting on the dance floor. The dance floor and walls were always wet, and the girls' hair had always fallen because we partied as hard as humanly possible. Males and females had zero problems interacting, and we did have fights, but that was just teen spirit, and yes, D.C. was a fight town. We grew up fighting, but it was all hands until crack came.

All of this influenced the song. We had the flyest girls on the East Coast. New York and Philly hustlers used to bring their girlfriends down here to get their hair done because D.C. girls could not be messed with when it came to their hair. Their girls were still wearing 'snatchbacks' and 'mushrooms,'" Davis chuckles and grins.

He sits back and explains, "That song helped me because I made money off of appearances. As a matter of fact, Sean Combs was one of my dancers. He was so greedy, always asking for more money. It was him, Ron Deberry, who became a promoter in D.C., and Obataye, who became a promoter in New York. I will share a funny story. Diddy had an apartment in N.E. while he went to Howard University. My cousin grew up with him in Mt. Vernon, N.Y., and he hooked us up. He always managed to be in the right place at the right time. He was broke and drove a VW. My little MONEY crew was always renting limos, and there was never enough room for the dancers because the money crew was deep, so the dancers rode in his GTI.

It's kind of funny but foul looking back. Dude had a lot of ambition. Respect to him. He extended opportunities while he was at Uptown/ MCA, and he did reach out when Bad Boy was on it's way while we were at Jack the Rapper [conference], but I was on some neo-soul funk jazz singing shit in Atlanta, happy with a band, and didn't capitalize." But, when one door closes, another will soon open, or so we all hope. It did for Davis. "My last big record deal was with Snoop Dogg in 2004 when MCA folded. They released 'Doggy Style All Stars Welcome to the House.' I have two songs on that one under the name Vinnie Bernard. One, 'Trouble' is all me. The other one, 'Just Get Carried Away' is Snoop, Uncle Reo, and me." And fast forward 35 years, from the time we first heard "$55 Motel" in 1987 to 2022, the years bring maturity. Davis responds that he has grown a lot since those days, "But we had a ball, and they will never party like we used to then- Never! Impossible! Come on Slim, the floors and walls were soaking wet! We did it all!"

Behind the Beat: Rare Essence PA Tape 8/5/1982 Highland
As told by Moe Gentry

The Rare Essence 8/5/1982 Highland PA Tape is probably the most sought-after PA Tape in the history of Go-Go. It's unbelievable to acknowledge that the recording is 40 years old. PA Tapes were how most Go-Go music was sold and purchased, and even a store named "PA Palace" was born from this unique method of selling music. Instead of going into the studio and recording product, the soundman would record the show through the PA system and sell the tape where there would be duplicate after duplicate and sold to the consumer. There are experts who can listen to a show and tell you, "Oh, that's so and so on a specific date at a specific location," and 99% of the time, a true Go-Go head is correct. There was something different about the Rare Essence Highland 8/5/1982 tape, though. Moe Gentry, a longtime sound engineer, was there the night this tape was recorded.

This is his account:

Rare Essence at this time consisted of Andre "Whiteboy" Johnson, Michael "Funky Ned" Neal, Anthony "Little Benny" Harley, Rory "DC" Felton, John "Big Horn" Jones, Marky Norris, Mark "Godfather" Lawson, "Scotty" Haskel, Roger "Jungle Boogie" Williams, Quentin "Footz" Davidson, David Green, and Mike Muse.

The show took place as one of the Showmobile events at the Washington Highland Dwellings which comprised Condon Terrace and Wahler Place at 8th and Yuma Street S.E. It was project housing, and there were several places to play over there. Bands could play at the skating rink, which was outside the loading dock, which was out back, or the auditorium in the Rec Center. Rare Essence had played everywhere there. This show, however, took place on a Thursday on the field since they were playing on the Showmobile. Why is this particular tape so popular and still talked about? It's because it was from a place in time when Rare Essence was dominating the whole Go-Go scene. On this show, Benny held it down by himself. Rare Essence's name, how they carried themselves as far as showmanship- no one else was doing that at the time. We came with a light show, and we had our own sound system. We were a self-contained unit. People are STILL buying this tape, now CD.

People that know this tape know that this is the night that there was not enough power to run everything that needed to be run for all of the

125

instruments, the lights, the sound, etc. There wasn't enough power because the Showmobile didn't drop off the generators- only the stage. The type of equipment Rare Essence had back then, the Hammond B3 organ, needed a line just for itself. We had to hook up the Hammond B3 with power amps that needed a 30-volt breaker. We had to run power cords all the way up to the Rec Center. We probably used 3, but they were all hooked on the same line. God was with us that day and that is why it is a classic. No matter the power situation, the band kept playing. Benny was doing what he was doing throughout the whole thing. The place was packed. People didn't even think that Rare Essence was going to play that show because of their status. This was the show where the infamous line "Tell Jungle Boogie to put the vocal mic on the congas" came from. Go-Go Heads know.

When Moe was setting up, he knew there wouldn't be enough voltage, but he and Vincent Green, a member of the crew, were told by manager Miss Sis to go down to Highland and set everything up. She had said to go down there and get it done.

She was the boss. Once we got down there and started to hook things up, Moe saw the lights dim on the Showmobile as he played music to test the equipment. Mike Hughes, another of the top sound engineers, showed up around that time. Moe explained the power situation to Mike, and they both knew they would have a problem. Mike's eyes grew wide in disbelief as he was shocked that the Showmobile didn't drop off the generator. Moe and Mike did all of the configurations that night and separated some things out and looked at what didn't need to be hooked up in order to conserve energy. Moe decided, Mike agreed, and the crew executed.

It was a very special night without a single incident after they figured out how to configure the power. And still, that very special night is still talked about 40 years later, sought after, and in every true Go-Go fan's collection.

Spotlight: Tom Goldfogle on Being Behind the Scenes in Go-Go

Tom Goldfogle, Chuck Brown's longtime manager and friend, prefers to stay behind the scenes, but in 2012, after the passing of legendary Chuck Brown, he kept Brown's band, The Chuck Brown Band, playing and doing tireless work with the Chuck Brown Foundation.

Goldfogle, born into a military family in Nebraska, spent time in the D.C. area between moves to Louisiana, Mississippi, Peru, and Michigan. "In between moves, my father would be at the Pentagon, so the DMV was the only place growing up that felt like home."

Although Goldfogle was aware of Go-Go in the late 70s with the release of "Bustin' Loose," it became ingrained in his life in the early 1980s while managing a record store in Landover Mall.

He describes the times, "The store was part of a chain based out of New York. I would call the head of operations and say that I needed to pay for 2,000 copies of a Go-Go 12" in cash, out of the register drawer on a Friday, but that I would sell all 2,000 copies by Monday. They thought I was completely out of my mind until Monday rolled around- pretty much had carte blanche after that and could bring in whatever local product I wanted."

With an extensive resume in the music business, Goldfogle recalls starting out working at a 3,000-seat concert hall in Gaithersburg, Maryland. "It was 7 days a week from age 14-18. There I was exposed to every major act in all genres of music and was hooked. I worked at Eclipse Jazz in college at the University of Michigan, then started my own concert promotion company, Double Shot Concerts, Inc., while in college and put talent in a 1,200-seat theatre. I also worked music retail after college, first managing record stores, then becoming the regional supervisor for the Mid-Atlantic, overseeing many stores."

In the 80s, Goldfogle started Liaison Records with Becky Marcus, "first as an independent label, then becoming a national independent urban distributor and one-stop. We did an annual music industry conference called the Music Business Forum for about 6 years and moved into talent booking, management, PR, and music publishing as the years went on," Goldfogle explains.

It was through Liaison that Goldfogle met Brown. He shares, "It started as helping Reo Edwards, his manager at the time, with Future Records and Chuck Brown products in the late 80s and early 90s. We initially met with Reo to try to elevate Go-Go music from its then-current state of being sold out of the trunk of a car at a low price to a few local stores, to regional and national distribution at a higher price through major chain stores, which we were able to do. Throughout the 90s, Liaison began helping Chuck in more ways. I took the lead on that work starting around 2000, and within a year or so, I was doing everything for him."

Leaving Liaison in 2004, Goldfogle continued managing Chuck Brown's career and focused on his own expanding roles in publishing, PR, marketing, booking, and consulting.

After Brown's death, it was essential for Goldfogle to keep the legacy alive. He states, "Chuck was always known to have some of the best musicians on the planet in his band. Greg Boyer, Brad Clements, Bryan Mills, Cherie Mitchell-Agurs, Kenny Gross, Maurice "Mighty Mo" Hagans, Karlston Ross, Marcus Young, Donnell Floyd and his daughter KK, along with stage manager Bobby Smoot and a great live engineer, Greg "Googie" Burton- these are all incredibly talented artists. They can stand toe to toe with the best of the best. This has always been the case, starting with the original Soul Searchers and on through the years- he has always had the best musicians in his band. Frank "Scooby" Marshall joined the band to fill in when Chuck was first not feeling well, adding so much. Each band member feels a loss in personality, mentorship, friendship, father figure, and band leader.

Keeping the band playing is a way to keep celebrating all that Chuck meant to this city and a part of a healing process for all who loved him, including the band. I've always tried to elevate the music. The series at the Howard made so much sense- having national artists join the band in celebration helps reinforce the tremendous impact Chuck Brown had on music as a whole, and the Howard was enthusiastic about making that happen on a regular basis. It also gives us a chance to celebrate some of the other legends of Go-Go. I would love to see something positive come from the Chuck Brown Band going forward. I am hopeful that I can help with that in some of the work I am just beginning now. I also hope his fans will continue to support the band and continue to celebrate Chuck Brown. His fans meant the world to him."

Another project developed after Brown's passing was a foundation in his name, The Chuck Brown Foundation, to address and assist with issues important to Chuck Brown- education, homelessness, and re-entry into society after incarceration.

"The Foundation came about at the Brown house when we first got a few people assembled to think about how we could put the homegoing services and viewing together in such a short time frame, and on the level Chuck and his fans and this city deserved. Mayor Vincent Gray was instrumental in making sure that happened. Darryll Brooks suggested it would be a good time to consider a foundation.

Over the years, I had countless requests for Chuck's time every day of the week. We always tried to fit in the schedule whatever we could, but there were a couple of things that we always made time for--helping the homeless, going to schools, and encouraging those who were incarcerated or recently re-entering society from incarceration. Chuck had such strong empathy for these causes because they all impacted his life in major ways. He had been homeless, even after having a hit record. He was not able to finish school until getting a GED while serving at Lorton, and he experienced firsthand the prejudice and difficulty someone has getting a second chance after incarceration. The Brown family all felt that continuing to help in these areas was a way to keep Chuck Brown's true spirit at work in the city he loved so much. Chuck and I spoke a number of times over the years about how he would like to be able to help more in these areas. People can donate by visiting www.thechuckbrownfoundation.com.

Chapter 9: Radio Play

Local radio support helps regional artists and genres reach a wider audience, but despite its popularity, Go-Go has never been as present on D.C. airwaves as one would think. The relationship between radio and Go-Go has always been complicated. From WOL-AM banning the area's unique sound in the 80s to local stations refusing to put the music in rotation in the '90s -- even when Go-Go artists recorded radio-friendly tracks – Go-Go music wasn't always given the same love from radio stations and local media as, say, Miami Bass or Baltimore House. Still, Go-Go caught ears and captured fans outside the region, with some bands even signing major label record deals.

The Go-Go/radio relationship has improved over the years, thanks in part to D.C. natives, such as DJ Rico and DJ Heat, securing jobs at local stations and playing the music they grew up on, as well as online platforms, like Go-Go Nico [Hobson]'s Go-Go Radio, which have allowed people at the center of the culture to play the music for a wider audience.

And even during the years when it was rare to hear Go-Go on a D.C. radio dial, there were people within the scene and outside of it, fighting for Go-Go to travel beyond D.C. Albie Dee, who worked at local urban radio stations in the 80s and 90s, George Harrell, former Radio Promotion Executive at Uptown/MCA Records, and James Funk of Rare Essence remember the battles that took place in the 80s, 90s, and into the 00s, as they fought for Go-Go to receive the widespread acclaim it deserves.

Albie Dee, radio personality and DJ, on hearing Go-Go for the first time: "I had just moved to the DMV from Connecticut and never heard Go-Go before. [I thought], What the hell is this crap? [But one day], I was at the Georgetown Library on M Street and saw a very diverse group of women just losing their minds to Go-Go. That's when I knew this was "mainstream" for D.C.
He was initially reluctant to play Go-Go during his timeslot on WPGC 95.5, the number 1 rated urban radio station in D.C., but he eventually relented. "I would meet record reps every Thursday. My first "open door" meeting with reps, maybe the second week at WPGC, in came [two representatives from a go-go promotion company]. [R]emember, I didn't understand Go-Go because I had just moved from Connecticut. I gave them major pushback, but they never gave up. They came week after week

to educate me, and, finally, I gave in."

Around the same time, legendary band Rare Essence was still fighting for local radio play, still upset that its 1982 single, "Body Moves," had been a hit in the Go-Gos, but was given little airplay. James Funk, Rare Essence: "I was the brainchild of that production, and I poured my heart into ["Body Moves"]. I just recently spoke to [radio host] Donnie Simpson about it because when he was program director up at [radio station] WKYS [at the time], he wouldn't touch it. I had three people in [my] plan, Chuck, to help me produce because it was my first production. He helped me put the groove and all of that together, Arthur "Maniac" McLeod, the number 1 DJ in the city, and Donnie Simpson. I got the first two on board. I could not reach Donnie Simpson. I thought "Body Moves" was a great record. I still think... it's my masterpiece. It's my masterpiece, and a lot of the older local fans love it. But I never could get him in there."

Years later, when Funk performed with another band, Proper Utensils, he received long overdue local radio love for the group's cover of Wreckx-N-Effect's "Rumpshaker." Gary Drew, who worked at KYS, put it in one of his mix shows...Gary had played "Rumpshaker," the original "Rumpshaker," and he had a mix because he was a great mixer, too, and played our record at the stroke of midnight. The Go-Go Rumpshaker lasted so long that I had to put it out [as a record]. I wasn't going to put it out because I really didn't want to interfere with Wreckx-N-Effect. But it gave their record life."

Funk says that, as time went on, other DJs, like Albie Dee, also began playing recordings of live Go-Go shows during their timeslots, which meant artists no longer had to record short, studio versions of their music to get radio play. The shift has its pros and its cons. From that point, Albie Dee, who was over at PGC, all he wanted then was live recordings from the groups. And that just, it peaked. But when it went down, it really went down because now the groups, all they have to do is make a live show from the CD, which saves money, but we're losing in the end because...[n]ow you're not going in the studio, re-tuning these songs up and making them quality records for people to hear."

Even though that change meant fewer Go-Go bands were recording studio albums from the '90s on, it didn't stop George Harrell (no relation to Andre Harrell, then-president of Uptown Records) from signing Rare Essence to a record deal in 1991. Sean "Diddy" Combs, who was working

131

at Uptown at the time and had recently attended Howard University, is primarily credited with bringing the group to the label's attention:

George Harrell: "I don't remember who did the formal introduction. I would want to say Sean Combs because he was the A&R at the label...Sean always stayed in front of the culture and turned to different things that were coming on. As a radio promotion person, I definitely promoted all of the music that was on the ["Strictly Business" movie] soundtrack [which included RE's hit "Lock It"]. But, if I'm going to talk about D.C., I've got to talk about my man Marc Barnes who was one of the regionals at Uptown, and it's a good possibility that he played a role in that as well because we had certain tastemakers around the country that we interfaced with all the time. I remember Spike Lee doing [EU's]"Da Butt" [on the "School Daze" soundtrack], and there was a cultural phenomenon at that moment around Go-Go. [Also], Doug E. Fresh, who's a dear friend of ours...he always spoke about Go-Go as well and was a big fan of the culture.

From the 2000s and beyond, the relationship between radio and Go-Go has remained fraught, but things have changed. Salih Williams, a Go-Go band member and radio personality, Chuck Chillout, a radio DJ on WBLS in New York and on Rock the Bells Sirius XM, and Funkregulata Celo, a radio and club DJ who has been playing Go-Go for decades, say things have improved. Williams, who was part of Simpson's show, says that Simpson has been supportive over the years and has incorporated more Go-Go into his show.

Salih Williams, AKA Bootsy Vegas: Donnie Simpson played Go-Go. When I was on the show, he played it. Donnie was one of the few people that played "Sunshine" when he was on PGC, he played "Sunshine." But I also know for a fact that he's been playing the new DJ Kool song and the remix and I know for a fact that he played Michelle Blackwell "Enjoy Yourself." Donnie can only control what's on his show. He can't control the whole station and what the music director plays. He's always been supportive. He's always had a great relationship with people in Go-Go bands. But I think sometimes people assume because he played it on his 4 hours, that it should be played all day. It's unrealistic. But I do believe that one thing that's not known is the fact that there's a lot of turnover in music directors and deejays, so it all depends on who the person is. I mean, since he's been on Majic 102.3, Deejay Rico plays Go-Go every day. Like literally. It depends on what deejay is there and what days he's on. But it's not supported on radio enough or very little and that's a great question. That's a legit question.

Radio is still relevant, but it's not the end all, be all as it was 10-15-20 years ago. Through the internet, hash tags, and all these streaming services, I think we've got to come up to the digital age because the way the average person consumes music is now different, and radio is only one form of that. You know, YouTube, I mean literally, there's just so many other streams- Reels and all that. Tik Tok. If you ask somebody how they want to hear music depending on their age range, they would say Tik Tok first and radio second. We've got to get creative and find creative ways to connect with our consumers. We've never had this great, cozy relationship with radio anyway.

Chuck Chillout, a radio personality from WBLS in New York and Rock the Bells Sirius XM, says he plays Go-Go regularly and has throughout his career. He remembers the hip-hop/Go-Go collaborations of the 80s and their appeal with radio listeners in D.C., NYC, and beyond.

Chuck Chillout: "I play Go-Go all the time. I play Chuck Brown, Junkyard Band, EU, Trouble Funk, and Rare Essence. I like the beats. Go-Go is a cousin of Hip Hop. I have a funny story. When I met Trouble Funk, they were in the studio in Brooklyn with Kurtis Blow. I was there when they put down the timbales. We were talking and I was like, 'Oh, I play all your stuff,' and they were like, 'Oh, really?' I was like 'Why do you think Kurt is doing the record with you? Because all the beats we played were part of hip hop, so y'all's stuff was part of that.' They were shocked. I never got a chance to meet Chuck Brown. I wanted to meet him. He was the first one we played in the 70s- the Bustin' Loose record. About a month ago, I opened for Doug E. Fresh and he had the Chuck Brown Band with him.

I think he's doing a couple of dates with them on tour. They sounded good. I remember when Russell Simmons signed Junkyard Band to Def Jam. They did one or two records. I don't think he knew what to do with them, but at least he signed them. One thing about Russell, he had an ear for stuff, so whatever was hot, he was signing them. The music business today goes by how many followers you've got, not if the music sounds good. We play all the break beats along with their (Go-Go) stuff too. 'Da Butt' was huge. And Chuck Brown's 'We Need Money.' I played that the other night on Rock the Bells radio. Doug E told me that he met Chuck and said he was cool. The foundation of Hip Hop was James Brown, Jimmy Castor,

George Clinton, Sly and the Family Stone, and Chuck Brown. That's all the music we heard growing up, so they put the blueprint in our heads for us to do the Hip Hop.

Funkregulata Celo, a radio and club DJ who got his start DJing in Go-Gos with Ken "Icy Ice" Moore, *says Go-Go has always gotten some radio play but thinks if the genre produced more original compositions, it might receive even more time on the airwaves.*

Leon "Funkregulata Celo" Ferguson: I think it's because they're not writing original songs. They might write some original songs, but to me Go-Go needs a Chucky Thompson. God rest his soul because ... look at Chuck's last album. He came out with "Chuck Baby." I was in Savannah (GA) when that song came out. I went to the Club in Savannah. I had just moved there so I went to the club. They were playing music and people were dancing, but the DJ slid "Chuck Baby" in, and everybody got up. I saw everybody put down their drinks and stop whatever they were doing, and women were taking their shoes off to go to the dance floor. It was amazing to me. It was in Savannah, Georgia. So Go-Go has a big influence in many places that people don't even know.

When I was coming into radio, it was under different circumstances. When I was coming into radio, it was to do a hip-hop show. DJ Iran put me on the radio and we had the first hip-hop show. It was on Saturday night for 2 hours. We were playing all hip-hop, so my focus at that time was hip-hop. To be honest with you, Hip Hop is my first. That's what made me want to become a DJ. Not to slight Go-Go at all, but for me, Hip Hop always came first. I could have been a drummer in a Go-Go band. I play drums. But I wanted to be different, Hip Hop was my way of being different, and DJing was my way of being different as a young mind. I came to WKYS and at WPGC at that time, yes. They were playing a lot of songs that had Go-Go remixes.

Mystro, DJ Mystro (Sean Mathers) was responsible for that, God rest his soul, and Charles the Mixologist made Go-Go remixes to everything. And KO Productions. When I came in, it was a little different. When I came in, after a while, when I was on KYS, probably about a year, they came to me and asked me to do a Go-Go show. Play an hour of Go-Go, and I did it for a little while, but then I went to them and said, "I know somebody who loves Go-Go a lot more than I do. And it's not that I don't love Go-Go, don't misunderstand me because I do love it, but I know somebody

134

who loves it way more than I do." And that was DJ Flexx, and I gave them a DJ Flexx tape, and that's how DJ Flexx got there. He got in, started doing the Go-Go thing, and then went to PGC. "Da Butt" is a universal record that will be played in every single location. It could be a Bar Mitzvah. It could be a wedding. It's always going to get played out of every Go-Go record.

From a DJ's standpoint. To me, if you listen to Hip Hop back in the day. It had Go-Go in it. They sampled it. Kurtis Blow used it. "Rock the Bells." "My Mic Sounds Nice." We can keep it going. Go-Go is unique to D.C. and everything, but it can be produced. For example, you've got [Junkyard's] "The Word" and "Sardines." That was a produced record. Even though the difference between that record and a whole lot of records that are being produced, that record sounded authentic. And when I say authentic, it sounds like that's how they would be playing it on the stage in front of people.

Spotlight: James Funk

In 2012, I had the privilege to sit down with the legendary James Funk of Rare Essence, a highly sought-after DJ, after one of his Saturday morning shows at WPFW 89.3 in Washington, D.C., where he has been a fixture for decades. I wanted to pick his brain about the decades-long success of Rare Essence from the beginning, his group, Proper Utensils, which he started as a project away from Rare Essence, and his thoughts on the music business in D.C. in general.

First, you've got to know the business and what it always looks like. It's not always that. At the end of the day, when you count your money and pay your expenses, it's that bottom line that makes sense. After you pay your bills, if your bills get paid, so we had a lot of great shows and we had a lot of miss shows and this is during in our best season. People left- some left because they thought the grass was greener on the other side, not knowing the business, and some left because of big heads. Everybody's ego inflates once it starts coming in, but you've got to know how to control it so you can continue on. But it's good to have an ego. I always tell them that, musicians, it's always good to have an ego. It kind of helps your persona. But then you've got to know the business. You've got to learn the business. That was the first thing I was told when I got in the business. Learn the business and learn the people who are in the business. Although at the time, I was going to school for business, I did eventually drop out because I thought I had it in hand, I made mistakes, but you learn from your mistakes. The one thing they could never say was that the books were ever closed to them. When we started, the parents were involved because they were boys, but when they became men, everybody else had to back up and let them handle their business to the best of their ability. We always had to bring lawyers in, corporate lawyers, entertainment lawyers, they're something else. They are more expensive than any other lawyer that I ever had to deal with. But all of that costs. Rent, daily upkeep, daily expenses, payroll, taxes, and everything like that, that has to be paid. I'm not trying to go to prison if you don't pay your taxes. Ain't nothing in jail for me.

Rare Essence was known for their red and white uniforms; Funk says they helped the band stand out, especially in the early days.
Footz, it was his brainstorm. He came up with the color. He came up with the name Rare Essence. He turned a perfume name around. It started with Young Dynamos, but those names don't last. It's alright for boys, but when you become men, you've got to drop that. But yeah, we had people making them (uniforms). And then they made some themselves. Like the tuxedos we had, I can't remember the name of that tuxedo shop, but they went out of business, so that was like a steal because they kind of gave them to us for nothing. We had to pay for some things and some things kind of fell in our lap.

Funk says that the band received community support early on, but he worked with them to develop their musicianship to have longevity as a group.
I guess most of the community was so amazed that the band being so young, having this big sound, so when I would hear them (the band), I would come down and try to teach them certain things. But the main thing I tried to instill in them was to learn to read and write the music. Learn to read and write. And own your own music. Right after Rare Essence, they took music out of the schools and that hurt. If you listen to some of the acts today, it's cool to play on feel if you know your instrument, but you've got to get the technical end of it that helps you get through the basic rudiments, the basic knowledge of music. That helps you get through. And then, Rare Essence came up in an era where I came up right after the big bands- I was the oldest. With my brother being in the house, there was always music in the house. There was always a band around our house, so we came up with bands, vocal groups, doo-wop groups, funk bands, big bands, so all that kind of music throughout our career, you can hear different genres of the different music- blues, all that, but now, today, since

everything is electronic, you just got a bass and maybe a drum machine, and then you don't have music in school, where they get the technical end from, that's why you hear a lot less. Even with national music that's been recorded, ain't nothing but a drum machine and maybe a one-note here. You don't hear chords and things like that no more, bridges— you don't hear none of that no more.

Funk on newer bands:
For my preference, I don't knock them because they're a part, a form of Go-Go, and they may be the one. Even though Go-Go is underground in a lot of cities, I think it's bigger in other countries, but it's still underground in a lot of cities in the United States. They may be the ones that can make it all over the globe. You never know because even when Rare Essence came in, though we were playing songs, we got to start creating our own music, and people think, some people, the older people thought the same thing that they think of the bands today. But that didn't stop us because whatever we had to do, we did it musically. Because we played songs that people could understand who we were until we got into our own thing. But I still don't have a problem playing songs and being an act myself. I don't have any other people playing other songs. It makes it fun for me. I always like to create my own, but I don't have a problem playing nobody else's.

Personally, my other group, Proper Utensils. Maybe L!SSEN. I can say Maybe, but you know, because I'm used to... even though I'm used to Trouble Funk, Experience Unlimited, Rare Essence, I'm a little older. I go back to the Young Senators, Black Heat, Corvettes, Aggression, and Brute. There were so many... D.C.'s always been a LIVE city with live entertainment, whether it's vocal groups or live bands. And I go so far back so these newer groups- to me, there's something missing. Something is missing, but like I said, I don't knock them for what they do.

Funk on how Go-Go can keep its integrity as music becomes more driven by computers than musicians playing instruments.
I hate to say, I don't know. I thought by now, the world would be completely computerized, and all you've got to do is just push buttons. It may not have a drum machine. It's definitely not going to have the feel of a live drummer. It's just two different feels. It's kind of good for a DJ because it's straight. You don't have too much fluctuation, even though it does move a little bit with a drum machine. But a drummer might speed up to 88 beats and drop back down to 82 beats during the course of a song,

but try to keep it steady, but I think as the world is changing, it's really only the old-school Go-Go fans that like that pocket the way that we used to arrange the songs. When we played up at the Black Hole, I noticed that the kids were in some of the songs when we played "Mr. Big Stuff," when we went into the breakdown, the kids liked it, and the younger bands saw how hyped the audience got with the timbale breakdown and how they got hyped any time we played it. That's why it transferred from the conga player to the timbale player with the newer groups, but to answer your question, I don't... you know, they're close, but they're not touching it, like I said. L!SSEN, that's the only other group I kind of listen to and I listen because I like that they were creative. They had creative juices flowing in there. It's kind of hard to say for some of the other groups.

I don't want to name, but when you're just playing R&B songs and just playing them and if you're not rearranging it, to make it feel like it's your own song, that's one of the things a lot of the groups got away with back in the day because there was a time we had to play the song exactly like the record. Then there came the era when you had to put your own feel to the record and that's not what most of these newer groups now, but L!SSEN, I think, is rather close. Tell you the truth, I can't think of all the groups. There're so many groups. Every 10 years, it seems like a flow of bands and only the strong stands. Out of the 10 bands, you might get only 2 or 3 that be a mainstay. I can't hardly answer that question.

In 1986, Rare Essence released the iconic album, Live at Breeze's Metro Club; Funk says that looking back, he wishes the sound quality would've matched the quality of the music.
That was my second thing I was involved in, even though I've always wanted to own a radio station and a record store, but I blew all that. That was a good production. But the sound people we used didn't come up with the best sound gear. It was a lot of stuff that they didn't do that they should have done to make that a better-sounding album. It was a good party album, but as far as sound, I'm always into the sound. You have people looking to compete. You've got the majors. You've got Quincey Jones, Stevie Wonder, and Michael Jackson, and if you want to get into that arena, you've got to be as technical to get there but yet don't lose your groove. If I give you something that just sounds half the sound, then especially it's almost as if we are a new artist even though we're based here and the number of years we're here, we don't have it like Michael Jackson... Like "Oh, let me see what that sounds like," "Oh, Rare Essence – tell me about this," and you have to go through all that again.

138

Funk on how a little "Little Benny" joins Rare Essence

Benny came up, and I was sitting on the porch the first time he came around. He was taking horn lessons from Mr. Harrington around the corner, and he came around. You think he was short now? He was a tiny little thing. He was carrying this big ol horn case, his trumpet case. "Can I join the band"? I said OK. He came out twice before we let him in because I told him. "Man, there's a little dude out here that wanna play horns." And at that time, I was just advising them. I wasn't in management just then. This was before they changed over to Rare Essence. So he came in, did his little thing, and I took them up, Ned, Footz, Whiteboy, and Godfather. I took them up one day to see Chuck because, at the time, I was kind of, I was real strict on them. I had always heard from James Brown that all band leaders- that you've got to be strict on your members and don't let up. And my mother used to beat down on me, saying to let up on them. They're kids. I always believed that if you want something, you have to work for it. And Benny, boy, he beat me up real bad because he was so short. I was maybe just 19 at the time myself. This was maybe 75, no, 76. Chuck was playing at the Maverick Room. Ned was the first to take off and start learning to play. My uncle was teaching Footz all the rudiments on the drums and all that. I think Whiteboy took guitar lessons too. I didn't know it was called dynamics at the time, but you weren't doing dynamics- you've got to play with clarity.

You have to compliment each other. I took them up to The Maverick Room. I had to ask Mr. Jones if it was okay to keep them with me because they were underage. They might have been 16. They might have been 15 or 16. They were like 4 years younger, but Benny was like 7 years younger. So, I took them up there to hear the band. They had never heard of the band. I said this is how a group is supposed to sound. They weren't even into concerts, and I was always going to concerts. Chuck was about the closest thing in town so I could give them an idea. See, this is how a band is supposed to sound. Before we came up there, I had already asked Chuck if we could play that percussion part. That was his idea. But he didn't know the group would be as tight as it was. He just thought it would be like EU or Trouble- someone just giving him a headache or something at the time, but so the next time. From that point on, you could see I really knew then that they were really interested in the groups because they were like on them when they took a break, I introduced them to the band, and they were on them like that, asking them all kinds of questions and that made me proud, but Benny on the other hand, he was mad as he could be

139

because he couldn't go so I don't know how, but somehow we slipped him in there. I don't know how. I think Godfather went with me and took them to see what a band is supposed to sound like, and I guess from that point on, we just set the sails, and they just went on. It's been interesting.

There are pressures of being in the public eye, and sometimes things don't always go as planned, but it's still family at the end of the day.
As far as Rare Essence, those that were in it like I told the group, one of the first, like it was told to me, I pass them two down. I always tell them, some of the people might be in the group to be in the group. They might be here for prestige or for right now- they're not in it for the business part of it, and it might not last. Somebody's gonna get big-headed, and somebody might get drugged out, a girl might turn them out... I lived it. Thank God I'm here today. I was telling a close friend of mine Benny is still...I'm still healing from that.

Because I know a lot of people, some of them mean well, and some of them, you just gotta, "Look, I can't talk about that right now." Even though I really think God took him from us to wake us up. Somebody that's in the midst of everybody...because it took everybody by surprise, so it's something God wants us to do, or he's trying to wake us up. That's how... Benny did, he had that We had an argument and everybody, that's the tape that everybody buys "The Fight Tape," that I was fighting [a fight occurred during a live show where Ned's bass was too loud and Ned and Funk had words while other band members instigated] and ... see what I do now when we perform, Let me say this first. I know I did it and admit to it and have to accept it like I did because, just like with drug addiction, I did it. I can't hide it. I did it. You know I did it. What's it gonna do? It's not gonna do me no good because when I talk about it and band members, I'm like, No, I'm gonna talk about it. I'm not talking about it cause I'm making fun of it. I'm not making fun of it, and I did it. And I'd be lying to you if I said I didn't do it. But the same thing with me and Benny. What angers me is they always wanna talk about the fascination of it. Some people's heads might not be clear enough to see, but we discussed it when we played with Proper Utensils. Look, yeah, we fussed a lot, but families do that. But look at us now.

We had to both laugh at ourselves- what were we mad about? But after that, during my drug addiction, I understood that the band had lost faith in me. Because their leader is now lunchin' out, I'm not mad at none of that. It was a wake-up call for me, and I had to learn. I don't place blame anywhere. If I blame anything, I start with me first. The thing about that fight thing is that, yes, we did argue. We weren't the ones fighting, and who I was fighting was not the issue here. The thing is how must stronger we grew and how much more we did since our brotherly love was there.

Chapter 10: The More You Know

This section is dedicated to and inspired by the untimely passing of Timothy "Shorty Tim" Glover at the age of 58 on January 6, 2022. He was a pioneering percussionist in the genre of Go-Go and left his mark! Most percussionists in our genre cite Shorty Tim as someone who they watched, followed, and strived to emulate his style, whether with the cowbell or the roto toms. After his passing, several people mentioned that Shorty Tim always felt terrible because although he had done so much, he remained under the radar for some reason. He never got his "just due." I know that many people in Go-Go have done a lot but are not among the significant topic of conversation, and I decided to change that. I never wanted anyone to feel unappreciated again. I started this "Spotlight" series a couple of days after Tim's passing on Facebook and Instagram. I shined the spotlight on a different person every day. We should all be able to get our flowers while we are here to enjoy them. These brief Spotlights only scratch the surface of the contributions of these talented individuals, and there are many, many other great talents involved in Go-Go who still aren't included.

(These Spotlights were written in 2022, so some featured may now be playing with different bands.)
Responses are listed in alphabetical order.

Chris Geronimoe Allen, percussion
Geronimoe is a musician, producer, manager, and consultant. He is also a sought-after percussionist with a decades-long footprint in Go-Go, having played with bands such as Mass Extinction, Redds and the Boys, Soul Patrol, Bela Dona, and Trouble Funk. He has recorded with and/ or performed with national recording artists Earth, Wind and Fire, Foo Fighters, Najee, Tony Terry, Frank McComb, and Sylver Logan Sharp, to name a very few. Now, the culmination of all of the years in the industry has brought Chris to his latest venture as the CEO of his own entertainment group- JUSS GUD Muzik LLC. His vision is to spread love, GUD energy, and GUD Muzik.

Darrell "Blue Eye" Arrington, drums
Darrell started on his musical journey playing the congas at age 11. After the band Trash Connection broke up, their equipment was stored in Arrington's basement, so he had unlimited access to practice on any of the

instruments. Congas was the first choice. While other 11-year-olds were out playing, he was in the house teaching himself how to play congas. Over the next few years, Blue Eye joined several neighborhood bands to hone his skills, such as Valley Green Groovers and Southeast Groovers, and then started the band Wahler Place Groovers along with Little Duke. He joined Ultimate Groove at 15 and then joined Physical Wunder on congas where he appeared on his first recording, "Let's Get Physical." Then came the move to Junkyard Band, where his versatility paid off as he spent some time playing both congas and drums during his many decades on and off with the band. Blue developed a great relationship with Roy Battle, opening the door to several bands and projects- Hot, Cold Sweat, Proper Utensils, and Rare Essence. In between his many years with JYB, Blue Eye played with 911 and EU. He then joined his former Physical Wunder bandmate, Doc Hughes' newer group, Faycez U Know, where he felt like he could recharge his spirit. During his career, Blue Eye played with 50 Cent as well. "I idolized Rare Essence as a child. I grew up sitting outside on the corner listening to all of them practice."

Wendell Bacon, guitar

Wendell was 7 years old growing up in NW D.C. when his mother made him play guitar and bass. He was enamored with guitarists Carlos Santana, Al DiMeola, George Benson, and Jimi Hendrix but did not even like Go-Go until he saw EU play at a Jack and Jill dance in 1978 at the age of 11. Wendell's older brother had made him go to the dance because he always sat in his room practicing every night. He heard Anthony "Redds" Williams of Redds and the Boys playing with Rare Essence while Andre "Whiteboy" Johnson was on a break. He thought it was Redd's band until he saw Rare Essence again at Emory Park in 1979. Wendell had the good fortune to meet another NW musician Greg "Googie" Burton, when he was 13 or 14 and played in the D.C. Youth Orchestra. They formed Reality Band and, from there, with Chris Walker, started Suttle Thoughts. Over the years, Wendell has played with bands such as Familiar Faces, Godfather and Friends, and Soul'A Movement, including several Reality Band members, Michael Benjamin, and Googie Burton.

Donald Barnes, vocals

Donald Barnes has been going to Go-Go s since 1981 but was blessed with the opportunity to start performing in 1998. At a Maiesha and the HipHuggers show, he was in the crowd when vocalist Junie Henderson "dared" him to get on the mic. Donnie surely caught the attention of Sugar Bear and Maiesha that night! That "dare" turned into a two-year, seven-night-a-week run! He has also been on the mic with Rare Form and Black Trax with Ivan Goff, the Formula, and Paridym Band. In 2021, he performed with All Access Band. 90% of Donnie's career has been as a vocalist/ rapper and hype man for EU. It has taken him across the country, "Doin' the Butt."

Roy Battle, musician, engineer, producer
Roy continues to have a decades-long career in Go-Go as a producer, audio engineer, and musician. Roy has teamed up with Charlie Fenwick for most, if not all, of Charlie's projects. He's worked extensively with Hot Cold Sweat and Huck-A-Bucks and was very instrumental in helping to put the all-female band Pleasure together. Roy spent many years with Proper Utensils before moving on to Rare Essence, where he has been for the past 20+ years. "Rare Essence brought me into the band in 2000 from Proper Utensils, but they've been very good to me and very accommodating when I have other ventures to partake in musically. They always welcome me back, so it's been a good relationship with them- great management team, great personalities, so it's never a dull moment with Rare Essence."

Michael Benjamin, keyboards
Michael started playing music while a student at John Bayne Elementary School. He first learned trumpet and then played the tuba in the marching band at Largo High School. He developed a love for keyboards after watching the "3 Kings": Rare Essence's Godfather, Scotty, and Marky. He was blessed to be taught by Largo High classmate Byron Jackson. They would go to the piano room at Prince Georges Community College and play for hours. In 1984, Mike played with Icee Hott, and in 1985, he joined Reality Band. In 1987 he played a short stint with RE. In 1993, Michael was a founding member of Suttle Thoughts. He was also a member of Soul'A Movement.

Archie Beslow, vocals, trombone
Archie Beslow got his start in 1983 with Black Nation Band. Black Nation Band was the first band to play at Chuck E. Cheese. In roles as lead talker, cowbell, and trombone, Archie can also get behind the congas. He's played with Ayre Rayde, Reality Band, Versatyle, Prophecy, Nexxx Level, and Sharmbe Mitchell Paradise Band. Currently, Archie can be seen and heard as the leader of the group Blacc Print Experience, who released their single, "Hey World." Archie is also a 2-time author and athletic coach as well.

Greg Boyer, trombone

Greg started his illustrious musical journey playing the alto sax, although he played his first gig on tenor sax at age 15! He switched to trombone when a band he played with in college already had two sax players. That was "all she wrote." A year later, in 1978, at 19, Greg joined Parliament-Funkadelic after the entire horn section had quit! Rodney "Skeet" Curtis, who played bass for P-Funk during the time, encouraged Greg Boyer, Bennie Cowan, and Greg Thomas to fill the vacant horn slots and became the horn section for years. He stayed with P-Funk until 1996. Greg played with Sluggo (1988) and Little Benny (1988-89). In 1989, he joined Chuck Brown, where Chuck gave him an open door to play whenever he wasn't on the road. He still plays with the Chuck Brown Band. In 1998, Greg joined saxophone great Maceo Parker until 2020. This led him to play with the late great legend Prince from 2002 to 2009.

Gerald Brooks, drums

As their drummer, Gerald started playing with the Pump Blenders in the summer of 1979. They enjoyed a three-year run at the Howard Theatre as the second headliner opening for Rare Essence. In 1985, Gerald recorded his first album with the Pump Blenders. In 1986 they met the late great Glenn Ellis, long-time bass player for Chuck Brown. Gerald was a member of the Pump Blenders when they recorded their second album with Glenn while they were all members of the Maxx Kidd camp. Maxx Kidd worked with Trouble Funk, EU, Chuck Brown and the Soul Searchers, Redds and the Boys, Sluggo, and the TTED All-Stars. Gerald performed with The Pump Blenders in New York on two notable shows- once at The Ritz for Madonna's Welcome Home Tour party with Redds and the Boys and then at the Palladium with all the bands with Maxx Kidd. In 1988 the Pump Blenders recorded "I Want You Back Now." Reo Edwards took the group under his wing and taught them a lot about the business and how to structure the band. Gerald left the Pump Blenders in 1993 and started playing drums for Reality Band and Crossover Band with Ricky "Rock Steady" Brown and the late Slickdaddy Rick. In 1994 he went on the 1994 SWV LONDON TOUR, where he was the drummer for the group Intro. He played for a month, returned home and married again in 95. In 1999, Gerald went back to playing with Crossover until 2004. A year before Mr. Busey Sr. passed away, he asked Gerald to work with his son, George Jr., to take over the band. After some time, he decided to do it. Gerald is the only original member of the Pump Blenders still with the band. He is also playing drums for Unity Baptist Church.

145

Ricky "Rocksteady" Brown, percussionist
Rocksteady started playing drums at the age of 10. By the time he was 14, he had landed a gig on the 1983 movie *The Big Chill*, which earned him a platinum album! Ricky's first Go-Go band was called Chuck and the Boys; he later played with a band called Crowd Pleaser and was eventually discovered by The Pump Blenders. He auditioned on a Thursday and was playing with the band at the Howard Theater by Friday. Ricky also played with Hot Cold Sweat and then started a band called Crossover, where he met Kenny Green from the platinum '90s R&B group Intro. Crossover toured with Intro for more than two years. Rocksteady has also toured with Patti LaBelle, CL Smooth, Maze, Ashanti, and many more. Once off the road, Ricky returned to D.C. and started The Sweat Band. After the passing of his good friend and longtime bandmate and collaborator, Brian "Slick Rick" Williams, he retired the name "The Sweat Band." However, he continued to play—his most recent endeavor is the Go-Go group The Rock Steady Project.

Tony "Oola Tony" Brown, vocalist, and percussionist
Oola Tony Brown has enjoyed time in the Go-Go genre as a former member of EU but was able to parley his talents onto the national scene touring with New Edition as their percussionist. In the early 90s, Tony used his vocal abilities to form a trio, and a successful audition with Showtime at the Apollo was the result. Back at home in D.C., Tony connected with Adrienne Burkley to form the group Horu releasing several popular singles.

John "JB" Buchanan, musician
JB can be seen and heard playing both the trombone and the keyboard (sometimes simultaneously) with Proper Utensils. As a member of The Soul Searchers from 1971 to 1986, JB earned a gold record for "Bustin' Loose" in 1979. Besides his long tenure with The Soul Searchers and writing or co-writing most of the songs on their first 3 albums, JB joined Rare Essence in 1986 at the request of James "Funk" Thomas. JB spent many years as a music and science teacher in the DCPS of which he was also a product. He continues to educate students through the Teach the Beat program. JB is also a certified diving instructor.

Tommy "Ko Ko" Burch, musician
Ko Ko displayed his gift for music at a young age, and his parents cultivated it. He showed immense promise as his parents watched him

"perform" on pots and pans in the middle of the kitchen floor before he was old enough to walk. He got his first professional drum set while he was in Preschool. Although he played with other bands, he had a special connection to the Young Experience Band, which his mother founded to give the youth in the community a way to cultivate their musical talents. They traveled all over and even played at the Apollo Theatre. Members of the Young Experience Band were Nicky, Ronnie, Taj, Gino, Erik, Pat, Sidney, Lavert Cole, Naa Naa, Clinton, Kenny, Marcellus, Shawn-B, Roland, and Harold B. Sadly, Ko Ko passed away in 2015.

Gregory "Googie" Burton, musician, sound engineer

When Gregory "Googie" Burton was 12, he picked up the bass. His father was a guitar player, but Googie didn't want to play the guitar. After watching a gentleman at church play the bass, he knew that was the instrument for him. At the time, he also cultivated his passion as a mechanically inclined young man by building minibikes. He traded his minibike for a bass guitar. Googie was splitting his time between playing the bass and also building cars. He had a car at age 14! As a young man, too young to get into the clubs, he and his friends hung out in front of the Creembo Palace at Georgia and Sheridan NW to listen to The Soul Searchers and Mixed Breed. At 13 or so, Googie had his first band called Crankshaft. They played Top 40. In 1976 Googie and Gerald Brooks formed Chase Band with several other guys. However, it wasn't until Googie saw Rare Essence that his thinking changed. He had seen Chuck Brown, but the way Rare Essence did their groove, and the fact that they were in their age group, he could relate more. At the time, Rare Essence was more of a groove band, not yet straight Go-Go. Although Googie is most well-known for his tenure with Reality Band, he also played with several other bands, including Busey Chase, Petworth, N2Deep, and Soul'A Movement, to name a few. In 1984, Googie got more interested in sound as a necessity. Reality was paying top dollar to sound technicians who weren't working out. Googie built his system and learned to run sound. He is currently one of the top sound engineers and runs sound for The Chuck Brown Band, Still Familiar, Rare Essence, Soundproof Band and E.U. and so many others. He has been working as a session musician in the studio and co-mixing some projects at Uptown Royalty Studio in Upper NW. Googie is also working on a significant project that is sure to change the game in 2022.

Eric "Bojack" Butcher, percussionist

Bojack, who has been in the scene since he was 11, started with Trash

Connection from Parkland in SE D.C. Trash Connection was the only Go-Go band to play in the Cherry Blossom Parade. Although Bojack began as a drummer, he soon mastered all things percussion. He actually brought the Latin sound to Go-Go in the timbales. He made the timbales more prevalent in Go-Go. He's also known for his top-notch skills on cowbell and conga. Bojack played with Junkyard on and off for years. During his 40+ year career, Bojack has played with Class Band, AM/FM, Rare Essence, Proper Utensils, 911, Familiar Faces, and Double Agent Rock. He has also recorded with Chuck Brown, Little Benny, Nonchalant, Doug E. Fresh, and Method Man to name a few. "Quentin "Footz" Davidson and Andre "Whiteboy" Johnson of RE asked if I knew how to play roto toms. They asked me to sit in for Mickey at the Metro Club one night. I started as the backup conga player, Mickey's back up. They auditioned me on the timbales and were impressed with my demonstration, and I became a member from then on. I dreamed of playing with Rare Essence, even as a little kid playing with Junkyard. I always wanted to play with them."

Garry Clark of the Peacemakers vocals
In the late 70s, Garry was a dynamic lead rapper of The Peacemakers. He managed the group, wrote songs, and was also a costume designer for the band. Today, Garry is involved in several organizations and founded Pep Rally for Peace in the Streets, an outreach entity. Garry still performs from time to time.

Lavert "TBob" Cole, vocals
TBob would turn to music as a career since he has been groomed for this since he was a baby. He would watch from his car seat in the rehearsal space as his father, Larry Cole, a soprano for Frankie Carter and the Dreams, would rehearse with his group. Lavert has been performing since 1989, when he was 11 years old. He started as a lead mic with Imperial Band. After a decline in his grades, his mother put her foot down, and he had to leave the band. Once he returned to the group, he was on the second mic as the hype man. At the time, Imperial Band was the youngest band on the circuit, and in 1991, they recorded their first PA tape at the Metro Club when Lavert was just 14 years old. He then went to Superior Funk, which soon changed the name to Pure Elegance. At the end of 1993, Lavert, KC, and Dre Dog were recruited by the Junkyard Band after the departure of Gene Pratt and Bruce Bailey. During that time, he played with Young Experience and Intimate Groove. Growing up in Southeast D.C., he attended both Ballou High School and The Duke Ellington School for the Arts. One of Lavert's first shows with Junkyard was at Ballou High

School. This versatile talent can sing, run mic 1 and mic 2, and play rototoms, congas, drums, and cowbell. He can also play the keyboards but has never done so with a band. He's also had two bands of his own, Da 1 Band and All4U Band. Lavert has worked with Lil Wayne and Jim Jones and, more recently, with CeeLo Green.

Steven "Too Tall" Coleman, trumpet

Coleman has lent his talents as a trumpet player across the Go-Go genre with the top bands. As part of the Wellman family dynasty in the DMV music scene, Steven started with Young Sound Band and Show which evolved into Fate's Destiny several years later. In the early 80s, Steven joined Experience Unlimited, an entirely different band than we currently know, where he could play in the same band with his cousin, Ricky Wellman. The lineup at that time featured one of the most well-respected horn sections in the area with Steven on trumpet, Carl "CJ" Jones on sax, and Mike "Go-Go Mike" Taylor on Trombone. They were known for "Somebody's Ringing That Doorbell," "Future Funk," and "Ooh La La La," to name a few. Steven then joined Redds and the Boys and appeared in the movie, "Good to Go." Steven went on to play with Chuck Brown again with his cousin Ricky Wellman and can be seen on Go-Go Live at the Capital Center! He also appeared on the Little Benny track "Who Comes to Boogie."

Stanley Cooper, guitar

Stan has been on the stage since the early 80s when he joined the band Prophecy. He has since played with a Who's Who in the industry! He has also performed and recorded with Little Benny & the Masters, CJ's Uptown Crew, Proper Utensils, The F.A.M. (featuring Shorty Corleone, Michelle Blackwell, and Gene Pratt, Backyard Band, L!SSEN, Chocolate City, the Legends of Go-Go, Trouble Funk, The Chuck Brown Band, Godfather and Friends, Suttle Thoughts, DJ Kool ("Just Be Thankful") Tony Wood, Northeast Groovers ("Sweetown"), Chuck Brown ("Can't Nobody Do Me Like Jesus"), Rare Essence, Experience Unlimited and Sweet Cherie/ Be'la Dona. His tenure with these bands laid the groundwork for Stan to parlay his talents into the jazz and R&B arena with his group 76 Degrees West. Their version of AWB's "School Boy Crush" may be better than the original. Stan has also toured and collaborated with other artists across genres, including Marcus Johnson.

Terrance "Coop" Cooper, manager

It was 1987 when Terrance "Coop" Cooper was 18 years old, living on

14th and Perry Place, NW. He was already an assistant manager at People's Drug Store. He woke up one Saturday morning to the sounds of music at the end of his block on Holmead Place NW and was intrigued after seeing a group of 11–13-year-olds playing on buckets. He asked their name, and they replied, "Back Yard." Soon Coop was managing the band and decided they should use real instruments. He already had managerial skills and was then promoted to Manager at People's Drug Store (now CVS) at 19. He had learned the music business through his friendship with the late Chucky Thompson and studied how Moe Shorter built Junkyard Band. After many years with Backyard Band, Coop shifted direction to work with AntFarMusic featuring Top 5. He is back on the radio with the Supa and Supa Midday show on Wednesdays from 2-4, along with DJ Supa Dan.

Derrick Leon Davis, also known as "China Boogie," saxophone
In childhood, Derrick's passion was ignited once he heard Trouble Funk's "Straight up Funk Go-Go Style." It prompted Derrick to join a neighborhood band where he honed his skills on the saxophone. Since he is a Maryland guy, through and through, it only made sense that in 1983, he would join Maryland's Ayre Rayde. In 1986, he joined EU and can be seen lighting up the stage with his saxophone, tambourine, and dance moves on Go-Go Live at the Capital Center. Just before EU went on tour to support their hit "Da Butt," Derrick was faced with the choice of a lifetime- go with EU or return to secure his college degree. He opted for the degree which has served him well. Once he obtained his degree, he returned to play with EU in the 90s. He also managed Y2K Band. He has also served PG County as a Councilman representing District 6.

Wayne Davis, bass and guitar
Wayne Davis has been playing music since the age of 8. He's a multi-genre, multi-instrumentalist and songwriter whose primary instrument is the bass. He started in Go-Go with a band called Double E, which later became The Mighty Groovers. He played bass and then switched to guitar. Wayne also played guitar for Chance Band, Certified Funk, Raw Production, Groove Masters, and others. He played bass with Whop N Em, Suttle Thoughts, Soul Patrol, and Proper Utensils to name a few. Wayne also has deep roots in funk, jazz, R&B, and gospel. He has performed and/or recorded with Citilites, Pookie Hudson & The Spaniels, the Midnight Movers, Keith Washington, and a host of others. Wayne released a solo CD, "A Childhood Dream," under the label Da.Bass.ics, to

showcase sounds that he's passionate about.

Rachelle "Chelle" Douglas, vocalist

Douglas has been involved in music since she was a child in elementary school. During her school-age years, she was a member of the D.C. All-City Choir and the PG County Public Schools' All-County Choir. When younger, Chelle was very bashful, but the moment arrived at a Faycez U Know show when Halima Peru shared the mic, and Chelle belted out Jill Scott's "Hate on Me." In 2007, a friend reached out about joining All 4 U, the first band Chelle joined. Later, she joined Anthony "Tom Tom" Talley and "Shorty Tim" Glover in the Vyntage Band. She then joined Go-Go Award-nominated Certified Funk Band. Things changed when Chelle joined G-Swagg Complete. Again, she joined "Tom Tom" Talley in this band and Mike Sharrieff, Marvin Brimage, Rodney Williams, and the late, great songstress Michele "Chel'e P" Perry. Chelle took a short break from performing, but by 2012, not only was she performing with G-Swagg, but she was also part of the management team where she was creating events alongside Smitty Productions, RED Productions, and OnFire Productions. In 2014, Chelle became the owner of G-Swagg. With an interest in radio, she also co-hosted The Cocktail Lounge DMV and Partymode Live, both on the Go-GoRadio.com platform.

Reo Edwards, producer, engineer

Reo Edwards is a producer, recording engineer, and songwriter, notably working with Trouble Funk and Chuck Brown. Most people know that Future Records is synonymous with the name Reo Edwards. Reo was the founder and manager of Trouble Band and Show, which later became Trouble Funk. He produced most, if not all, of the Trouble Funk classic hits in the mid-80s and many of the classic Chuck Brown hits. He also worked with Hot, Cold Sweat, Nature Boys, Northeast Groovers, Backyard, Pure Elegance, Physical Wunder, Mass Extinction, The Pumpblenders, and Publicity solidifying his production work and relevancy of his label, Future Records and Tapes, throughout the 90s. In the 2000s, Reo continued providing sound, this time for the next generation- the Bounce Beat bands. It has been said numerous times that the sound system that Reo built was made especially for Go-Go because the bass cabinets had the "thump" that made Go-Go famous. He continues to make an impact on the sound of Go-Go today.

Brandon "Blue" Epps, keyboards

Blue has always had an ear for music. He grew up in Southview, and after finding his older brother's Junkyard and Northeast Groovers CDs, he was immediately inspired to play in a band. Brandon was 18 when he started playing with Black Impression with his cousin. He started off playing percussion- timbales and blocks. It was during this time that he picked up the keyboards. He earned the nickname "Blue" because of the light on his keyboard. He stayed with Black Impression from 1999 to 2001, and then from 2001 to 2008, Brandon played with True Definition. He then went to MCB in 2008, where he stayed until 2011, briefly leaving to play with Da One Band and Real Live. Realizing that MCB was where we wanted to be, he returned and has remained there since.

Mercyle "Butchie" Farrell, CEO of Distinguished Entertainment
Butchie was a mere 12 years old when he produced his first event in the basement of his mother's house in NE, D.C. 12! At 14, he played keyboards for the band Sound Production Band and Show. Butchie also managed 2 bands during his career- Side Show and Bad Boys. As a student at Norfolk State University, he was entrusted by the student government to develop events, so he created the College Weekend at King's Dominion and various concerts and bus trips. During this time, he decided that promoting was the path that he wanted to take- and that's just what he's been doing. Just about 25 years ago, Distinguished Entertainment was born. Butchie has produced and promoted shows and events under his company/ brand. His first foray with a national act was The Isley Brothers, Angela Winbush, and Suttle Thoughts at DAR Constitution Hall. He has worked with just about every band in the DMV. Starting next month, all these years later, Butchie embarks on a new venture with Distinguished Entertainment with The Consortium at Capitol Hill in NE D.C., where it all started for Butchie Farrell at 12.

Charlie Fenwick, bass, studio owner
Charlie Fenwick has had an exciting career playing bass with the legendary Otis Redding and The Winstons. He and his wife, LeOra, then created Hot Cold Sweat, a famous group on the Go-Go Live at the Capitol Centre. The group was responsible for the hits "Meet Me at the Go-Go" and "Wiggle Your Body." As time passed, Charlie created and managed both Pleasure, the all-girl Go-Go band, and The Huck-A-Bucks. Both groups enjoyed successful runs. All-N-One and Dazzle were two other groups that Charlie had affiliations with. He is still going strong as the owner of Thump Studios, one of the prominent studios in the Washington, D.C., area.

Donnell "D. Floyd" Floyd, rapper, saxophone
Donnell "D. Floyd" Floyd played saxophone and rapped with Rare
Essence for 18 years between 1983 and 2001. He has also returned a time
or two to grace the stage with Rare Essence during the 2000s. Troy
Marshall and Bobby Smoot, who had the group Chance Band, introduced
him to Go-Go at the Duke Ellington School of the Arts. "I played with
Chance. Anyone familiar with Go-Go knew that Rare Essence was the
greatest band, and an opportunity arose when the sax player, Rory 'DC'
Felton, was quitting. I auditioned off of the song 'Mr. Magic' and played
with RE until 2001." Floyd then left to create several other bands,
including 911, Familiar Faces, Team Familiar, and Push Play. He is
definitely one of the most energetic frontmen in all of Go-Go.

Adebayo De De Folarin, vocalist
De De got his start in 1986. The first band that he worked with was the
Pumpblenders. As a versatile vocalist, he has performed with Let It Flow,
Brencore All Stars, S.O.U.L.O, 911, A Touch of Essence, Trouble Funk,
Round of Applause Band, and Suttle Thoughts. It's so great to see him
back with Rare Essence these days!! He appeared on RE's studio album
released in 1999, RE-2000.

Darrin "X" Frazier, keyboards, manager
Darrin X has been uniquely positioned to play, create and elevate both
classic Go-Go and Bounce Beat. As a musician and producer with Rare
Essence throughout the 90s, Darrin appeared on many of the most popular
hits. He also went on to manage TCB, the Bounce Beat Kings. Currently,
Darrin is working with some of D.C.'s professional sports teams behind
the scenes, and no doubt that some of the event pairings between the sports
and Go-Go were introduced by Darrin.

"Lil" Mickey Freeman, percussion
Mickey became interested in music at the age of 3. Of course, it's in his
blood as his father is the famous "Go-Go Mickey" Freeman, and his
grandfather is Mickey of the 60s group Mickey and the Blazers. By age
10, Mickey was playing trumpet in his elementary school band. At 14, he
played in his first Go-Go band, Mad Collision Band. Mickey can play all
percussion instruments and the trumpet. He's graced the stage with such
bands as EU, Suttle, and Team Familiar, to name just a few. Besides
seeing Mickey onstage, he is more focused now behind the camera lens,
where his photos and videos tap into more creativity from Mickey
Freeman.

Moe Gentry, sound engineer

Moe Gentry appeared on the scene in 1979. He is a highly sought-after sound engineer still over 40 years later. His contributions helped to create the sound. Over the years, Moe has worked with Rare Essence, Little Benny and the Masters, Junkyard, and Backyard Band to name a few. After a 6-year hiatus during the 2010s, Moe burst back onto the scene with not only his sound technology skills, but the development of G3 Entertainment which encompasses a management element as well. Moe is working across genres and has expanded into business and creative aspects of the genre. He can also get behind the congas if needed. He is known for the famous statement in the Rare Essence Highland August 5, 1982, PA Tape "Tell Jungle Boogie to put the vocal mic on the conga!" Fans know!

Boneita "Bunny" Glenn, vocalist

The first female member of Rare Essence, Boneita "Bunny" Glenn, joined the band in 1977. Boneita and founding RE member/ drummer Quentin "Footz" Davidson were in the same Spanish class together when she was in the 10th grade. She was always singing or humming, and it caught Davidson's attention; he mentioned to Boneita that he was in a band and that they were looking for a female singer. Boneita tried out and secured her spot on the front line, where she remained for about 2 years. After Boneita left the band, they asked her back to record several early Rare Essence hits, including "Body Moves," "Shoo Be Do Wop," and "Back Up Against the Wall," forever linking her voice with the band.

Tom Goldfogle, manager

Tom has been the man behind the scenes making things happen for decades. He became aware of Go-Go in the late 70s with the release of "Bustin' Loose" and in the early 80s when managing a record store in Landover Mall. In the 80s, Tom started Liaison Records with Becky Marcus as an independent label and became a national independent urban distributor and one-stop shop. Liaison then provided talent booking, management, PR, and music publishing. Most Go-Go products at some point went through Liaison during those years. It was through Liaison that Tom met Chuck Brown. In 2004, Tom left Liaison and created Full Circle Entertainment. He continued managing Chuck Brown's career and still manages the Chuck Brown Band. Tom is involved in many aspects of the business of Go-Go.

David Green, percussionist and vocalist

David started his musical journey at 12 on Xenia Street SE, the home of Rare Essence. David, the cousin of Jas. Funk and the late Quentin "Footz" Davidson attended St. Thomas Moore Catholic School. After class, the nuns allowed students to play instruments, and between David, Andre "Whiteboy" Johnson, Quentin "Footz" Davidson, John "Big Horn" Jones, and Michael "Funky Ned" Neal, they realized their musical talent and formed the Young Dynamos, the group that would eventually become Rare Essence. David and the group participated in talent shows and performed on the Showmobile, a traveling musical stage that was one of then-Mayor Marion Barry's Summer Youth opportunities, and at various schools. Admission was always 75 cents and a canned good. David also played with the Legends and Little Benny. When David started, he said no one was using the rototoms and timbales, and RE was the first. Most people know David as a seasoned percussionist, but few know he's also a vocalist. He says the highlight of his career was the first time he ever played at the Capital Center, and what brings him the most joy is making people happy with his talents and being a trendsetter. He loves seeing the kids watching him and picking up the sticks rather than hanging out in the streets.

Kenny "Kwick" Gross, drummer

Kwick was introduced to the drums at the age of 4. Starting in church, he also learned piano and organ. By 14, he was the drummer for the top 40 band "Expressions." Being well-versed in various genres, such as gospel, rock, R&B, Go-Go, and jazz, has prepared Kenny for many opportunities. He's been able to share the stage with Keith Sweat, Anthony Hamilton, Jon B., Chico Debarge, Kanye West, Ginuwine, Candy Dulfer, Spur of the Moment, John Legend, Salt-N-Pepa, Doug E Fresh, Jada Kiss, Marcus Johnson, and many others. He's also worked with Chuck Brown, Wale, Heaven Sent, and Godisheus. He's currently still playing in the church and also with Trouble Funk, DCVybe, and Chalyss Band. Kenny has also toured internationally with X-Factor's David Correy.

Sean "Kal-El" Gross, vocals, producer, sound engineer

Sean "Kal-El" Gross has been in various roles for many years. Not only is he a singer, songwriter, drummer, and producer, but he is also a trained recording engineer. Kal-El has worked extensively as an engineer in many area studios and does beats and vocal arrangements for many local artists. He is a four-time WAMA's Wammie Award winner. With Kal-El's versatile style, he played with and won a Wammie with the funk rock band

GODISHEUS. Kal-El also spent time on the stage with Familiar Faces, Faycez U Know, and E.U. He has worked with a Who's Who of national recording artists such as Gerald Levert, Johnny Gill, Mint Condition, and Patti Labelle, and that scratches the tip of the iceberg. He has graced many local stages, including the prestigious Kennedy Center and locations in New York, The Rock and Roll Hall of Fame in Ohio, and Disney World's BET Soundstage in Florida.

David Gussom, guitar
David has been on the scene since the 80s, showcasing his talents with everyone from the real, first, original Familiar Faces, Double Agent Rock, Chuck Brown, EU, Pure Elegance, Little Benny and the Masters, Trouble Funk, and Fayces U Know. Dave has worked both on stage and behind the scenes in the studio and production work. David spent a lot of time collaborating with the late Ivan Goff, even holding a position with Goff's Big City Records. This only scratches the surface of the contributions of David Gussom.

Maurice "Mighty Moe" Hagans, percussion
Mighty Moe has shared his talents behind the congas for 30 years. Not only has he played with Chuck Brown and The Chuck Brown Band, but he's also been a steady member of EU for many of those years. He has also performed with the unique Go-Go Symphony!! Mighty Moe also released his own single titled "Mighty Moe."

Benjamin "Scotty" Haskel, keyboards
Scotty was just 7 years old when he became interested in music playing congas, bongos, and drums in church. In 1979, when he was about 16/17 years old, he tested several positions with Rare Essence. He joined just after the Young Dynamos had reorganized before adopting the name, Rare Essence. Scotty started as a sound man but is the first to admit that he wasn't very good. He soon moved into a role with the crew setting up the keyboards. He learned that Darrien Grice would leave the band and started preparing to take his place. One evening, as the band was set to play at Northwest Gardens, Scotty began to play during sound check. Jas. Funk approached him, giving him a rundown of the set he would play that night and the next gig. He became a band member. Rare Essence was the first band Scotty played in and the first band where he would play keyboards. He was a member of Rare Essence from 1979 to 1985. Over the years, he's played with Little Benny, Pure Elegance, Exodus Gospel Go-Go, and Raw Production. "One of my best memories was being promoted from crew to

band member."

Edward "Junie" Henderson, vocalist

Junie is best known as a vocalist with EU appearing on some of their most significant hits, notably "Taste of Your Love" and "Don't Turn Around." These were released at the height of EU's popularity when they were signed to Virgin Records. Junie also performed with Double Agent Rock, Maiesha and the Hip Huggers and spent many years performing with The House Band at The Fish Market. Junie also appeared with EU in Spike Lee's film "School Daze" during the performance of the mega-hit, "Da Butt"! Most recently, Junie can be seen performing with his All-Star Purple Party, where he performs as Prince! It's a fantastic show and highly recommended!

Derrick Holmes, vocalist

Derrick has repeatedly proven to be a versatile leader heading up Vybe or DC Vybe. His vocal abilities, as well as his showmanship, lend themselves to keeping Vybe as one of the steadily working bands. He is always very professional.

Quentin "Shorty Dud" Ivey, drums

On the scene for over 35 years, Shorty Dud was a percussionist with the original Familiar Faces, formed in 1985. He also performed with AM/FM alongside Mike Hughes. Shorty Dud is well known for being a fixture with Rare Essence for many years. He is currently playing with several bands.

Malachai Jones, manager, booking agent, musician

Malachai's contributions to Go-Go are immeasurable. As a musician playing with bands such as Northeast Groovers and OP Tribe (and others) to managing Mambo Sauce, co-writing and producing "Welcome to D.C.," Malachai has a wealth of knowledge. He also served as the Entertainment Manager at Maryland Live! creating Go-Go Night, where Go-Go bands were able to hit the stage. He continues as a booking agent as he created Allive Agency and is the founder of GoGoTix.co. He is the creator of the band Crank Caviar. This scratches the surface of his contributions as a musician and businessman who has used his talents to push the genre further.

Allyson "Allycat" Johnson, keyboards

Allyson started out in 1989 with the band Klyxx and remained on the scene for decades. From Klyxx, this talented keyboardist spent time with the all-girl group Pleasure. Pleasure was responsible for the #1 Go-Go Christmas song, "Santa Claus is Coming to Town." In 2006, Allyson joined the pioneering group Trouble Funk before she retired in 2021. Thirty-three years is quite a long time as one of the first female musicians in the male-dominated industry of Go-Go.

Curtis Johnson, keyboards
Curtis Johnson was playing music before there was such a thing as Go-Go. Prior to joining The Soul Searchers in 1977, he played with Skip Mahoney and the Casuals and with the Dynamic Corvettes. After the release of "Bustin' Loose," the Soul Searchers became Chuck Brown and the Soul Searchers. Curtis appears on Chuck Brown and the Soul Searchers' hits on organ and backing vocals from 1977 through the 80s. In February 2011, the D.C. City Council gave a Proclamation on Chuck Brown and the Soul Searchers, which Curtis was named in this prestigious honor. Curtis can now be seen and heard with his group, Eternity.

Esther "Justice Jay" Jones, vocalist
Justice is no stranger to music, as she began writing music at the age of 11 and poetry at the age of 12. She was always involved in any opportunity for a singer, whether school musicals or plays. Although she began singing in church at a young age, she did her first R&B performance at 12 and recorded her first studio album at 15. When she was 19 years old, Go-Go was calling her name. After trying to find the right fit for her sound with multiple bands such as Class Band, NStyle, Drastic Measures, Smokin' Aces, Dynasty, and Project Stars, she found her home with Mental Attraction Band (MAB) in 2012. She decided to spread her wings and move on for several years with Mature Clientele and Band of Brothers but soon returned home again to MAB in 2019. She is most known for her vocal range and energy on stage, bringing her a solid fan base over the years.

Khalid Keene of K.O. Productionz, producer
Khalid started his first band, The Funk Invaders, in his basement in Lanham, MD, when he was 12. He played the drums. His first professional show was at the Chapter II (which became Chapter III then The Mirage) for the kiddie cabaret on Easter Sunday. Years later, the band morphed into The Stratus Band, where they were popular, playing Mayor Marion Barry's Inauguration at Tracks and opening for bands such as Pieces of a Dream and E. U. They had the honor of playing at the Music Radio Convention in Atlanta- Jack the Rapper. Their first single, "You're the

One," got nightly play on the Kevin James slow jams on 93.9 WKYS. Soon, as the music landscape changed, Khalid began writing raps, and his childhood friend, Clemont, started the group The Pretty Boy$. They released two singles, "Protection" and "Chillin at the Go-Go," on their label Cold Crushin' Records. Later, keyboardist Brian O. and Khalid moved behind the scenes to start KO Productionz and opened a studio in the basement. They hooked up with iconic On- Air Personality Albie Dee at WPGC and produced remixes. They soon signed with Madonna's label, Maverick/ Warner Brothers, and released "Booty Call." As time went on, Khalid has been involved in production work across genres, including Monica's "Don't Take It Personal" remix with Biz Markie for Dallas Austin's Rowdy Records and Yolanda Adams' "Gotta Have Love" featuring Tony Terry, which was nominated for a Dove Award. Later, they became in- house producers for Big 3 Records out of Tampa.

Randy Kilpatrick, bass
Randy Kilpatrick, also known as "Hollywood," is one of the genre's pioneers. This talented bass player graced the stages with Players Choice, the original Familiar Faces, Ivan Goff and BlaccTrax and Soul Patrol. His most notable tenure was with Redds & the Boys appearing on the group's hit "Movin' and Groovin'," where he can also be seen in the video. Randy also appeared in the Island Pictures film "Good to Go" (renamed "Short Fuse"), which was a controversial film. Currently, Randy is behind the scenes with his modification and repair shop for basses, Bassworx, where he has a Who's Who list of clients.

Dwayne Lee, musician
You can see Dwayne mostly playing guitar onstage, but he is also a drummer, bass player, and keyboard player! He is a recording engineer and a music producer with his company D.LEE PRODUCTIONS. Dwayne was the drummer for Redds and the Boys during their success and has played guitar with Fayces U Know, EU, Familiar Faces, MVP Band, No Sins with Lady Day and also played music and did production work with the Super Producers group, The A-Team. He also won a Wammie award for Best Rap Duo or Group with Godisheus, an honor bestowed on musicians from the Washington Area Music Association and also five-time Wammie award-winning group 3LG. He has also worked with Ashanti and J Holiday. Dwayne used his vast music business knowledge to host a radio show called DeBizNest. He works with Marcus Johnson on Johnson's Crank and Flo project.

Ras Lidj, Regg'Go creator

Larae King-Day, better known as Ras Lidj, has performed since age 5. In 1985, when Ras was a drum major in the Ballou High School marching band, he caught the attention of Go-Go veteran Kenny "Doc" Hughes. Doc invited him to audition for the band Physical Wunder, where he became a fixture on the frontline. Throughout his career, Ras –given his name by Rastafari elders in 1991 – has remained committed to and grounded in the foundation, beliefs, and roots of his Rastafarian way of life. He became focused as a songwriter, telling stories with a socially conscious edge. Ras Lidj's live music experience was branded Regg'Go—the unique combination of reggae and Go-Go fused roots and dancehall reggae with a strong Go-Go pocket beat. Ras Lidj and his Regg'Go traveled the US college and music festival circuit. In 2004, he released the EP "Baptismal," in 2007, Ras Lidj Regg'Go Band received the Dennis Brown Achievement Award at the D.C. area Reggae Music Awards. In 2019, the title track for his EP "All to the East" became the official theme song for the Pan African Federalist Movement's repatriation campaign, leading to Ras receiving its "Cultural Ambassador" title in the fall of 2020. In 2021, he traveled to Ghana to record the historical Regg'Go mini documentary featuring him performing at the Oak Plaza Hotel poolside bar "JamRock." Ras Lidj believes it's the Go-Go in Regg'Go that keeps the party in reggae.

Harold Little, trumpet

As a graduate of the famed Duke Ellington School of the Arts, trumpeter Harold Little fuses jazz, funk, and R&B from a Go-Go perspective. Not only is he a musician, but also a songwriter and producer. Harold has a large body of music showcasing his talents and has also worked with a "who's who" of D.C. area musicians, including Randy "Hollywood" Kilpatrick, Derek "Redfootz" Freeman, Milton "Go-Go Mickey" Freeman, Tony Cothran, and many others to create Go-Go infused music.

John "Cabalou" Locust, vocalist

John "Cabalou" started in Go-Go in 1978/79 with Leon Gassaway in a group called Warlocks. He played the roto toms because he really didn't want to be on the mic. Cabalou was more interested in doing what Rare Essence's David Green was doing as he was a beast on the roto toms. Gassaway said he didn't have time to train Cabalou on the roto toms and told him to go on the mic. The group had something at 14th, and Irving Street NW, and it was packed. Cabalou didn't want to do it, but again Gassaway told Cab to get back on the mic. Cabalou wasn't even sure what to say, so he was told to talk about his Mom or the Redskins. He did just that and hyped the crowd. It went on from there. But he still wasn't satisfied. Cabalou relays, "We ended up linking up with Petworth. Kenny and I were up there together, and I told him to do his thing, and I would back him up like how Funk and them were doing with Rare Essence. I ended up having to take over because Kenny had to leave the band. I stayed with Petworth briefly and then went to Heavy Connection. Binky from Peacemakers called me and asked me to go with them. Ju Ju [House] and I went to Peacemakers, and then I left, and I went back to Petworth for a while. Moe Gentry reached out to me to go with Ayre Rayde. I stayed with Ayre Rayde briefly, but while there, I did the vocals on their hit song, "Sock It to Me." I then went to play with Reality. In 1986, Reality was opening for Rare Essence at HD Woodson, and they didn't have anyone up there with them on the mic, so Donnell and Mickey reached out and said that Footz wanted me to play with them that night, and then they asked me to come to rehearsal. Rare Essence had a lot of shows, and I had a job where I had to be in at 4 am. I would leave the Metro Club and go straight to work. That wasn't working. Then in 1987, Tom Tom reached out from Hot Cold Sweat. I played with them for a little while. We played at the Capital Centre for Go-Go Live at the Capitol Centre. After that, I just left it alone. People were reaching out for me to return, but it wasn't what I wanted to do. People liked me on the mic, but I didn't think I was that good and I really wanted to play the roto toms."

Nathaniel "Go-Go Bouncey" Marshall Lucas Sr., percussion

Born in Washington, D.C., and performing under the name of "Go-Go Bouncey," Lucas has been involved in D.C.'s homegrown sound, Go-Go, for several decades. Known for his energetic style on the congas and roto toms, he has shared the stage as a member of Grammy-nominated recording artist EU. Over the years, he has performed with Little Benny and the Masters, 1-LUV, High Potential Band, and The Godfather of Go-Go, Chuck Brown. Lucas has also lent his talents to Jonny B, Hip Hop Artist Trip Star, Horu Music Experience, The 202 Project, and Proper Utensils. Lucas can be heard on recordings, "Ho Ho Santa," a 1989 release from High Potential Band, "Getting Funky Up in Here," and "Take Me Out To The Go-Go" releases from Little Benny and the Masters, and "Fire" and "Make Money" from EU. The album release of Little Benny and the Masters' Get Your Drink On (Get Your Freak On) featured a host of the Go-Go genre's luminaries, including the legendary Chuck Brown, James "Jas. Funk" Thomas, William "Ju Ju" House, Milton "Go-Go Mickey" Freeman and more. In 2002, Lucas debuted as an actor in a Crystal Restaurant and Bar commercial in Hyattsville, Maryland. He has also appeared in the TMOTTGo-Go Documentary performing with Little Benny and the Masters. Most recently, Lucas appeared as the drum teacher in the film Residue, released in 2020, written and directed by Merawi Gerima.

Liza Figueroa Kravinsky, musician
Liza was 8 years old when she moved to the D.C. area. She had an interest in music and honed her skills in classical music over those years. In 1985, while playing with pop group "The Answer," Liza was introduced to Go-Go as the group began to add songs to their setlist. In 1998, Liza received a visit at her home studio from Bob Pitts, the road manager for Motown recording artist and D.C. native Stacy Lattisaw. She was invited to tour with Stacy. Initially, she declined the offer, but when offered again a short time later, she accepted and went on tour as a member of Stacy's band. Over the next few years, Liza played with an all-female Go-Go band, Pleasure, and a faction of Trouble Funk, TRJ. In 1991, Liza composed for, directed, and performed with "Robin Power and the Uptown Dames," a Paisley Park project created by Prince. In 2010, after spending years immersed in various styles of music, Liza came up with the amazing idea to intertwine her training in classical and Go-Go, and The Go-Go Symphony was born. She is the founder and artistic director. Liza has been joined by Go-Go luminaries Stinky Dink, Ju Ju House, and Mighty Mo Hagans, to name a few. Liza is also a filmmaker and actress.

Frank SiRiUS "Scooby" Marshall, vocals, guitar
Scooby honed his musical talents starting at the age of 10 with various neighborhood bands. After solidifying his skills as a vocalist and guitar player, he played with 3rd Dimension, OP Tribe, UCB, LISSEN, Lissen Da Grewp, and Familiar Faces/ Team Familiar. Currently, he splits his time between Chuck Brown Band, 76 Degrees West, and, most often, Sirius Company, where they've just released new material, "On Top of the Moon," on all streaming platforms. At the age of 18, Frank had a publishing deal, and in 2010, he won a regional MTV award for Breakout Artist of the Year. He also founded The Go-Go Music Collective, a nonprofit organization to assist with educating our youth and advancing Go-Go music. Frank has also performed with a who's who of national artists, including Stevie Wonder, Fantasia, and John Legend.

Ihkand Mason, drums, engineer
With D.C. musical fixture Ignatius Mason as a father, it's unsurprising that Ihkand Mason has been around music his whole life. He was introduced

to the music industry at birth in 1976 and started playing drums at the age of 10. By 1989, Ihkand had formed Optimystic Tribe and became the backup drummer for Backyard Band from 1994 to 1998. Sound was always a big deal for Ihkand; in 1991, he started his career in audio engineering. He was the setup and monitor for Infant Eyes Productions, providing sound for OP Tribe, Raheem Devaughn, Glenn Jones, Dick Gregory, and many others. In 2002, he became Lissen's house engineer until he moved to Atlanta in 2005. While in Atlanta, Ihkand joined XO Band along with Ricky Angles from the Huckabucks and Off Script, with Khari Pratt from NEG as the drummer for both. He created the Cranklanta movement. In 2008, he created the Crank Brothers franchise with the help of Preston Blue under the Bag of Beats label. In 2010, Ihkand released his debut CD, "Welcome to Cranksville." He has made a career and life for himself in Atlanta, working for various sound companies, leading him to become the House Engineer for Q Parker of 112. This led to other opportunities with Ceelo Green, Jagged Edge, and more. He has a significant song placement led by a "certain" major artist that he will soon reveal…

Kenny McSwain, Trumpet
It was 1981, and trumpeter Kenny McSwain was just coming out of Shaw Junior High School when Boogie West approached him about auditioning for Mass Extinction. From there, he was hooked! Kenny had gone to Shaw Junior High and Dunbar High School with the late, great Carl "Chucky" Thompson. Chucky had been playing with Petworth Band and recruited him to join the group. Kenny graced the stage with Petworth from 1984 through the early 90s. At the time, he was also attending UDC, so from 1985-1987, he was a member of the UDC Jazz Ensemble. When Kenny left Petworth in the early 90s, he created the group, Colours along with bassist Gary Smith. In 2000 he joined Maniac and the Soldiers, and in 2010, A Touch of Essence. 2016 led Kenny to his project, B-Dock. He also played with Paradigm and Déjà Vu. He has also been on stage with Godfather and Friends in more recent years.

Kermit Meredith, aka CongoKermit, percussion
Kermit, also known as Congo Kermit, fell in love with percussion in elementary school, "playing beats" on the classroom desk. By the age of 14, he played with the Little Rascals, a local band that opened for Junkyard, Pleasure and Hot Cold Sweat, and other Go-Go legends at Holy Comforter School. After playing with Reality Band and Soundproof Band, Kermit played with Ayre Rayde and Vybe. He credits legendary conga

163

player Milton "Go-Go Mickey" Freeman as a mentor. In 2000, Kermit went on tour with R&B artist Ginuwine and continued to tour with him occasionally. Kermit credits his musical journey as helping him stay out of trouble when D.C. was known as the murder capital. In 2009, he tried his hand at acting, appearing in several movies, such as Mitch Credle's "Boss1" and "Boss2," Hannibal Chancellor's "Transitions" and Russ Parr's film "The Big Fifty," featuring Tank and Remy Ma. Kermit also appeared in Ben's Chili Bowl commercials with Russ Parr and Donnie Simpson.

Jeno Meyer, keyboards
Jeno Meyer is a self-taught keyboardist born and raised in NE, D.C. At a young age, he developed a passion for music and performed throughout the city with Go-Go bands such as Progressive Groove, 3rd Dimension (from Potomac Gardens), and the Young Experience Band. Jeno was always attracted to various genres of music, including jazz, R&B, and gospel. In 1996, he played with an R&B trio of ladies called "Amari." Then, in 1999, Jeno could tour for a couple of years with the funk band, Heatwave. Then, starting in 2002, Jeno spent the next 13 years touring with The Stylistics, which took him all around the world. After his run with The Stylistics, Jeno came home and toured stateside with various legendary groups working with Keith Busey's Unit Band backing a Who's Who of National Recording artists. He was thrilled to have the opportunity to work with Maiesha and the Hiphuggers for a reunion show. After that show, Jeno performed with EU, and his first performance with them was at the opening of the Smithsonian's African American Museum for a Who's Who list of attendees. He continues to perform with EU.

Bryan Mills, musician
Bryan Mills, a well-known saxophone and keyboard player, has had the honor of playing with "Pops"- Chuck Brown. He has also worked with Suttle Thoughts, Proper Utensils, and the Chuck Brown Band. In 2008, Secret Society, the brainchild of Bryan, was born. Bryan is also part of The Crank Jam All-Star Band for the World's only Go-Go Jam Session at City Winery in D.C.! This only scratches the surface of Bryan's accomplishments.

"Sweet" Cherie Mitchell Agurs, keyboards, musical director
Cherie is not only the keyboardist and musical director for her all-women's group Bela Dona, but she is also a songwriter, producer, arranger, and composer. Anyone who has seen Cherie perform knows the high energy

she brings to the stage. As a participant in the "Teach the Beat" program, Cherie is also an educator. She has performed with a Who's Who across musical genres, including Nile Rogers and Chic, Sir Elton John, Stevie Nicks, Chuck Brown, Maiesha and the HipHuggers, Howard Hewett, and George Duke, to name a handful of the many artists.

Montu Mitchell, Love DC Go-Go Clothing

Montu's history in Go-Go started as a fan and then a "hyper consumer." He wanted everyone to experience Go-Go the way he saw it and experienced it. He wanted people to see it through his clothes, through his art. "These are not just clothes, but these are walking messages. I can sell you a piece of art and charge you $2,000, and it can stay in your house or office, but that art would be much better suited on the front and back and walked around with that message to any and everybody in the experience so that's the message, that's the goal." Mitchell is a seed of the Madness Connection. I've never known a world without Madness (Connection). I see Madness as the Yankees. The game is better when the Yankees are playing. The game of urban clothing and D.C. clothing is better when Madness is in position.

We share designs in a lot of instances. There are designs that I have helped recover from their archives and refurbish and have those ready to put back out, so those I have done and I saw those in some instances, the "Run Joe" and some of the other vintage prints- Mickey and Minnie, but then in another instance we share Love DC Go-Go. We have had an awesome history together because our stories are so intertwined. Not long after I created it, they helped me promote it. I started in 2018 after returning from Africa with Backyard Band. I went to Africa with Backyard to help them produce their stage show. A stage show we did at the Howard Theatre was so good that it landed a grant for us to go to Africa. It was me and Anwan Glover that put that piece together.

Ms. Margarine Neal, manager

Ms. Neal has been integral to Rare Essence since the group's inception in 1976. Along with Ms. Mack and Ms. Sis, Ms. Neal impacted the business of Go-Go as these three strong women held their own in a male-dominated genre. Not only were they the band's managers, but also their booking agents, promoters, and chaperones. Because of the foundation that they set up for Rare Essence, the group is still in business today. Ms. Neal met patrons at the door, counted the money, and ensured everyone got paid. 45+ years later, Ms. Neal is still involved in the business operations of

Rare Essence as treasurer and executive assistant- a steadfast fixture in Go-Go for decades.

Emmett Nixon, drums

Emmett Nixon is one of the founders of the group Trouble Funk. Growing up on the Eastern Shore of Maryland, Rick picked up his first set of drumsticks at the age of 7 and, by age 14, was playing professionally as the drummer/ vocalist for The Tempos, an R&B group on Maryland's Eastern Shore. The Tempos became the vehicle that allowed him to perform locally as an opening act for artists that came through the area- Kool & the Gang, Johnnie Taylor, Parliament Funkadelic, King Floyd, and others. This helped to hone his craft as a professional musician. Upon moving to the D.C. area, Rick quickly joined a four-man singing group, The Day-Tons as drummer for their backing band and recorded a few songs without any real traction. Upon their departure, the band morphed into Trouble Band & Show, playing cover tunes at cabarets and outdoor events. Personnel changes in the group later led to the advent of Trouble Funk, his introduction to a new and evolving genre of music, Go-Go. As a founding member of Trouble Funk, Rick was able to contribute as co-writer and create original beats as drummer/vocalist for their early signature recordings- "E-Flat Boogie,' 'Straight Up Funk Go-Go Style,' 'Drop the Bomb,' 'Super Grit,' 'Let's Get Small,' 'Pump Me Up,' 'Hey Fellas,' 'The Beat,' 'Get on Up' and 'Get Down with your Get Down' among others.

Kobina Pobee Orleans, trumpet

Kobina Pobee Orleans, the trumpet player for the legendary Pump Blenders, juggles music and his electrical engineering studies at Morgan State University. He started with the group in 2016 when he started playing the trumpet. He returned in 2018 and started playing more regularly with the group. It all started with Gerald Brooks, drummer for the Pump Blenders for several decades, who happens to be Kobe's drum mentor.
Orleans states, "Since elementary school, I've watched him on the drums. In High School, he started introducing me to certain legends and certain Pump Blenders band musicians and getting me to play the trumpet with the band." This multi-talented musician plays trumpet, drums, and keyboards.

Derek Paige, trumpet

Derek Paige was 13 years old when he got on the stage with his trumpet. He first joined Chance Band with his cousin, Donnell Floyd, a saxophonist making up a rich horn section. When Derek was in high school, he joined Ayre Rayde in 1982/83, where he also lent his talents to enrich their horn sound. In 1985, he joined Rare Essence and joined his cousin Donnell again. Derek was there for 15 years during some of the most iconic songs and videos that Rare Essence released- "Work the Walls" and "Lock It," with "Lock It" appearing on the soundtrack for the film "Strictly Business." In 2000, Derek left the group to start the band 911, which later became Familiar Faces. He stayed until 2019, when he decided to retire. He has played Rare Essence reunion shows but no longer wants to play night after night. Derek shares, "All of the cover tunes have taken the soul out of Go-Go. It's different music now than when we were playing. You can see three bands and hear the same songs. Coming up, everyone had their own defining sound. My son plays, and I am glad he does it."

Derek Paige Jr., keyboards
Derek started playing music when he was 3 years old! His father, Derek Paige (Rare Essence, 911, and Familiar Faces), would practice the trumpet around the house and started teaching very early. Derek started playing saxophone in the school band in the 3rd grade and sang in the church choir. When he got to high school, he played trombone in the school marching band and saxophone in the school jazz band. Derek taught himself piano in his junior year of high school. That's when he helped start the gospel Go-Go band Walk By Faith. During this time, he played with several gospel Go-Go bands, including Xodus, Higher Heights, and Tru Potential. In 2011, Derek left Walk By Faith to play with Mission, another gospel Go-Go band. While with Mission, he played with a band called IGB that later became Finesse Sounds. In 2013, Derek joined Mental Attraction. From there, he played with Changing Phaces, Project 71, Mature Clientele, Black Passion, Band of Brothers, Peacemakers, LOUD, FAZE2, and Say No More. He also played bass for Timeless Vision for a while. In 2017, he returned to playing with Mental Attraction until later that year. Derek joined Suttle in late 2017, and he's been there ever since.

Halima Peru, vocalist
Halima Peru is the quintessential singer with the group Fayces U Know. She has been a constant on the stage for years, and she's not only a performer with the group but also a co-owner and business partner. She is a true professional who puts on a dynamic performance. According to her Fayces U Know partner, Doc Hughes, "Her talents have made it easy for us all to take on new challenges over the years. She is a strong, amazing vocalist that gets the job done." She is well-respected by her peers and

167

fans alike.

Vernell "Winko" Powell of Junkyard Band, percussion

Winko was only 9 years old, one of the youngest members, when the Junkyard Band was created in 1980. With humble yet persistent beginnings, he and his original bandmates from the Barry Farms Housing Project were determined to have their band. Their tenacity led them to make music replicating the sounds they heard on instruments by making do with what was available plastic 5-gallon buckets, Quaker State oil cans, hubcap rims, plastic toy horns, and other "junk." When they finally got "real" instruments, Winko gained notoriety on congas. Junkyard caught the attention of Def Jam and was signed to a record deal releasing "Sardines" and "The Word." He's played at The Kennedy Center and the Apollo and appeared in movies "Tougher Than Leather" and "D.C. Cab." Although he has enjoyed many guest opportunities, Winko Powell has remained a member of JYB. He is still among the top conga players today, over 40 years later.

Gene Pratt, vocalist

One of the golden voices in Go-Go belongs to Gene Pratt. Pratt gained notoriety as a member of the Junkyard Band when he was just a kid. Growing up in Go-Go, he has played with several versions of Junkyard and Suttle Thoughts, lending his voice to several other groups. After some medical challenges forced him to slow down, Pratt's determination and drive have kept him going over the years, still gracing the stages as a prominent member of whichever band he is with.

Antonio Robinson, drummer

1979 is the year that Antonio Robinson started as the drummer with Mass Extension/Extinction, the band that brought us the song and dance craze "Happy Feet." That's 42 years on the scene! During those 42 years, Antonio has been behind the drums driving the beat with bands such as Rare 4orm, Allure Band, Proper Utensils, Godfather and Friends, and Blacc Print- some of those simultaneously!

Steve Roy, vocalist, rapper, talker

Steve comes from a family of singers- his parents and 3 older sisters are vocally gifted. Although he could sing and was a fan of Go-Go, it wasn't until he was in his late 20s that Steve decided to investigate music as a career option. He was introduced to the Go-Go stage when the singers from Dynasty didn't show up at the start of a gig. He stepped in, and it all started from there! After a stint with Y2K, Steve joined After Hours, where he worked on harmonies with Steve Swann and then transitioned into the rapping and lead-talking roles. Steve wasn't very comfortable, but this would open the doors to a richer vocal experience and open more doors. Over the years, Steve has been a member of DaMixx and Vybe, but Suttle Thoughts was a game-changer for him. During his 10-year reign in Suttle, Steve learned from Chi Ali and developed his comfort level as a rapper and lead talker. He had grown into his own and was ready when he received a call from Donnell Floyd to join Familiar as he was preparing for his retirement. Steve is still learning and developing to this day. He continues with Still Familiar and currently runs the "one," although he comfortably handles the 2 and 3 like a pro.

Brion "BJ" Scott, percussionist

It would only be natural that Brion "BJ" Scott would get involved in music in some capacity! After all, his grandfather was a well-known band leader in the 60s with Mickey and the Blazers, his father is Go-Go Mickey, and his brother, Mickey Freeman, is also a musician. Back in 1998, his father gave Brion his first drum set. By 2002, he played in a concert band at his middle school. By the time Brion was 14, he was playing with a school band, Expanding Horizons. We regularly see Brion playing congas, timbales, and roto toms onstage, but he has mastered several other instruments during his musical journey. He's been seen over the years playing with such bands as Rare Essence, L.O.U.D., Sirius Company, and UCB, just to name a few.

Mia Scott, vocalist

Mia was always destined to be involved in music! Her mother was the lead vocalist for Expression Band and Show, and her father was a drummer, keyboardist, producer, disc jockey, sound man and band leader for his band, "The Kosmo Defacto Band and Show," which originally included Junie from EU. At age 6, her mother gave her the mic during a show, and she was bitten by the bug. Mia remembers always singing while accompanying her mom to band practice or sitting in her father's studio. She's entered and won numerous talent shows. Mia can also connect and work every board in a studio!! In 1997, after high school, one of her good friends, LuShawn "Drummachick," mentioned Mia's name to Precise, where she was the drummer. Mia became the lead vocalist alongside Sweet Michelle. Before joining EU, she was with SOS Ladies of Go-Go, Steele Band, Red Carpet Affair, and Mature Clientele. In 2018, Mia released her first single, "Here With Me."

Donald Doc Spencer, drummer
When Doc was 11 years old, he took drum lessons from the Clark music store and joined the District Heights Avengers, a marching band. In 1976, His band Funk Funk Smoke was created. The music crossed genres as the band perfected hits by Edgar Winter and Fatback band, to name a few. This set him on his musical path as a co-founder (along with his brother, Darryl) of Maryland's #1 Go-Go band, Ayre Rayde, in 1978. Doc, of course, played drums, and Darryl managed the band. Ayre Rayde had a hit song, "Sock it to Me," which made it to radio rotation and became the daily opening song for WDJY 100.3's morning DJ, Brut Bailey.

Vincent Tabbs, bass
Tabbs got his first bass at age 10, but by the age of 12, he'd caught the attention of Gregory "Sugar Bear" Elliott, who took him under his wing. At 14, Anthony "Redds" Williams asked Tabbs to help form Redds & the Boys and built the band with members of Vincent's original band, Transin. This led Vincent to be the original bass player for Redds & the Boys. By the age of 16, Vincent was recruited by Mike Hughes to join AM/FM. Through his affiliation with AM/FM, he worked with R&B legends Charlie Wilson and Glenn Jones. He also enjoyed opportunities to play with Little Benny and the Masters and CJ's Uptown Crew for many years, traveling to Japan five times to perform. Vincent also joined Citilites after the departure of bassist Wayne Davis. As a freelance bassist for many years, Vincent has created a new group, After-U Band.

Milton "Pep" Talley, Check One Check Two Sound Company
During a chance meeting in 1980 on a NE D.C. basketball court, Milton "Pep" Talley met the West Family of Mass Extinction fame. Pep was 14 years old. They discovered that they lived on the same street in NE, and the Wests invited Pep to see them perform at Coolidge High School. He was hooked! For the next 5 years, Pep was a roadie for Mass until he left for college in 1985. Soon after the initial meeting, Pep's brother Anthony "Tom Tom" Talley joined Mass Extinction on the keyboards. Over the years, Pep continued to work with the band, particularly during the height of the popularity of their song "Happy Feet." He always helped behind the scenes at a lot of the gigs and college tours. Pep absorbed all he could working behind the scenes with Mass, working in church, and taking classes at the National Association of Music Merchants (NAMM). In 2012, he launched his own sound company, CheckOne CheckTwo Sound,

providing sound for many DMV artists. Pep has also engineered national acts such as Harold Melvin's Blue Notes, K. Michelle, Jada Kiss, Beanie Siegel, and Pastor Troy. In 2019, he started Blast Entertainment to provide promoting services.

Michael Taylor, trombone
Michael first picked up the horn in Jr. High, but it wasn't until high school at HD Woodson that he began to get serious about his talents. Initially, Mike joined the band Black Love, but in 1981, he joined EU, where he stayed until joining Little Benny and the Masters. Mike rejoined EU and toured extensively with them to support "Da Butt" and the two albums EU released. He appeared in the movie "School Daze" along with his EU bandmates. After retiring, he was enticed back to the stage and returned to play with 4 Sho Band, NeXxx Level, Familiar Faces, and Let It Flow, and after a stint with EU, Mike played with Blacc Print. Not only is Mike known for his musical talents but also for his steps onstage. He credits Benny as being his blueprint. Interestingly, Mike is known by not one but two stage names- EU's Sugar Bear named him "Go-Go Mike," and he earned the name "Hardstep" with Little Benny and the Masters.

Donald Tillery, trumpet
As a trumpeter and singer, Tillery was a member of the Soul Searchers from 1972 to 1986. Tillery has often performed playing 2 trumpets at 1 time. Tillery was on the scene prior to the inception of Go-Go with his group, The Epsilons. He also played with the El Corals. After the Soul Searchers, Tillery played with Truth Groove and, most recently, with The New Soul Searchers. Listen to the title track from the 1972 album "We the People" to hear some exquisite trumpeting.

Jacques "Joc" Vaughan, percussionist, manager
Jacques was one of the original members of Central Groove, hailing from the Langley Park/Riggs Road/Hyattsville area. The group started in the early 80s when most members were in their teens. Jacques went on to play with AM/FM, Ayre Rayde, Hot, Cold Sweat, Chuck Brown, Proper Utensils, Wisdom Speaks, Familiar Faces, and Trouble Funk. 40 years later, since the inception of Central Groove, Jacques is STILL gracing the stages- currently with Trouble Funk while managing supergroup Push Play.

Derrick Ward, vocalist

Singer-Songwriter Derrick "Dirty D" Ward was born in Washington, D.C., where he started singing at age 5. He honed his vocal skills performing in church and school choirs. Derrick began his Go-Go journey in 1995 when he joined Ricky "Rock Steady" Brown" and the Crossover Band until 2003 when he returned to active duty to finish his military career. In April 2009, after safely returning home from Iraq (Operation Iraqi Freedom), Derrick returned to the Go-Go scene and was scooped up by Big Tony Fisher, joining Trouble Funk. He has had the privilege of performing on local and national stages as a member of the historical Go-Go Band Trouble Funk and is credited for providing vocals on Trouble Funk's "Hump Day," "Trouble Funk Live: Ultimate Crank," "Trouble Funk's 35th Anniversary Album and Trouble Funk's performance on the "Tiny Desk Concert" which has garnered over 1.2M views. He is also credited as a co-writer on TF's "Whatcha Sippin." Staying true to his R&B roots, in 2018, Derrick released his first solo album, "D. Ward The Journey." His music has been used in the soundtrack of the award-winning web series "Differences." He gives much credit to Big Tony for adding historical content to his musical career. Derrick is performing with Archie Beslow & The Blacc Print Experience and has co-written their first single, "Hey World."

Pammy Pam Ward-Godbold, vocalist
Pam Ward- Godbold is a native Washingtonian. As a child, she began singing in church and then spent years singing in various choirs, gospel, and R&B groups. This has allowed her to be able to sing in various styles of music. In September 2007, she joined Let It Flow and has never looked back. She remains with Let It Flow to this day. She sang with Lissen briefly after Y'Anna "Yanni" Crawley left and Pink Palish. Pam is a musical theatre actress performing in "Little Shop of Horrors," "Chicago," and "Sincerely, Holidays!" Pam has been fortunate that music and theatre has afforded her to perform with and for many international and national artists and tour. She is currently a member of the new R&B group Push Play where she is happy to be able to work with such amazing legends.

Dwayne "Kiggo" Wellman, drums
A member of the Wellman family, it would only be natural that Kiggo would excel in his talent for drumming. Spending time playing with Chuck Brown, EU and Little Benny and the Masters, he has been on the Go-Go scene for decades. As a matter of fact, Kiggo played with Chuck longer than his cousins Ricky Wellman, and Steve Coleman.

172

Gerald West, guitar

Gerald started performing with his family's band, Mass Extinction as the lead guitarist 43 years ago in 1979, when he was just 13. In 1985, they released the hit song "Happy Feet," which introduced the dance craze of the same name. Island Records eventually picked up the song. In 1987, Gerald was signed to MCA as a writer and producer, producing songs for Eric B., Brett Lover, Omar Chandler, Al B. Sure, and the Girlz. In 1993, after The Godfather of Soul, James Brown saw the band playing during one of his trips to D.C., he was thoroughly impressed. Brown signed Gerald and other West family members as his band, The New JBs. Gerald traveled the country as the guitarist with James Brown. Amazing! Locally, Gerald has performed with Mass Extension/ Mass Extinction, Good Kemistry, and Posse for Christ, and currently, he plays with The WestMob Band.

Al Winkler, sound engineer

The name Al Winkler is synonymous with quality sound. As one of the most prominent sound engineers in Go-Go, Al is one of the veterans. He has provided sound for almost every Go-Go band and is still on the scene.

Raenell Williams, manager

Williams' management experience in Go-Go began in the early 90s with Krucial Elements. She has since managed ReaZon BanD, LMG, Kaddy Musik Band, Azure Live, and worked with Finesse Sounds, Sounds of Unity, and LIT Band. Her ultimate goal in the DMV is to promote UNITY and show the masses that everyone can work together for the greater good. Love Over Violent Energy is her non-profit that promotes self-love. She has also been a stage manager, worked the door for different promotors, and has worked in promotions and marketing. In 2019, she received the 'Big City of Dreams-Sexy Female- Behind the Scenes' award."

Salih Williams, radio personality, rapper/talker

Most know Salih (aka Bootsy Vegas, aka "E" aka The Fifth Letter, aka Fidel Cashflow) as a member of OP Tribe, LISSEN, or Obsession, and a cohost of Da Blend radio show. There is so much more! His most important role is as an educator and mentor, helping young people navigate broadcasting and journalism. He also spent some time on The Donnie Simpson Show and Rise and Grind, his morning show in Charlottesville, VA, and is currently working on the Marc Clarke show. He was also mentored by Earth, Wind, and Fire while spending time on the road with them during their extensive and elaborate tours. He is currently performing with Crank Crusaders featuring Raheem DeVaughn. Salih also takes the time to help his friends on their various health journeys.

Spotlight: Jacques Johnson

Jacques Johnson comes from a musical family—his sister is a multi-instrumentalist and singer, Me'Shell Ndegeocello (formerly Michelle Johnson of Prophecy Band and Little Benny and the Masters), and his father, saxophonist Jacques Johnson, Sr. taught quite a few Go-Go musicians as a music teacher at D.C.'s Eastern High School. It was only natural for Jacques to develop his talents and hold a decades-long spot as a sought-after guitarist.

In my 11th grade year, 1981, the guys were beating on the desks at Oxon Hill High School. And they would bring these cassettes in, and during that time, I was just learning how to play guitar. I was listening to Funkadelic, Rick James, and everything else, so it was kinda new to me. The first Trouble Funk record I heard was "E Flat Boogie." Then E U Freeze came out on the radio, and it caught my attention. The first Go-Go I saw was Trouble Funk at Cheiry's, which blew my mind. I always wanted to play music. Music was in the blood. I'd go to school, come home and listen to records. When I heard Go-Go, I was hooked after that. My first band ... I could play some chords back then, so I got in this group called Hot Property which was managed by Joe Quarterman of Joe Quarterman and the Free Souls. His son had the group, and he played drums. I learned a whole lot from Joe. That was my first encounter playing Go-Go.

I graduated from High School and went to Howard. The Reed Brothers from Trouble Funk were still in school, and I always saw them on campus. Ivan Goff and I and a cat named Tony De'Tiege, we were all freshman together at Howard. Tony started the group Reality- he was the sax player. During that time, Ivan, I think, was playing with Redds and the Boys. That's where I met Roy Battle. Roy was at Howard. I knew Roy as a drummer and a writer. None of us got much work done during my few years at Howard. Roy took me under his wing, and I ended up playing with Hot Cold Sweat. During that time, Charlie [Fenwick] was still playing bass then. Rock Steady was playing then. My father said I was f***ing up in school so we are going to send you down to Virginia State in Petersburg, Virginia. While I was playing in Hot Cold Sweat, we had a show at RFK, and Chuck Brown played Family Affair. It was my first time hearing "Family Affair," and it blew me away.

Chuck came out of this white limousine… All I heard was that Hammond B3. Curtis Johnson to this day…classic rock and classic soul is beautiful, but playing that organ on "Family Affair.." and they hadn't recorded it yet, so… I was an RE head too – Godfather, Marky, Scotty, and all of them, Whiteboy and Ned. Those were actually my idols musically, trying to play like them. I got down to Virginia State and met this cat Rodney Lewis, and he was from here [D.C.], and I was hanging out in his room, and he had all these tapes, all these PA cassette tapes. I found Chuck Brown's "Go-Go Swing" on that tape. OH MY GOD. I said, "What is THIS?" I probably failed that whole semester because that was all that was on my mind. We would ride around campus in his little car, blasting Go-Go at Virginia State. I wasn't doing too well down there. There was a group called Code Red, and they had a single out called "Virginia has gone Go-Go." I left school and went out to California. We got into a club in San Bernadino every Friday and Saturday night. We did R&B; in fact, EU, "Da Butt" had just come out… "Drop the Bomb" a lot of folks out of state knew about "Drop the Bomb," and "Da Butt" had just come out, and the whole- any state you were in knew "Da Butt" so we would play a whole Go-Go set at the end of our first set and the end of our second set. Folks were like, "What is this beat?"

We were like, "D.C., man. D.C." I spent 3 or 4 years out there doing what I call Grown and Sexy. We were playing R&B and then mixing the R&B with the Go-Go beat. I came home in 1992. I met up with Roy again, and Roy was playing with Proper Utensils. I was there for a couple of years during the whole Rumpshaker thing. Funk was one of my idols. We used to get into it all the time, but years down the line, a lot of that, I deserved. I wasn't well disciplined. I think that after I left to go to school, Ned took Michelle under his wing. A lot of Michelle's playing and stuff came from being around Michael Neal, Federico Pena, and BJ (Byron Jackson). They were close. They were really, really close. If you listen to Michelle's playing, from her keyboard playing to bass playing, and the way she arranges things, she developed her own style. I was an outsider because I'd leave town and return, but Go-Go was always in my blood. I dealt with Prop [Proper Utensils], and Michelle had finally gotten her record deal, and Ned and I ended up going out at the end of her first album tour, which was great. We experimented with some Go-Go stuff on her tour- me, Fred… I came back and hooked up again with L-Rod from Virginia State,

175

and we started a group called Pure Natural, which was more of smooth jazz. Everybody was doing the jazz thing, too, back then, and I wanted to do things people were familiar with. We had a little run at Takoma Station in the mid or late 90s. We got fired, and Maiesha and the Hip Huggers came in. We had a good relationship with Takoma Station. My father and Margie with the Motown. They played up there too. I learned a lot from my father too. All genres of music, I love. If it's good, I'm in it. I'd wondered why we got fired, but Maieisha, they did their thing!

I got into a casino band and did a lot of traveling on the casino circuit. I came back into town. Maieisha and them left from Takoma Station, and Walker Redds and them- Suttle Thoughts- I think Funk and Benny were playing with them then. Michelle Blackwell and a whole bunch were playing. I was like, "Wow!" Right before Katrina, I moved to New Orleans and played on Bourbon Street for about 2 ½ years. I came back up here and ended up playing with Suttle Thoughts for a minute and then played with What? Band with Rah [Chris Black]. During the 90s, the Northeast Groovers blew me away too. I was like what young band is going to proceed after RE and groups like that. When I heard Northeast, the "Water Dance," I was like, "Damn." After I left Suttle, Rah started a band called What? And Michelle Blackwell, I was always fascinated because she was the first woman I heard doing the Go-Go thing, doing a rap like a Lauren Hill type thing. She said we needed a guitar player, and I played with What? for about a year and a half, maybe 2 years. I screwed that gig up. I learned a lot from Chris (Rah), another icon to me. I said, "For this person to have this much power over a lot of people in the audience, I was like, Wowwww! This man, to this day, can command a crowd. After What? Band, I ended back with Suttle Thoughts and then I did 13 years with Vybe Band. Derrick is a great businessman. We had the same vision. We knew that Chuck was getting older, and we wanted to be the next Chuck Brown and the Soul Searchers type thing. He would get the horn players to come in from Chuck. I got fired right before COVID hit. I've been freelancing around. During COVID, I hooked up with Chester Reis, Big Chess, and have been helping him produce his stuff since COVID. We've been in the studio. I hooked up with Whop [Craig/Wisdom Speeks]. He is very passionate about his music. I told him that I was there to help with his music. I've played with Shorty Corleone. It was Shorty, Me, Shorty Dud, Whitey, Mike Baker, and Godfather. That was a nice little unit too. I messed that up because I was still playing with Vybe.

The Reed Brothers were mentors to me too. I met Dyke, and Dyke got me into the computer thing- making music off of the computer. He showed me a whole lot of things before he passed.

Dyke made that sound with Trouble. He was the perfect person to come into my life. He and my father were friends. My father did some horn stuff with Trouble. They had a real good relationship. He took me under his wing. A lot of my production stuff and how he worked in the studio, just watching how he worked in the studio- to this day, if I am working with other people, some of the stuff that he taught me still applies to this day. He was one of the nicest people—a real cool cat. I was so surprised that he had passed. He introduced me to the Paul Reed Smith guitar that hadn't come out yet. He asked if I wanted one. He explained that you could get all of these different tones off it.

Ju Ju is another one who influenced me and Michelle. When Arrested Development came out, Michelle, Ju Ju, and BJ did that Saturday Night Live thing with them. I think Michelle played bass, and BJ played keyboards.

ABOUT MICHELLE [MeShell Ndegeocello]:
I was the big brother and became familiar with Go-Go first. I had a garage band in high school, and the drummer kept his drums at our house. I always told Michelle to go back upstairs because she didn't belong there. She probably still holds that over my head. Michelle would go downstairs when the guy would leave his drum set over at the house, and Michelle would go down there. She really had something. She learned the drums real quick. I was like, Wowwwww. I think Michelle was playing clarinet back then. We are 5 years apart. She learned to play drums, but my Mom said, "No! We're not having all that noise in the house." When I hooked up with Hot Property, the bass player had this short-scale bass, a Fender Mustang, and he left it over the house. Michelle picked that thing up like she had been playing for 20 years. She grabbed it, and that's all she wrote. I was like, Pop! She played by ear. We both started playing by ear. She picked the thing up, and it just came naturally to her. I don't know how she and Ned hooked up. They would hang out and come back to the house and be downstairs woodshedding. Ms. Mack and Funk and them took to Michelle. I think she ended up being Michael Neal's backup player. There are some tapes out there with Michelle subbing for Mike if you can find them.

177

Prophecy was Michelle's first band. That was with Stan Cooper, the keyboard player named Dawoo, Kevin Jackson played the drums, and Howdy Doody played congas. It was a really good band, then. Syed. It was a good band. Then she ended up going to [Little] Benny. She was with Benny after that. I think I was at Virginia State then. She and Benny were tight. Quentin ["Footz" Davidson] and Donnell [Floyd] had their own record company [Kolossal Records]. If you remember the song, "If That's Your Boyfriend, He Wasn't Last Night." A lot of her first album was done at Steve Franco's studio over behind Eastover. Ned was working out of there. I think "$55 Motel" was recorded there.

I was doing stuff with my father. His first album was done off the way Michelle did her demo. All of that production stuff was done down in our basement.

Spotlight: Carl "CJ" Jones

Known as "Big Brother" CJ or "Blow Your Horn" CJ, saxophonist Carl "CJ" Jones is a veteran in Go-Go. As a pioneering member of Redds and the Boys and appearing onstage as a notable part of both EU's and Little Benny and the Masters' horn sections, Jones also performed with his own group CJ's Uptown Crew. A nationally syndicated radio personality, he has created voiceovers for events and products and owns CJ Jones Audio Productions. He shares his thoughts on the Go-Go sound.

Go-Go is like Jazz. It's how one perceives it. It's an open art form that you can create anything on top of that beat as long as you don't get away from that essence of Go-Go. And it happens a lot. I don't think people in D.C. get it, but I go back to "Movin and Groovin" (Redds & the Boys). "Movin and Groovin" didn't sound like "Bustin Loose." It didn't sound like "Da Butt" because this guy mixed that song, and it made it sound- we were hittin' Go-Go, but it sounded like this is how Go-Go is supposed to sound. Not putting that song on a pedestal, but if you listen to the big-sounding drum and bass, that happens when you take it to someone else. Because if you notice everything that comes out of Go-Go now, everything sounds the same here. Now we get mad when a dude from Atlanta comes up because he hears it totally different. We've got to hear it totally different too for it to chart on Billboard. Everybody uses the formula. What's that cat that did Beyonce's "Crazy in Love"? Rich Harrison. That would've scared the s**t out of me. It had the Go-Go in it but look what he did to it!

I don't know if our level of thinking is limited. There's 2 kinds of Go-Go- inside the beltway, or you're going to go outside the beltway. And I fought with my cousin Redds about this. Instead of all that "Wooo Weee Baby," you're gonna say something. You're gonna sing. And he trusted me, and that's how we did "Movin and Groovin" because Redds just wanted to keep it all Arthur Caper and Howard Theater, you know, "Ohh weee baby, what's up now?" Don't nobody know what the hell you're talking about in Kansas. But they'll know what you're talking about if you've got a hook- "Movin and Groovin" .... Back to my point. Go-Go is like Jazz. It's how one perceives it. Go back to Tye Tribbett and Kirk Franklin and Beyonce, even Grace Jones. They just added their own thing over top of it. Some of it worked, and some of it didn't. And here in D.C., we're like, oh, the hell with that. That ain't Go-Go.

You can't have all these people up front (on the front line). What are yall doing? A protest march? That's not entertaining to watch because you're not doing anything and just standing there. There needs to be a show to that, just like with Redds. We told him that we weren't going to be upfront with him. Lil Beats will be on one riser, the horn section will be on another, and it will just be you by yourself. When it's time for me to do my sax solo, I'll come up front and blow for 60 seconds and then go back because it's Redds... and the Boys. That's what made him different from everybody else. I wonder what we would be doing if that boy was still living. It reminds me of that documentary "5 Feet from Stardom."

I came so close because Redds and the Boys, they wanted them to be the face. Redds and Lil Beats had that look. We were supposed to be the ones. And the next one, I think, was Mass Extention because they were very handsome fellas, well-choreographed, but Redds and Lil Beats, that was the ticket for Go-Go. It didn't work out, but I tried to take it as far as possible with CJ's Uptown Crew. We went around the world and on USO tours, and I knew when it was time to know when to hold em and fold em. But like Sugar Bear, I'm like you are the voice man because they have this song "Peace Gone Away." I'm thinking, that's a campaign, Playa.

Just like Donnell (Floyd). We know Donnell is brilliant. That group of his, Push Play, they sound great!! He has a whole new crew of musicians, and it reminds me of what we used to do with the black tie and played everything, "Mustang Sally," Aretha Franklin. Donnell's doing the same thing, and it sounds great! I salute him.

179

That's one thing I loved about Chuck. His songs were structured. I need a bridge, I need this, and it worked. It had a chorus. My song, "Satisfaction Guaranteed," it was structured.

During a mid-'80s recording session with EU, CJ found his voice, discovering he could use his deep voice on the local hit "Future Funk" as an instrument. But because of EU's construct, he was limited to blowing his saxophone while in the band.

By 1987, CJ knew it was time to step out on his own. Seeking to develop a cabaret-style band focused on melodies, horn arrangements, and strong singing, he enlisted D Pearson, Terry Stubbs, Al Johnson, and TomTom 84 of Earth Wind & Fire fame —all accomplished songwriters and producers. By 1988, this team would record and release the remarkable album *CJ's Uptown Crew*. The album's tracks included "Sexy Girls," "Satisfaction Guaranteed," and "Get Real," all club banger hits around the U.S. and in the UK.

The band that recorded the album consisted of some of the most known and respected Go-Go musicians of that time. Together, Anthony "Little Benny" Harley, Steve "Too Tall" Coleman, Michael "Go-Go Mike" Taylor, The Legendary DJ Kool, William "Ju Ju" House (EU), Mike Scott (Prince & Justin Timberlake), Ricky "Sugarfoot" Wellman (Miles Davis) and Lisa "Sylver" Logan (Chic and Kid Rock) recorded songs that did not fit the typical Go-Go sound at that time. More than a decade before Go-Go's "grown 'n' sexy" style took off, CJ also toured the USO traveling the world performing for Presidents, military groups, and various high-profile dignitaries and politicians. His band was the key band for Mayor Marion Barry, the most powerful local politician of his generation with the most significant political comeback. Along with CJ, the local/traveling band included Roxy Carter, Stan Cooper, Vincent Tabbs, Elliot Levine, Jacques Johnson, Paul Smith, Melvin "Mail Man" Rich, Felecia Manns, Reggie Baker, Shawn Allen, Anissa Twinky-Hargrove, LaDawn Brown, Farnetta Baker, and Rodney "LRod" Lewis.

CJ was looking to expand to a more mature Go-Go audience with his diverse experience in radio, television, stage, film, and music, and this multiple award-winning talent has been described as radical, revolutionary, innovative, and cutting-edge (CJ's Uptown Crew). As one of the founding fathers of the "Go-Go" movement is a three-time

"WAMMIE" (Washington Area Music Association) award winner, has more than 55 sound recordings under his belt, From Peace Makers, Shady Groove, Little Benny, EU, Pump Blenders and Redds & The Boys who charted nationally on Billboard's top 25 ("Movin' and Groovin' ") and is an NAACP and United Black Fund award recipient.

Blow Your Horn CJ has also been featured and starred in several films and documentaries alongside award-winning actors. Among such are "The BBC: Welcome to the Go-Go," Island Film's "Good to Go/Short Fuse," "Streetwise," "Middle Passage n Roots," "Melodies From Heaven," and "Straight Up Go-Go," and "The Legend Of Cool Disco Dan" landing him features in books such as Billboard's "The Beat," and hosting several of his own TV shows.

Over time, CJ became increasingly interested in impacting the community. With drugs and violence becoming real problems in the city, CJ wanted to do something to help. In 1987, CJ's Uptown Crew partnered with Dr. Calvin Rolark, CEO of the United Black Fund, to record the single "It's Good to Go Drug-Free," which helped fight the war on drugs, and lent this song added poignance and urgency.

A longtime presence on local radio, Big Brother CJ played Go-Go and hip-hop discs on "CJ's Wake-Up Club" on Flava 1580, and when the station switched formats, he played oldies as well. Later, he served as an on-air personality for WPGC-AM's Heaven 1580 new gospel station, CJ's Uptown Crew, which remains versatile and popular. On stage and on his syndicated radio shows, CJ did his best to use his platform to change and touch lives while ensuring his listeners are WOKE and fighting the good fight of faith in the community.

Spotlight: Ms. Neal

Three people who stand out to me as pioneers and icons of Go-Go are Ms. Annie Mack Thomas (Ms. Mack), her mother, Ms. Mattie Lee Mack (Miss Sis), and Ms. Margarine Neal. These three strong women held their own in a male-dominated genre. They were all integral to Rare Essence since its inception in 1976. Sadly, Miss Sis passed away in July of 1998 and Ms. Mack in January 2003, but their impact remains firmly tied to Rare Essence and Go-Go. They were the band's managers, booking agents, promoters, and chaperones. Because of the foundation that they set up for Rare Essence, the group is still in business today. They spent time meeting patrons at the door, collecting the money, and ensuring everyone got paid properly. 45+ years later, Ms. Neal is still involved in the business operations of Rare Essence as treasurer and executive assistant- a steadfast fixture in Go-Go for decades.

Ms. Neal on working with Ms. Mack and Miss Sis

"It was fun. It was a little difficult because we were always up against the men. We were three ladies that didn't let that bother us. We had our ways to keep [Rare Essence] in line. It was real hard sometimes, but we had our ways to keep them in line. It wasn't easy when it came to those guys because they were something else. They were young, and sometimes they weren't used to a lot of things that they were getting. It was a little tough. We had meetings every Monday to iron out how we would do something, making it easier for us because they had to follow our rules and regulations. We made rules but did it with them, not without them.

Ms. Neal on working with Maxx Kidd and Darryll Brooks

Ms. Neal chuckled when asked about working with people like Maxx Kidd and Darryll Brooks. "It was a lot of fun because they always tried to be slick. A lot of things I learned were things that they wouldn't have learned because a lot of people didn't know me. They knew Ms. Mack and they knew Miss Sis, but they didn't know me. People would talk around me and say things around where I was, but they didn't know who I was... and I didn't bother to tell them. You just listen. Keep your mouth closed and just listen."

Ms. Neal on how Go-Go has changed over the decades

It's changed a lot [from when Rare Essence started to now]. First of all, the whole world has changed since then. Like we used to play in a lot of schools. You can't play in the schools now and they are closing a lot of clubs and the rules in the clubs have changed too. People that go to the clubs have changed. They've got all of these guns out here now. I don't even go out with them anymore. I saw them for the first time in a long time when they were at MGM last year. I don't go out. I can't run that fast anymore.

Ms. Neal on the most valuable lesson learned from Ms. Mack and Miss Sis

Friendship. Working together. I knew how to work together, but I had never worked out in a world with anybody that I didn't know. I came from the country to the city, and it was a little different being raised in the country than it was being raised in the city. People in the country have a different lifestyle and treat each other differently from the city people. When we got together and started working with the group- the kids got it started over at St. Thomas Moore- they were practicing over there. Then they started practicing from one house to another because they even practiced at my place a couple of times, and I don't know what made Ms. Mack decide to let them practice at her place all the time, and it got started like that, and we got together and decided that we would talk to a lawyer, and we decided to organize. It took a lot of time, and we made a lot of mistakes because we didn't know anything about the entertainment world. At least I didn't, anyway.

You know what I miss? See y'all call Ms. Mack- everybody calls her Ms. Mack, but actually her name is Annie Thomas. Miss Mack was the mother, and people didn't know. Miss Sis was Ms. Mack, and then they called Ms. Mack, but that was Annie Thomas. But most people don't know that, but I miss them. I really miss them because Miss Sis and I were always together—all the time. Anyone will tell you that. Ms. Mack would go and do the negotiating and things with the contracts, most of it, and Miss Sis and I would often go and get them signed. And we would always be the first ones at wherever we were going to work, and Miss Sis and I would be the first ones to go. Sometimes, we would have to drive the truck because the guys were too young, and the other older ones that could drive-James and another couple of guys that worked with us, they would have to work, so we had to take the truck and go on. I used to drive that 24-footer and loved doing it because I wanted the guys to think I was crazy with that truck. It was a lot of fun. We did a lot of things to keep it going.

Spotlight: Allyson Gilbert Johnson

My career started when I was in the 3rd grade. My mom said, "Pick one: violin or piano." I said, "piano," and sooner than later, I started taking piano lessons at the Music and Art Center in Marlow Heights, MD. I have participated in many classical recitals and competitions in my day. I never won, but I always had an Honorable Mention. In ninth grade, I entered another county competition. This time I was determined. I told myself if I got another Honorable Mention, I quit. I was getting frustrated. I'm playing my heart out, and when I thought I won, someone else was always chosen. Well, this time, I won. Prize was to perform the winning piece with the Prince George's County Orchestra at the Oxon Hill Manor in Oxon Hill, MD. I played with all that I had within me. I received a nice trophy, took pictures, saw myself in the local newspaper, and still quit. The stress and anxiety were paying its toll on me so I chose to focus on something else.

My dad bought me a keyboard for Christmas one year, and now the story begins. Go-Go has always been in my soul since I bought my first 12" single for a 6th-grade school party where I was in charge of bringing some music. I went to a record store and bought "E-U Freeze/Knock 'Em out Sugar Ray" by Experience Unlimited. I would keep buying Go-Go albums and try to play along with them. My idols are "Godfava" from Rare Essence and were "Syke" Dyke (RIP) from Trouble Funk and Ivan Goff (RIP) from EU. I don't even know, if they knew, how much they affected me, but I still see them as the best. So, when I play sometimes, you can hear the influence.

Moving on….33 years ago, I made my debut in June 1989 with the Klyxx Band. Miss Ivory called me, as we graduated from high school together, so she knew I played piano. The band was small, with only about 6 members, including Miss Ivory and Karis Hill (from Bela Dona), but we had ambitious goals to make a mark in this culture. We were making some noise in this city with the help of Ms. Mack, Ms. Sis, Ms. Neal, James Funk, and Rare Essence. We would practice at Reo Edwards' studio, sometimes in the basement of Rare Essence Enterprises on Xenia Street, SE, and then we would open for Rare Essence when they played out of town or here in D.C. We all thought we made it the day we saw our name on one of those Globe posters on the trees. I have snatched down a few of those in my life. LOL! As soon as we made it to being nominated at the Go-Go Awards in 1990, egos kicked in, and then we broke up.

A week later, I got a call from Charlie Fenwick, the manager of Pleasure All-Girl Band and Show, asking me if I was playing with anybody. I said, "No." He asked if I wanted to audition. I said, "Sure," and then, "When?" He said, "Now." LOL! I looked at the clock, and it was about 11 pm. I left home and was on my way. The next day, I received a phone call from Charlie, who asked if I could come to practice the next day. I was so excited. During my very first practice, I think I am about to start learning the music. Nope. All the girls hopped in the Pleasure/Hot Cold Sweat van, and we were headed to Chris Biondo Studios, and that is where we created Santa Claus is Coming to Town for Liaison Records, or we used to say, Becky and Tom. And we all know how that song turned out. Still #1 in the DMV at Christmas time today. But that actual first practice, there was this little hook that Pleasure used to do that involved everyone in the band's name.

The rapper, Tam, tried to fit my name in the hook then. She did not like saying Allyson, so she created the nickname, AllyCat. I didn't like it at first. It made me think of cats in an alley. LOL! Once I changed the spelling to match part of my first name, I felt better about it, and it has stuck with me since. It took a few minutes to find my niche, and the girls took a minute to embrace me since I was coming from another girl band. I quickly made them feel like we were in this together, and I just wanted to be a part of it. I had a good run with these ladies for 9 years. Great girls turned into family, and we're all still friends today. We showed these guys that girls can do it too!!! Now, why did we break up? That ego thing again, and some real-life situations kicked in.

So now, what do I do? I tried a few practices with Precise All-Girl Band, owned by the first rapper with Pleasure All-Girl Band, "Sweet Chelle," but I wasn't feeling a fit with them. The funny thing though, is that we're still best friends today. So, within my hiatus, I graduated from college twice, got married, had twin boys, and became a soccer, basketball, and lacrosse mom. But within me, something was missing. Sure, I can play keyboards in the house, but I just missed that stage, the crowd, watching everyone have an enjoyable time, and the feel of that high energy.

One day, in 2006, one of my friends, David "Smitty" Smith, asked me if I wanted to try out for Trouble Funk. He was already playing with them but needed someone to help with missing parts. I was so reluctant. I was so nervous. I tried out and could not tell by Big Tony's face whether I did well. He was like, "Oh, okay, thanks." In my head, I was like, dag, I did awful. Then Smitty called and told me to come to practice the next day. And that was my opportunity to continue being in this Go-Go culture.

At first practice, I'm seeing all the guys that I had admired throughout the years. I believe I have every Trouble Funk album that exists, or at least extremely close. I met everyone, and they were all so nice to me. They are very personable dudes, and I'm feeling like a fan. It took a while for me to get out of that mindset and come to grips with the fact that I am a part of a major band. I have stories for days, stories of major shows, met a lot of celebrities, and even helped out on the administrative side. I've met a lot of people in Go-Go, men and ladies, and I must say, the DMV is extremely talented. Trouble Funk made me feel like I'm one of the fellas: the original and the new band. For most of my time with them, I was the only female, but at times, Trouble Funk tried some female singers, but after a few shows, they would quit; they all had different reasons. One came through, whom I will always see as the best fit, Donielle "Diva" Graves. She handled the spot well. She's the voice on Trouble Funk's "Hump Day," and I'm the one doing my best Milli Vanilli impersonation in the video. LOL! She left due to a significant opportunity in Germany, and luckily, we still keep in contact. As a whole, Trouble Funk produced fascinating opportunities. I could talk about this band for hours, from my experiences in playing for a less than 30 crowd to playing for over 20,000 to playing to all the smiling faces in different parts of D.C. to all the smiling faces in California to London, to meeting the originators of hip-hop like Afrika Bambaataa and Grandmaster Flash to rock stars like Dave Grohl. I can go on and on.

Then in 2010, being curious, feeling like I think I know all the elements to making a band work, I wanted to try. I and Charles "Junie" Jackson, Jr. (RIP), sound engineer for Rare Essence, put together a band. The concept was to have an all-female front line where they could all sing. The musicians could be male or female, whatever worked. I call her "The Voice," Kim Scott named the band, and now we have Love District Live! With my experience dealing with women, I chose to stay in the background, play, and run the business while Junie would be the contact. This was a great band. I even leaned on some players from Trouble Funk to help me. We sounded good and started being known in these streets. I hadn't quit Trouble Funk, and it was just something else to do when Trouble Funk didn't have any performances on the books. So now, I'm full-blown in the culture. I was playing with a legendary band and created a Top 40 band. This was the best of both worlds for a while. It was a great band, had great laughs, and met a lot of nice people. But, due to some differences, we broke up after about 2-3 years, and I just chose to focus on Trouble Funk.

Being back with Trouble Funk 100%, a family started to build. I've seen many guys come and go within this band, but the last unit, which I call "The Tiny Desk" unit are, all my brothers. We've been through it all, and it was a great run. These are my brothers for life. All of them hold a special place in my heart. I was the mother, the big sister, human resources, the counselor, the psychiatrist, the voice of reason, and the listening ear to all of them. Even found some time for myself and grabbed a Master's Degree in Accounting & Information Systems and graduated with one of the band members getting their Bachelor's Degree, Derrick "Dirty D" Ward, on the same day at UMUC in 2017.

I thank Big Tony for giving me a chance. I have had an awesome time with Trouble Funk on the performing side and the business side. Although we've bumped heads a few times, he always heard me out. The times I have had with Trouble Funk have been epic and indescribable. I have so many memories that I could write a book about it. Again, thank him for allowing me to share the stage with him.

All I can say now is, THANK YOU, DMV!!! Thanks for embracing me in this Go-Go culture. I hope I left a lasting impression on all females out here who think they don't have a place in this male-dominated culture. Just look at me because, in the words of my big brother D. Floyd, "I gave my whole life!" One can never say never, but you may see me back someday. Who knows? ☺

Chapter 11: Women Rule

Women have always played a pivotal role in Go-Go, both onstage and behind the scenes, as managers, journalists, record label owners, promoters, advocates, and much more.

This chapter will share the insight from influential women within Go-Go on the challenges or advantages of being a woman in this male-dominated industry.

"Sweet" Cherie Mitchell-Agurs, keyboards, vocalist, owner of the all-female group, Bela Dona

"I think it strengthened me. To play with "the fellas," I had to sometimes think like "the fellas." In my opinion, the guys are very passionate and competitive about their craft. Not saying that we women aren't. But I find myself in "combat" mode at times with the guys. I'm the first and only female instrumentalist in Chuck's band. I'm also the first in EU, but not the only one. During the mid-2000s, Sugar Bear used my lil buddy Steph Jones on keys."

Yes, the Hiphuggers started that Grown and Sexy era. We dressed up in 70s attire playing 70s-style music over a Go-Go beat. It became a hit. The lines were wrapped around the buildings at every show. Grown and sexy is taking covers and applying Go-Go rhythms underneath. It also appealed to an older/ mature audience. Many Go-Go critics call the "Grown and Sexy" era the demise of Go-Go because it lacks original music. Some people thought that I was Maiesha because I performed the Lil Kim rap on "Um Bop Bop." Also, when she got ill and wasn't present on stage, I was the only female, so most assumed I was Maiesha.

Becky Marcus, owner of Liaison Records

"I could say that it was challenging at times. The industry as a whole has always been male dominated in Go-Go. I think, regardless of gender, people come into their own and choose their path by the passion that drives them, making those challenges less evident. After 40 years of living this passion, I have been blessed to still be working with talented people with similar mindsets that aren't looking at gender but as a trusted business partner.

Victoria "Cookie" Mayo, Door Manager

"There are many challenges working in a male-dominated business. Because of stereotypes and gender bias, women are often in supporting roles. People praise the sound of Go-Go and who did it best, particularly with predominantly male singers and musicians. But there's not a lot said about how the Go-Go genre has survived 50 years from a business perspective. In my almost 40 years of working behind the scenes in Go-Go, I've observed, in many cases, its women who are key in building a structured foundation in organizing the business side of Go-Go, from promoting the events to managing the administration of securing venues, hiring adequate staff, ensuring front door operations are in order and the expenses are adequately allotted at the end of the event. Yes, the music and its sound are amazing without debate. But the business side of Go-Go goes hand in hand with the overall success of Go-Go, and as "they" say, "Behind every great man is a smart woman.""

Esther "Justice Jay" Jones, vocalist of Mental Attraction Band
"Being a woman in Go-Go has been challenging. You're expected to be strong but not too strong. Speak up, but don't have your own opinion that goes against the popular opinion of the men you're around. Sound sexy on the mic, but make sure you're loud and put bass in your voice. Be yourself but be sexier. Dress desirable, but don't be desired. Talk to people, but don't be too friendly. Hold your own but be the mother of the group as well. Everything is a contradiction when it comes to women in Go-Go. The expectation for a woman is higher for a female than that of a male because we are looked at as the "sex symbol." Our talents are mostly overlooked, and we must work 10 times harder than the men we work with to prove we can hold our own weight. God forbid we start to outshine the men we work with, and then we are seen as trying to take over and make Go-Go about us. It's crazy because nothing we ever do is ever good enough, but I continue to do it because I love the stage and the feeling Go-Go gives when I perform it. There's a lack of respect for women, so instead of asking for it, we take it by going all out on stage and behind the scenes."

Kapri Monique Curtis, On Stage Hostess and Owner of Voice of the People podcast.
"Being a woman in this business is a double-edged sword. If you are strict about business and its practices, you are viewed as a bitch. If you let them tell you anything and don't stand with integrity, they'll think you're sweet. Being a woman in this genre and business requires you to be even keeled and emotionally sound at all times, even when the masculine counterparts

189

around you are not. The life lessons are swift, hard, immediate, and extremely life changing. Moving with integrity and not emotion is a must. The love will make you want to nurture all things you see potential and growth in, but the reality will make you see that you can't force your dream for someone on them. They have to do the work and want it for themselves more than you do. This is a ride I wouldn't trade for the world. Go-Go is a lifestyle. It's a culture. It's a movement."

Raenell Williams, Manager, Advocate
"Being a woman in Go-Go is a blessing. Having a voice in a male-dominated community is a wonderful thing, and I'm thankful to have been accepted to keep the community informed on decisions being made and to update everyone on the planned future in Go-Go."

Bobbie Westmoreland, Advocate, Writer, and Organizer
"I've seen women have to fight for certain things. I remember the first year that WKYS did the Go-Go Awards. They had [categories] Best Lead Talker, Best Conga Player, and then Sexiest Female. And you know Michelle Blackwell was pissed. And you know then they felt some kinda way like we're doing this for you. Be appreciative. In the end, I think they ended up changing it. The following year they developed Female categories. And then in the years after that, the Peaceoholics took over, and I think they did 3 of them so I can say being the only female, and I don't know if it's because I have 5 brothers and 2 sisters, it wasn't a huge deal for me. I think, in a lot of ways it worked to my advantage and I know a lot of times with the work of the Go-Go Coalition, a lot of stuff, I'd end up doing. I think in that aspect, especially things that were administrative, I'd end up doing it. A lot of times in groups like that, people look for the women to do that type of stuff, whether it's the typing, the copying, the keeping track of things which honestly when the Go-Go Coalition started, Chi Ali put the word out to come to a meeting at Thump Studios when Club U was closed down. I brought a pencil and paper for everyone to put down their contact information on a list and I'd be the one to contact people and that became the Go-Go Coalition.

I didn't even know I was nominated the first year that Ronald Moten did the Go-Go awards until someone said Congratulations, and I asked, "What are you talking about?" They had posted it online, so the following year, I worked with him after that part was done, but the following year, I created a letter and email template to email to people saying that they had been nominated and a letter, something nice, that people might want to

190

frame. I don't know if that's being a female or just me being creative and organized about doing that type of thing.

I can say that I've always had people say Yes to me. I don't know if it's personality because, for so long, people would say there's no unity in the Go-Go community- Soldierette used to say that all the time. When I got involved, I found that many people like Sugar Bear or Donnell Floyd-some bands work more like as families, and it could be with a female head. Donnell Floyd's attitude was like most of my band members aren't going somewhere where they're not getting paid. Sugar Bear just wouldn't bother to tell his band members. This is how I developed many relationships and amassed so many phone numbers from these bands because I would reach out to people individually because I knew their band heads weren't reaching out to them. So certain people like Earl from Backyard, JT from Junkyard- he came out to every single thing I told him about. They would always ensure that I had an updated number when they saw me keep them in the loop of what was happening. When I reached out, I rarely got NO, only if it was timing- not because they weren't interested. I feel like people from the top to the bottom bands, all you had to do was ask them. They liked to be included in being a part of the Community, especially when you reached out to them individually.

The What? Band, and that could be because they had a female co-lead, even though Rapper was probably the CEO, Michelle Blackwell was the COO. When they came out, they came out en mass. They came out as a group. And it could be because they were like a family, and that attitude could be because they had a female head. Backyard works like that in a lot of ways. I know a lot is due to longevity, how long the group has been together, and a brotherhood there or like with the What? Band with Michelle in charge, they just always came out as a group. It may not have been all of them, but it was pretty much the bulk of them. When we did the calendar, one of the calendar signings, some bands had one or two people, but Michelle had the whole What? Band. And a lot of that, too, was her strong personality. She comes from a long line of strong, accomplished women.

Michelle Blackwell, vocalist, writer, producer, manager
Michelle was asked about her role as a woman in Go-Go and whether she has impacted the culture.

I am inspired and proud of every woman who represents this business and who is doing their best to move the culture forward in their own unique way.

My role as a woman in Go-Go is based on the things that I do in Go-Go which is perform, write, produce, manage. All I've done in this business is what I was moved to do based on circumstances outside of my job titles that I've had.

I have performed with many groups. The bands I've actually been a part of would-be Suttle Thoughts, Northeast Groovers, and What? Band, and my own band. And Chocolate City was not the only band that I did solo work with. I formed Chocolate City, and then after my album came out, I just performed as a Go-Go artist and had musicians play with me the same as Chuck Brown did.

In every role I've played in Go-Go, there was someone who played that role before me. The only thing I feel I may have done differently was that I self- produced an all original all Go-Go album. There were women managers in Go-Go before I joined the scene. I'm not sure if my role as manager was any more impactful on the culture than theirs was because they became an example before I became a manager. If I've done my job correctly, I'm sure the answer would be yes, but that's not a question I can answer. That's only a question that other women in Go-Go could answer if they chose or women in the culture from fans to crowd or what have you. I can only hope that my presence and my work in Go-Go has made a positive impact.

That's really all I can do is hope that it has. I know what I've been told and I know what my goal has been to represent women, black women in particular, in this business, and honestly, the entirety of my walk in this business has not always been every move I make. I'm being intentional about representation. Some of it is just circumstantial. Again, I hope my work here has done some good. Other than that, I can't make assumptions, but as far as role models for me, every woman that's been in this business from the stage to behind the scenes has been an influence one way or the other for me. It's not like I studied at the knee of every woman in Go-Go before I joined the business, but I observed on different levels their roles, and sometimes it's just being made aware of the role that exists whether I have a close connection with them or am able to be in proximity to see what it is they are doing correctly or incorrectly. It's just the very idea of them being there is enough, quite honestly.

Adrienne "Dre Dre" Burkley, Manager HORU Band

"A male-dominated culture is definitely where Go-Go lands.
Indeed there are many women in Go-Go- from fans, promoters, managers, musicians, and singers- even an all-female Go-Go band (Bela Dona). But the culture consists primarily of men, and it's saturated with male fans with an "exchange of respect" being offered between the gentlemen of Go-Go and their fans.
This leads to my experience in the genre.

Initially, as a fan myself, my encounter with the genre was with me wanting to exchange dialog with my peers about it. However, the ones most willing to discuss it with me were men. They seemed to appreciate my engagement with it more than my female peers, but even with that, the respect level still wasn't like it would be with a male-to-male conversation.

My next interaction was on a much higher tier- managing two pioneers of Go-Go. The full-time engagement with the male pioneer and, admittedly, the respect level was much better than I had encountered in my past years. Additionally, the acceptance of my knowledge about the genre was also embraced. However, many of my concepts and ideas were overlooked and even dismissed.

Eventually, these rejections would lead me to move on to my next venture-promoting an entire band. Finally, my skill sets were so highly embraced that within one month, I would become the manager of this band and land myself a home. Throughout my tenure, I would move into a Partner role and additionally become a primary vocalist of the band, songwriter, and producer of some of the music.

With each tier, I have unfortunately encountered and still encounter a lack of respect from some of my male counterparts, sometimes second-guessing my business models, proposals, and ideas/ concepts. The odd thing is how they would fully embrace a male's perspective before they would mine until they realize that my business models work and work well. In a nutshell, I have to work twice as hard to convince this culture that I have the skill set to own/operate a business within this genre. Admittedly, some male colleagues dub me a "Baby Miss Mack" because of my sternness and business-minded behavior. However, there's still a lack of full level respect from many despite the aforementioned offerings."

Spotlight: Chris Biondo on Being "Behind the Boards" in Go-Go

Chris Biondo was "that" guy. He was the guy that had the studio that everyone went to because he was such a great sound engineer.
Chris's story is unique as he did not start in Go-Go.

"A guy and his wife and his kids lived in the house in Rockville. He was an art rock musician guy. His name was Tom Scott. He got a loan for a 24-track recorder and mixing console and built a studio in his basement. Around 1983 he decided to move to Canada with his wife and family, do some farming up there and learn about organic healing methods using plants. He didn't want to sell his house, and I had recorded at his home, and he asked me if I wanted to move in and take over the business and the money generated from the recordings in the basement. I would send him a percentage of the money, and I would get to live in the house and record my own stuff. And probably in the first couple of times, I went over there to watch him work and how the place was set up, Junkyard was recording there. And I do not know what they were recording at the time. I don't remember the song or the session, but that was the first Go-Go band I saw. After he moved out and I moved in, I started doing primarily punk rock. Mostly the Washington area bands- this was their place before I started recording there. They liked the guy there before me, and I was working with these people, and then one day, I got a call from Ivan Goff, and I had never heard of him or too much about the Go-Go. I'd heard of EU. I'd heard of Trouble Funk, and I'd heard of Chuck and Rare Essence, but I didn't know anybody. He came in and recorded Tina Brown, a singer, and made a couple of singles with her. One of the funny things about one of the singles he made with her was he got Junie from EU to do the artwork for the cover. The name of the single was "Tina Brown and Ivan Goff keyboardist, and he spelled keyboardist wrong and they printed up a couple thousand of these, and keyboardist was misspelled.

So, I started working with Ivan, and he brought in EU one night, and they did "Go Ju Ju Go," and that's where I met Ju Ju and Kent (Wood). And that was really good. That was a good record, and I really enjoyed working with those guys. Kent wasn't at the original session during the day and came that night to put his keyboards on. I didn't know he was coming, and he was banging on the basement door, and I was upstairs. By the time I got downstairs, he had gone around to the front to knock on the front door, but he leaned his keyboard up against the back door, so when I opened the door, the thing fell down and smashed, and a couple of the keys fell out so when he came around, and he looked at me, and I looked at him, instead of him being mad or anything, he started laughing, and I thought, "I'm really glad he's laughing about this because this could have been a problem." He had a couple of keys missing, but he laid his tracks with a few missing keys, and Ivan, Kent, and Ju Ju came in a lot. I'd say about once a week for the next couple of years with different bands like Little Benny and the Masters doing "Cat in the Hat" and Go-Go Lorenzo and Pleasure. Pleasure came in with Reo Edwards and Roy Battle. Roy was so quiet. I wish he would've talked more. But they came in because Ivan had come in, and then I met Chuck. He came in to do "Hoochie Coochie Man," and we hit it off. I was hanging around Ivan, Kent, Ju Ju and Chuck, and Reo, and they were bringing in all these bands. Bands like Hot Cold Sweat and Benny had another band besides Little Benny and the Masters-The Groovemasters. Ayre Rayde did a Christmas record for Liaison with all of the groups, and then Rare Essence came in and remixed "Lock It" in my studio. Donnell came in, and I worked with him, and we did "Work the Walls," then I moved my studio to Prince George's County (Glendale). I loved the music and how the guys knew who all the best people were in all the bands, and everybody knew where they stood. Everybody knew that Rare Essence was the best band; even if you played in another band, you went to see Rare Essence playing. And Benny.

I spent some time with Benny and worked with him a lot. But it was a strange time. Recording a band that's got as many people as a Go-Go band has is not easy. There's a lot going on. It's noisy. It's loud. The songs last a whole lot longer than regular songs. But I made some friends that I still have today. Obviously, many of them are dead- Ivan, Kent, and Chuck are dead. And Benny. I always thought Benny was a sweet guy. A really nice guy. And that's pretty much my whole Go-Go thing. I kind of pulled away from doing almost anything except for Go-Go and R&B and Rap for the last 5 or 6 years of my engineering, recording career ending in 99. I don't know if you know Lenny, but Chuck made a Jazz album, and Lenny and I produced it for him.

Do you remember Eva [Cassidy]? He played piano with Eva. Another thing we did was we got Chuck and Eva to do a duet record. It was a great record. That's pretty much everything. Near the end of the whole thing, I just thought the whole scene was getting a little out of hand. I think Ivan was starting to spend more time on the West Coast. EU was going through some changes. Kent left and went to play with Rare Essence. And Ju Ju was playing with Chuck, and I'm trying to think… It's been a long time. I cut the cord in 1999. That's when I stopped doing the engineering thing. I like what I'm doing now. It's peaceful work. It's more structured. I'm not having to listen to loud music all of the time. I didn't mind it, but as you get older, you can't keep listening to loud music all the time, or you will lose your hearing or get tinnitus, which I know many people have gotten. I make my living off of being able to hear, so I can't let that happen to my ears.

Chapter 12: Voices from the Industry

Some people will classify Go-Go as the cousin of Rap music. Similarly, both Go-Go and Rap were born of the street for the street. Both were designed to bring unity and serve as a voice for the voiceless. Differently, Rap went way further than Go-Go did to become mainstream and the artists household names.

I asked Darryll Brooks, promoter and former manager of Salt n Pepa, why he thought that was. He replied, "They had more money behind it. That's real simple."

Voices from the Industry are those voices of people who have worked with Go-Go bands to create music, like Kurtis Blow and Salt n Pepa, or sometimes having the difficult task of performing on the same bill.

Although Doug E. Fresh was unreachable for this book, we certainly can't leave him out as one of the biggest supporters of Go-Go. He's another entertainer from the hip-hop camp who has always shown love to D.C., Go-Go, Chuck Brown, and Rare Essence in particular. As a matter of fact, wouldn't you consider his beat boxing an extension of percussion? One of the basic foundations of Go-Go is percussion.

Doug has been entrenched in Go-Go for decades and has appeared on tracks with Rare Essence and Chuck Brown and, in 2022, appeared on some shows with The Chuck Brown Band.

In 2022, Doug released a project entitled "This One's for Chuck Brown." It contains 9 tracks, one aptly called "Chuck Brown."
This section will contain remarks and interviews from some entertainers and other industry insiders sharing their thoughts on Go-Go.

"Go-Go Music, like Hip Hop, is the voice of the people. It's a unique combination of funk, soul, and hip-hop that is unrivaled in its ability to make people move, get down and bob your head. It's the pulse of the city and a true representation of the culture of Washington, D.C. I will always love Go-Go Music!"- **Kurtis Blow, Rap Artist**

Cheryl "Salt" James of Salt n Pepa shared her thoughts on Go-Go and what it was like working with some of our great musicians who were raised in Go-Go.

Jill Greenleigh: When was the first time you ever heard Go-Go music?
Cheryl James: The first time I heard Go-Go music is when we began to travel to D.C. in the early days. I think Rare Essence was playing in a club, if I recall correctly.

JG: What were your thoughts?

CJ: I thought, wow, this isn't just music. It was a movement. I was amazed at how the crowd reacted in the club and how much the people loved it. The groove and the vibe were undeniable. I thought live music was so underrated but so good.

JG: Why do you think rap went so much further than Go-Go?

CJ: I often wondered that myself, possibly because rap is a wide variety of sounds from r&b to pop, including Go-Go. Go-Go is a very particular sound that people grew up listening to in the D.C., MD area, and there's a lot of city pride that comes with it.

JG: How did the "Shake Your Thang" collaboration with Experience Unlimited come about?

CJ: "Da Butt" was a great song, and EU and Sugar Bear were killing it on a commercial level; Hurby knew Sugar Bear, and the collaboration was a no-brainer, especially since we had already done "My Mic Sounds Nice" with a hint of Go-Go.

JG: What was it like working with Experience Unlimited?

CJ: Working with EU was a pleasure; whenever we played in D.C., we would bring Sugar Bear up to sing his part on "Shake your Thang," and the crowd always lost their minds; they were like our secret weapon because D.C. was completely about that Go-Go life.

JG: Do you have any stories to tell about those times? Anything that stands out that was fun or funny?

CJ: We hated headlining in D.C. because Go-Go is all they really wanted to hear, I used to be confused because the audience was always full, and they knew we were headlining, but the reaction was always mediocre. Pep and I wanted to switch places with whichever Go-Go band was on the bill, and there always was… any artist will tell you it's tough headlining in D.C.

JG: I understand that at one point, during one of the Salt n Pepa tours, you toured with a live band, Go-Go's all-female band, Pleasure. How did that come about? Who's idea was that?

CJ: Meeting Pleasure in D.C. and wanting to empower female musicians and support live music and Go-Go. It just made sense that we'd have an "all-girl band," like it says in "Expression," a platinum single I wrote and produced on my own btw. Toot Toot.

JG: Do you have any favorite Go-Go groups/ songs?

CJ: Chuck Brown is my favorite.

George Harrell, who worked in radio promotions and as a tour manager with Uptown Records, a label Rare Essence once had a deal with, shares his thoughts on Go-Go.

Jill Greenleigh: What is Go-Go to you?
George Harrell: Go-Go is an expression of live music with all kinds of incredible sounds, different than anything else out there, and the home of D.C. is the foundation of it. But it's an incredible music. To be in the room when it's playing, you have to be there to experience it, and I think it's an amazing art form. I love Go-Go.

JG: Do you feel that you have contributed to Go-Go in any way?

GH: I think I am a pebble in the sand to the people who founded it, and we [Uptown Records] played a part for that moment, but that's a cultural D.C. legacy. It's like talking about me contributing to Stevie Wonder. Go-Go and the people who founded it and love the culture and built it are the lead people, and I would never say I was in that lane. Did we sign Rare Essence and make an effort to contribute to the culture? Yes. We were there, and we did our part. I don't know exactly why we never got a

platinum record on them because sometimes records would come...
records come out of A&R and sometimes a record – the thing about a
group coming to Uptown at that time, there're only so many slots to come
out so you've got a Heavy D., a Jodeci, a Mary J. Blige, a Lost Boys, and
Rare Essence. And nobody can come out at one time. So, it was stiff
competition, them coming out, and we were sitting in meetings talking
about who's got the biggest record- that's only business. And the one that
would perform the best- the streets would say that's the biggest record,
and that's the record that came out.

JG: Was Rare Essence supposed to do any other work on Uptown or just
"Lock It" for the Strictly Business soundtrack?

GH: I am radio promotions and that's more of an A&R question. I don't
remember who was the A&R assigned to the project at that time, but what
I do know as a radio promotion person, sometimes it's hard to get a live
performance to work on radio, and I think that that was one of the
challenges in finding the right record that radio was going to be receptive
to and as well, have a big enough budget to promote it national. Those are
just standard things that have to happen, and again, I didn't sit in those
meetings with that particular artist. They would only bring it to me once
they had worked out all of that stuff and say what the budget was, but I
knew that they were stable in D.C., and I don't remember the name of the
radio station, but they were kind of like a Go-Go radio station in D.C.

JG: What are your thoughts about Uptown's acts playing before the Go-
Go bands on the big shows in D.C.? I know that Uptown groups were
used to being headliners anywhere else.

GH: One thing about us at Uptown, we were on the pulse of the culture,
and guys like Jimmy Jenkins, who was the Sr. VP, and Marc Barnes, and
me, we would explain the mentality to our artists and teach them the
structure of respecting the art form, and again, I got a lot of these artists,
i.e., Mary J. Blige and those guys when they were baby acts so again, I'm
explaining those kinds of things to them so they would understand so it
wasn't really like a hatred, they were learning something.

JG: Why do you think that rap went so much further than Go-Go?

GH: I think that in Go-Go, they didn't find that record that was going to
be more mainstream like "Doin the Butt," ["Da Butt"] which I would think

would be one of the biggest records that I can think of that came out of that genre, but that doesn't mean that it wasn't great and you need a certain level of expertise that has to go into it for it to have transferred into the mainstream: the right record, the budget, the styling of the artist, and the vision. And a company, and someone has to believe in it and want to bring it home.

JG: Would you say there is room for Go-Go to become mainstream, or has that ship sailed?

GH: I'd never say never, and I'd have to go to one of my newer guys, that's my guy Raheem DeVaughan. My friend Craig Davis is the manager for Raheem who was an independent promotion person at Uptown, and I've seen him do a phenomenal show in D.C. and turn the spot out. I did the Kennedy Center with Raheem and did not know that the famous actor, [Anwan Glover] Slim, from The Wire, was a Go-Go guy. I saw them (Backyard Band) perform at the Kennedy Center that night, and they were amazing. Somebody has to come with the money, the budget, and the vision. That's another thing, Mary J. Blige, You Remind Me took 28 weeks to break in the beginning and it broke out of a mix show. Red Alert and Chuck Chillout played it before the program directors. When you look at a record that's new like that, you've got to stick with the record until it breaks. And somebody has to understand that concept and be willing to make the investment to do that.

Grandmaster D of Whodini (Drew Carter), DeeJay
There ain't no beat like a Go-Go beat. To me, Go-Go is a funky drum beat, and saying it's a drum beat, to me, Go-Go was a part of hip hop because when you are a hip-hop artist, you rap off of drum beats. But Go-Go was a drum beat that was always funky. Big Tony from Trouble Funk became one of my good friends. I connected with them. They were the first- between them and Chuck Brown- those are the ones I was playing in New York back in the day, you know, "Bustin' Loose" and "We Need Some Money," but Big Tony had put me on to it because I was scratching back in the days Trouble Funk "Drop the Bomb" and stuff like that, "Let's Get Small." We had a show in Washington, and I think it was one of the Go-Go bands, I think it was EU or somebody on the show, and Big Tony told me backstage, I had invited him to the show, "Tell the crowd when you get up there, 'Where y'all from?'" and I said that, and they went crazy. And I dropped "Bustin' Loose," "We Need Some Money," and "Let's Get Small." The Go-Go sound to me was incredible. It was always funky to

me. But as my band, I've got to say, Chuck Brown, one of my all-time, Trouble Funk, EU, Rare Essence, Little Benny- that was my Go-Go connect. We owe a lot to Chuck Brown. Chuck Brown was the Godfather. You've got to give him the credit, man.

I really feel some people in the industry really feel that Go-Go should just stay in D.C., which I didn't. To me, any beat is good as long as it is funky. You can't go to D.C. without playing Go-Go. But I really feel like it crossed over through the south, you know, like North Carolina, Virginia, and some parts of New York. Crossing over all around the United States, it didn't. I think what went mainstream was with EU "Da Butt." That really crossed over. That opened the door more, but old heads that really know Go-Go, you've got to go back to the history of Chuck Brown. And you can't talk about or explain it; you had to be there to witness it live. It's like being at a jam session. They get down. They bring it. And it's just not just the drum beat. They've got the horn section too! At the time, we were as hot as a firecracker, so every song we had was going to play well. And they (the crowd) knew the words. But not only that, a couple of Go-Go groups covered the song "Freaks Come Out at Night" in a live session. I've seen it a couple of times on a video. Other than that, we were very hot so we blended it right with the Go-Go. It was a great experience.

Davey Shark, a former member of Doug E. Fresh and the Get Fresh Crew
"Go-Go is a movement forged by fire and the hardships of people in the ghetto. Go-Go came about through that fire through a man, Chuck Brown, who literally did prison time, and through his hardship, his prison bid became not a way to be bitter but a way to be better. In his artistic genius, he came up with a different style of beats which transformed into what we know as Go-Go. What Go-Go means to me is that no matter how down a person is in life, a part of them is willing to create and form something good or create and form something that's not good. So Go-Go is showing you how a person who's wanting to transform themselves into something better and not only makes them feel good, but everyone who listens feels good. They wanted to make everybody a part of this movement. So, in Go-Go, you have basically the Master of Ceremonies, or Lead Talker, telling you what to do. Everybody is doing it in accord with one another which brings forth unity. Where there's unity, there's power. That power could be used for good, or it could be used for evil. But then there are the powers that be that have been against Go-Go. When these people see this movement, and they see people coming together, predominantly black and

brown people, that scares the powers that be, so they have to make Go-Go into a villain, and that was done in D.C. Go-Go was villainized. They fought to unvillainize it. They started thinking about a Museum for Go-Go only a few years ago, but this should have been done decades ago. But they spent so much time trying to make an enemy for D.C. that it's only now recognized for the art that it's been.

As a New Yorker, you would think of white hippies in Go-Go boots when you think of Go-Go. When you go to your first Go-Go, and the crowd is really familiar, it takes on a whole new meaning once you see that. When you see everyone in unison and in sync with the lead talker and the fun everyone is having. Going from being on tour with Doug E. Fresh, who is a champion for Go-Go, and I think that it is really noble of him to stand behind Go-Go as he's done over the decades and is still doing. I have been blessed to be in his company to understand why he's doing what he is doing as we both recognize that it is unity, a movement and it's an art that is going to be lost."

Jalil Hutchins of Whodini:
"Go-Go didn't make it as far as rap, in my opinion, because on a wide scale, they lacked subject matter. We (Whodini) played around the world because a lot of our subject matter was global. Whodini headlined in D.C., and D.C. always showed us mad love. When asked if he had a favorite group or song, he replied, "I have jams that I like. I didn't have a special group."

The business end would have happened if the music had been directed at a wider audience like "Da Butt." "Da Butt" wasn't watered down Go-Go. It understood the assignment and was done. "Bustin Loose" wasn't the rawest Go-Go. Salute to the Godfather Chuck Brown.

If you play for the backyard that's who is coming. If you play for home and other people, that's who is coming.

"Planet Rock," "The Breaks," "The Message," "Friends," "Freaks Come Out at Night," "The Show," and "It's Like That" all excelled hip hop to different audiences. Salt n Pepa is a good example. Kurtis tried to make Go-Go- they made a jam and fit Go-Go into it. There's a difference.

When asked what he thought about Doug E. Fresh doing an entire album paying homage to Chuck Brown, he said, "That was his people. Chuck deserves it. He studied Chuck, and he was accepted early in D.C."

"I have songs I like. It can go from "Pump Me Up" to "Let's Get Small" to "Run Joe" to "Da Butt" to "Sardines.""

Bo Sampson, **CEO of Bodacious One**, an entertainment firm, has been in the music industry for over 3 decades- many years with MCA working with Mary J Blige, Jodeci, and New Edition, to name a few.

"Being from Washington, D.C. and knowing the sound of Go-Go has never really gotten its "just due" nationally, I put some things together because God gave me the opportunity to work with superstars who like Go-Go, so I knew the music was at the same level as the music of some of these artists that I've worked with so I celebrate Go-Go. Trouble Funk was one of my favorite groups growing up."

Spotlight: Ju Ju House

On April 24, 2011, I published the article below on examiner.com. The article was prompted by negative comments on an internet program called "The Drummer's Breakfast," where some participants questioned the commitment of one of Washington, D.C.'s premier drummers, William "Ju Ju" House. Ju Ju had played all over the world by this time with both Go-Go and International recording artists, one being Jazz great Mr. David Sanborn, for which Ju Ju earned a Gold record recording and touring with him. He sat down with me to complete this interview to get some things off his chest.

I sat with him again in September 2022, 11 years later, to review this article and see if anything had changed in these years. He asked me to use this article as is, don't add or subtract, as it still speaks the truth. He joked that we were able to see into the future in 2011 as this is as relevant today as it was then. Here it is.

The Drummer's Beat: Ju Ju House, The Legend Speaks
When William "Ju Ju" House was six years old, he picked up his first set of drumsticks to play drums at his father's church. Coming from a musical family, his grandfather played guitar for the church band, and Ju Ju's father played drums, saxophone, and bass. Ju Ju watched his father play with the greats, including Otis Redding and James Brown, and knew he would follow in his father's footsteps. Ju Ju's own son would follow in his playing with the Air Force Marching Band.

Fast forward several decades and Ju Ju is still going strong and has developed a drumming style all his own, positioning himself as one of the most sought-after drummers on the worldwide music scene.

Ju Ju, who has traveled the world playing with David Sanborn, Chaka Khan, Roberta Flack, and D.C.'s own E.U., is honored to discuss his contribution to the D.C. Go-Go scene as one of the pioneers of this homegrown music. "I can honestly say the first gig where I made what I consider a lot of money was when I first played with The Peacemakers. The Peacemakers are another lost group. This was when Go-Go was really Go-Go. This is the biggest problem that I see with the D.C. musicians and the music in D.C. now. You go to a Go-Go and you hear the first band so you've heard all of the bands that's playing there that night. And this is where we lost our flavor."

He elaborates, "Back in the day when you would go see a band like The Peacemakers, Trouble Funk, E.U., Rare Essence- each one of these groups had an identity. Whether you liked them or you didn't, you knew E.U. was E.U. You knew Trouble was Trouble. You knew Chuck (Brown) was Chuck. You knew Essence was Rare Essence. You knew the groups. You knew (Little) Benny. You could tell. They each had a different flavor, a different style, a different image. Everything was different about the groups."

"The Peacemakers were a group that came up with a lot of the old Go-Go chants. There are a lot of things that's happening that these young groups are playing, and they don't realize that many of these older groups brought that creation. They brought it to the table."

Developing your identity is the key to success in the music industry, and Ju Ju encourages younger bands to do so. He credits Chuck Brown, Trouble Funk, and Junkyard Band as three who developed and maintained their own identity away from the other D.C.-centered bands. He offers, "I have never seen a group of people, a group of musicians from out of Washington, D.C., that are supposed to be the best musicians in the world break their necks to rehearse Beyonce. Break their necks to rehearse Jay Z. Break their necks to rehearse someone else making money from the song. They don't have any creativity anymore, any writing ability anymore- they call it Go-Go. This is what they call Go-Go now- playing somebody else's material. They call that Go-Go. Bounce. Bounce what?

205

What are you bouncing? Bouncing checks, that's about it because you're playing somebody else's music, basically."

Ju Ju understands that the style of music the younger bands from the DMV are playing, Bounce Beat, is both a blessing and a curse. He explains, "When I came back home (from touring), there were no bands even playing. The only bands still playing were Proper Utensils, Rare Essence, and Chuck. We put a group together called Maiesha and the Hiphuggers. We came out with a song 'Um Bop Bop' and 'Bounce.' The clubs weren't letting the bands play in there, and what Maiesha was able to do was take that transition of some Top 40 and some 70's and mix it in with the Go-Go which was a good thing, but it ended up being a disaster because the bands lost their identity. They didn't have the ability to say, 'Hey, you know what? There's a limit to playing someone else's stuff.' It's ok to play somebody else's song, but when you do it all night when you've got 2 hours and out of that 2 hours, you played 99% of somebody else's stuff, with a beat, and you talk about a bounce beat, a Go-Go beat- there's no such thing. I mean, it's- the identity is not even there."

When asked if Bounce Beat is Go-Go, "Go-Go has made money. Go-Go has traveled around the world. Bounce hasn't gotten out of D.C. yet. That's the difference. It's what the pioneers created. How can you take the pocket from Go-Go and call it Go-Go? What the young kids are doing that's cool. Hey, that's every bit of cool, but where do you draw the line? When will there be songs on the same level as "Da Butt," "Buckwild," "Drop the Bomb," "Misty," and all the things Chuck did. Back in the day, we had the strength because of the fact that we did Go-Go. We created our own- 'Ooh La La La,' 'Knock em out Sugar Ray,' 'Drop the Bomb,' 'Cat in the Hat,' 'Go Ju Ju Go.' We had the ability. We had the strength because we wrote, we put out our stuff, and radio stations didn't have to play it. Now the groups depend on these little radio stations. Things have changed, and we look at these local Deejays that never made a career for any of us. *We* made *their* careers by giving them the records to play. There wouldn't have been a DJ Flexx or a Rico or Tigger on the radio if it wasn't for 'Cat in the Hat,' 'Go Ju Ju Go,' 'Um Bop Bop,' 'Bounce,' and the rest of this stuff. We made a path for them to be on the radio.

So many people have used Go-Go to get their platform, to get their foot in the door, and after they use it, they abuse it, and this is with everything that everyone has touched- even with these clubs. The clubs will start going down, and their income is going down, so what they do is they get the Go-Go bands to come in there and play- pump it out for a good month or two, build their franchise back up, remodel the club and then tell the bands, 'Oh we're not gonna have Go-Go bands in here anymore.' Well, no one was coming in here before we got here. So many people have used Go-Go for so many years, and the young people don't even realize it. They have no clue that it's bigger than D.C. because they haven't been anywhere. It's much bigger than D.C."

With success often comes jealousy, and Ju Ju is not immune to this phenomenon. Some of his detractors have publicly questioned his level of commitment to Go-Go. "Go-Go has lost its ability to even be called Go-Go. People wonder, 'Ju Ju, don't you want to play Go-Go anymore? Have you lost your interest in Go-Go?' I say, 'Hell no! I don't want to play Beyonce anymore. I don't want to play Jay-Z anymore. Hell no! That's not what I have based my career on for 30 years to play Jay-Z. I played with Jay-Z, so what do I want to play Jay-Z's song for?"

Ju Ju adds some insight, "I've played with Chaka (Khan), I've played with David Sanborn, played with Marcus (Miller), George Duke, Grace Jones, Soul II Soul, played with Roberta Flack, Jon Secada, with Arrested Development on MTV Unplugged, played for the Pope when he came to Central Park. How many brothers do you know who was standing next to the Pope and the Mayor in Central Park? I've been around the world and toured for 26 years nonstop. When you start talking about Japan- Japan knows a lot about Go-Go. They know more about Go-Go than the people that are actually playing it in this City. But, they look at it and say what we've heard in the past is great, but what's coming out of D.C. now, it's disgusting because they are hearing us play everyone else's songs."

"I remember when I played with Chaka. We did this song, "Through the Fire' and at the end of it, she said 'I want you to go into that Go-Go thing.' And this is Chaka Khan, and she plays drums- go into that Go-Go thing. So it's bigger than D.C. And understand that playing drums is a big part of D.C., congas is a big part of D.C., so no matter if you're doing bounce or pocket, it doesn't matter. Have you had the ability to be identified? You can identify me. You know who I am, and you know how I play. That's my style. I don't want to sound like anybody else. That's why they call me Ju Ju. My identity is worth more to me than trying to play like somebody else. That's why they hire me for the big gigs."

JuJu respects those legendary people that were there beside him as the

207

genre was being developed. "I've been in the trenches. Sugarfoot's (Rick Wellman) been in the trenches, Glenn Ellis has been in the trenches, Sugar Bear has been in the trenches, Benny's been in the trenches, Chuck's been in the trenches, James Funk's been in the trenches. Footz (Quentin Davidson) has been in the trenches. Heavy One (Willie Gaston) has been in the trenches. And Godfather (Mark Lawson). Godfather is one of the cats- that's another one they have to have the utmost respect for that has an identity- not just ability. He's another one that people overlook and, to a point, try to treat him like he's a little peon, but they have no idea what this cat has done. Godfather is a legend. I have the utmost respect for that man, and he's a creator. He's bad as shit. Tino, Big Tony, Rock Steady, Jungle Boogie, Go-Go Mickey, and Buggs (Steven Herrion). We've been in the trenches. There's only a handful of us living."

Ju Ju credits Cherie Mitchell- Agurs with understanding true musicianship. "I'm really proud of Cherie. Cherie stepped up her game. She's toured. She's actually been out there, and she was able to see what the other side is like, and she came back home and did her thing and put Be'la Dona together. And Cherie is not afraid to write a song. Nobody in that band is afraid to write a song. I'm impressed with that. When I see people like that, I'm impressed. You're showing me something."

"I made a living off of playing drums, not just D.C. I've never worked a job in 35-40 years. I played drums all my life. And I've got proceeds to prove that I've played drums. The important thing is to be able to teach these youngins. I don't care what you're playing, personally, but at the end of the day, can you pay your bills? Can you take care of your home? Can you pay your rent? Can you pay your car note? Can you go to the ATM, and it doesn't say 0 balance? I'm talking about just playing drums."

Ju Ju offers some advice, "What's important is being able to get out here and experience the world. It's more important than you sitting here thinking you're gonna hit gold playing Go-Go. Go-Go is a beautiful thing and I made a living off of Go-Go, but you're not gonna hit gold playing Go-Go. You're not gonna reach the top of the mountain playing Go-Go. You're not gonna reach the top of the mountain playing anything. You will reach the top of the mountain by having an identity and being able to do what you do better than anyone else, but it has to be you. You have to have that ability to do that. There's no band, nobody in the world that can help you do that. You have to have that ability to stand up on that stage and play in front of 20,000 people when that band walks off the stage and leaves you up there by yourself. If you've got that ability, you will survive in this. If you don't have that ability, you'll be working from 8-4 playing Wednesdays, Fridays, and Saturdays at the little clubs at the little rec centers for the rest of your life, and if that's what you are looking forward to, then so be it. That's not what I was looking forward to."

Ju Ju has reached out to the up-and-coming drummers in the DMV to teach them, the way that Ricky "Sugarfoot" Wellman did for him. Ju Ju remembers, "Darrell 'Blue Eye' Arrington used to sit behind me, and Blue would be right there watching when I would play. I'm quite sure he has implemented some of what he learned from watching me. I did the same thing with Rick, so I'm quite sure he has. Rick Wellman has the ability and he also has the identity, and that's what's so important. Sugarfoot has an identity. Sugarfoot has a style. And that's why he has played with Miles Davis."

Sharing some of the main things to remember in this business, Ju Ju concludes, "If you have that ability and knowledge, be a musician, not just a Go-Go musician. Not just a Go-Go drummer. Not just a Go-Go guitar player. If you have the ability to play music, be a CREATOR. This is why God gave you this gift, to be a creator- not just Go-Go. Chuck plays Blues just as well as he plays Go-Go. Sugar Bear can do Rock and Roll as well as he plays Go-Go. So, what I'm trying to tell these young people out here it's not just about playing a pocket, a bounce beat, but be able to… I play Country music, Hank Williams Jr., and I can play a Bar Mitzvah. Eva Cassidy, I played with Eva. I played with the Boston Pops, the only black kid onstage with the Boston Pops Orchestra. I played with the Dallas Symphony. I did the Boston Symphony. I walk in there looking like Snoop Dog, the people looking at me, and they're thinking, 'Who is this young kid coming in here with plaits? He's got his book in his hand.' And they know I can read music when they see me pull my stuff out, look at those charts, and hit it."

"Instead of talking, the young people should be asking me questions about how to be successful. How has it been that I have been able to play drums all my life and not work? How I've been able to send 3 kids to college and not work a job? How I've been able to buy 3 houses and not work a job? That's what they should be asking. I have a heart for all these young people. D.C. has been good to me. And the people in D.C. have been good to me. It's just the younger people and the younger musicians that are coming up. There's always something new that people are gonna try, and that's natural, and it's a good thing, but you can never change history or the fact of where Go-Go came from. You can't ever change the fact of what Go-Go was built on because you can never go back and change Grover Washington- you'll never go back and change Mr. Magic."

"And at the end of the day," Ju Ju relays, "I've got drum magazine, Billboard magazines, Japanese magazines with me and Chuck, drummer magazines, Arrested Development, MTV, MTV Unplugged with Arrested Development. I have Gold records- one from David Sanborn, one from Grace Jones 'Slave to the Rhythm,' EU's 'Da Butt,' another one for 'Buckwild.'"

He confidently adds, "When we're gone, I would hope that these young kids can carry on the legacy of the identity and tell the young kids the story of how Go-Go got started, what Go-Go is about, what Go-Go has been about, and what we've done in our own separate journeys away from D.C., what we've accomplished. Until you experience what it's like, I'm still sitting on top of the mountain."

Chapter 13: Leaving D.C.

There is no question that Go-Go has birthed some extremely talented musicians who have parlayed their "training" (so to speak) with Go-Go bands into a platform to take their talents to a national and international platform. We have had many people who started out playing in Go-Go bands, honing their abilities, and then went on tour with major acts, and some have even returned home to play with Go-Go bands.

Some of the national acts that have been introduced to our Go-Go sound and hired the musicians include Miles Davis, Prince, Parliament Funkadelic, Maceo Parker, James Brown, Patti LaBelle, Maze, Chic, Wale, Keith Sweat, Jon B., Anthony Hamilton, Keith Washington, DeBarge, Kanye West, Candy Dulfer, Doug E Fresh, Salt n Pepa, Charlie Wilson, Glenn Jones, Pookie Hudson and the Spaniels, members of Earth, Wind and Fire, Skip Mahoney and the Casuals, Grace Jones, Arrested Development, David Sanbourn, Tony Terry, SWV, Stacy Lattisaw, George Duke, Howard Hewett, Elton John, Stevie Nicks, Stevie Wonder, Fantasia, Foo Fighters, Najee, and Gerald Levert.

Below are stories, memories, and thoughts from some Go-Go musicians who have toured nationally and internationally with prominent acts.

"One of Miles Davis' roadies was from the Washington, D.C. area, and Miles was playing in D.C. He walked into soundcheck, and a Chuck Brown PA tape was playing. Miles asked who was playing the drums. Ricky's personality came through his drums. You would know that if you ever shook his hand. Miles got ahold of Ricky's number and called him up, and he was sleeping. His wife, Vicky, answered the phone and didn't wake Ricky. The following day, she told Ricky that Miles Davis had called. He thought it was the guys playing a joke. The next night, Miles' manager called and spoke with Ricky. It was then that he knew it was real. He went to play with Miles Davis. **Steve Coleman, trumpet, Chuck Brown and the Soul Searchers, EU, and Redds & the Boys**

"I quit school after my third semester at St. Mary's College to pursue music full-time. Three months later, I auditioned for and got the Parliament/ Funkadelic gig at 19.

Over that time, Boyer played with some of the heavy hitters of funk and

R&B, who were leaving James Brown's band to join Parliament Funkadelic. Boyer explains, "The pipeline from James Brown to Parliament Funkadelic included Maceo Parker, Fred Wesley, and Kush Griffith, collectively known as The Horny Horns, Bootsy Collins, and his brother Catfish Collins, as well as Mallia Franklin, who was known as the Queen of Funk."

During a lull in activity, I joined up with my section mates Bennie Cowan and Greg Thomas to round out the horn section for Slug-Go. The section moved around in the Go-Go community, landing a gig with Little Benny and the Masters.

Chuck Brown heard us playing with Benny and told us verbatim, 'I'm the only one in town qualified to pay you.' Anyone that brazen deserves my attention, at the very least! So, in 1989, the P-Funk horns became the section for Chuck. He understood our obligation to P-Funk, so we were allowed to join back up with Chuck after touring was over. Eventually, Bennie and Greg stopped playing with Chuck while I continued under the arrangement I'd play when not on the road. I've been playing with the Chuck Brown Band ever since.

In 1998, after leaving Parliament Funkadelic, Boyer rejoined his former bandmate, the sought-after saxophonist Maceo Parker, as Parker had started his own band. One evening, the band got a visit from Prince. "Prince kept asking the sax players that he worked with to 'do it like Maceo,' and after many a futile attempt, he got an idea- hire Maceo," recalled Boyer. Prince saw a chemistry between Parker and Boyer and invited them to join the New Power Generation, where Boyer remained from 2001 to 2008.

Prince asked Maceo to join his band (the NPG) after failing to find a sax player to groove like Maceo. When Prince saw us live, he also asked Maceo to 'bring that trombone player with him,' taking note of the chemistry Maceo and I had together. So, from 2002, I was a trombonist and horn arranger with Prince, playing with Maceo in between tours until I left in 2009.

Besides Go-Go, Boyer has played many styles of music, from Jazz to Salsa. Recalling playing with the salsa groups Orquestra La Romana and Sin Miedo, he enthusiastically states, "As a bone player, it doesn't get any better than salsa. All those hot, jazzy brass lines over an extremely hot

212

groove." As a member of the Chuck Brown Band, Boyer continues to play with them as his time permits.

After a 25-year hiatus, Greg is back with Parliament/ Funkadelic- taking the Farewell Tour with George Clinton and a reunion with the P-Funk Horns.

It's good to see the world; it's an education you cannot obtain through TV, an app, or a trip to the library! Rule number one for any citizen- get a Passport. Rule number two- use it! And when you do, your appreciation of home is no longer taken for granted."- **Greg Boyer, trombonist Slug-Go, Chuck Brown, Parliament/ Funkadelic, Maceo Parker, and Prince (to name a few).**

"Being in Go-Go has been an honor because growing up in D.C., you were either surrounded by the wrong crowd of people, played sports, or became a musician. The music kept me busy and out of trouble. I've performed with many bands over the years, but the most recognizable band was EU. There is a big difference between performing locally and touring. Preparing for your performance when you are doing local shows is that you know that it's usually going to be the same show, but maybe a different format weekly, so it's based on how you are feeling the audience. When you are on tour, it's an all-day thing including rest, travel, arrival, check into a hotel, sound check, lunch/dinner, little rest, lobby call, travel to the venue, prepare for show, showtime, back to the hotel, rest for the night, lobby call to leave the hotel, off to the next city and all of this is in one day. It's the life of a musician."- **Jeno Meyer, keyboardist for The Stylistics, Heatwave, EU.**

"We love to be the big fish in the little pond. And we can't get passed this mentality of working to grow. And unfortunately, the wrong people try to do the right thing and that creates the problem. I know this for a fact. I've been deeply immersed in it. And as much as I try to help people, they get in their own way. I'm still here working to expand on a different level, and that's in film. How many people are really trying to get out of their own way? I applaud Trouble Funk. Trouble Funk was all over the world. They left in the 80s to pursue, to push the platform of Go-Go, and they did it. They traveled the world. They did what musicians were supposed to do. It's hard because you don't have the right managers… sometimes, it's about timing. You have Trouble's music in all kinds of movies. Even Rick Rubin (Def Jam) had Trouble Funk in LL Cool J's 'Rock the Bells'-

Tarek Stevens, Whistle
"I was discovered by the Stylistics from posting youtube clips of me singing their songs on live shows after I stepped away from Go-Go. Keith Busey, who is my friend and the musical director for the 70s Soul Tour band also put in good words for me. I got the call from my friend John Johnson who is also in the Delfonics with me now. He told me that the Stylistics needed a new lead, so the audition was set up, and the rest is history. I toured overseas with them, then left and now sing with the Delfonics."- **Michael Muse, vocalist, Rare Essence, The Stylistics, and The Delfonics.**

"James Brown was in D.C. getting the key to the city, and we were asked to perform. He was there. At the time, we had a song on the radio that was pretty hot called 'Thank You for letting me be Myself,' and he was in the car going back to the airport when the song came on the radio. He liked the song and wanted to know who it was. When he found out that it was the band that he had just seen playing, the next thing we knew, we were on a plane headed to Augusta, Georgia, to personally audition for him. He treated us very well. We learned a lot from him. The Godfather of Soul."- **Gerald West, Mass Extension**

"I was in California and got word that Klymaxx was looking for a bass player. I tried to get Michelle out to California, but my mother wasn't having it. I was staying on a ranch, and there was plenty of room. Michelle had gotten an offer to audition for the group Living Color. She went to New York. She ended up getting a meeting with Madonna's lawyer. Madonna had just started her own label. Michelle ended up getting signed the next day for her own deal. I knew she was going to get signed one way or another. Even before that…with Kevin Jackson and Night Flight (studios). I would have to say that Michelle was part of that Night Flight. They just really clicked musically."- **Jacques Johnson on his sister Michelle Johnson aka Meshell Ndegeocello.**

"I am a true native of Washington, D.C.—Son of Ignatius Mason, who introduced me to the music industry at birth in 1976. I started playing drums at 10 and formed Optimystic Tribe in 1989. While performing throughout the city and playing at the Ibex [Club] every Tuesday, I became the backup drummer in Backyard from 1994 til 1998. I started my career in Audio Engineering around 1991 as the setup and monitor man for Infant Eyes Production, who provided sound for OP TRIBE and various celebrities like Raheem Devaughn, Glenn Jones, Dick Gregory, Iyanla

Vanzant, and others. After years of paying dues, I became L!ssen's house engineer in 2002 until I moved to Atlanta in 2005. While in ATL, I joined XO Band(which I brought Ricky Angles from the Huckabucks) and the Off Script (which I brought Khari Pratt from NEG) as the drummer for both. I created the Cranklanta movement as all bands came to Atlanta through me because I was the lead engineer for a sound company. In 2008, I created the Crank Brothers franchise with the help of my then-manager, Preston Blue, under the Bag of Beats Record Label. In 2010, I released my debut cd...'Welcome to Cranksville' Being a part of the Go-Go scene in Atlanta and working for various sound companies, I was blessed with the opportunity to become the House Engineer for Q Parker of 112 (which granted many opportunities to engineer artists like Ceelo Green, Jagged Edge, J Holiday, Xscape and many more)."- **Ikhand Mason**

"In 94, I went on the 1994 SWV LONDON TOUR. I was the drummer for Intro."- **Gerald Brooks, Pumpblenders**

Spotlight: The Beat that Ricky "Sugarfoot" Wellman Built

Ricky "Sugarfoot" Wellman had contributed vitally to the original Go-Go pocket, the percussive beat prevalent in Go-Go when he joined Chuck Brown and the Soul Searchers in the mid-70s. At Brown's request, he continued to play drums between songs in an effort to keep people on the dance floor.

Wellman's father, Frank Wellman, along with Lloyd Pinchback, John Euell, and Chuck Brown made up the original Soul Searchers. According to Chuck Brown in a 2011 interview, "Ricky joined in 1976 and started playing the beat that I was trying to put together."

Ricky Wellman was born in Bethesda, Maryland, and grew up in Washington, D.C., and Prince Georges County. His father, Frank, taught him to play drums on grandma's front porch, where, according to cousin Steve "Too Tall" Coleman, a musician himself, the whole family learned to play drums on that drum kit. He recorded his first 45 record when he was 11 years old with the Famous Jaguars called "Crazy Thing" and "Banana Fana." The record was very well received, garnering a tremendous amount of airplay. He appeared on his first gospel album at 14, "Save Thyself," with D.C. gospel artist Myrna Summers. In High School, Wellman was playing with Peaches and Herb. Wellman inspired

215

other drummers to study his craft to elevate their careers, learning from the master himself.

Robert "Mousey" Thompson, drummer for the late James Brown, explains, "Ricky came first! I was a vocalist for a local group impersonating James Brown. I used to go to the Panorama Room because I lived in Southeast and would be right up front watching Rick with the Jaguars before Chuck Brown and New Breed. In my group, the drummer couldn't give me what I needed to be in the music, so I got behind the kit. God gave me Rick as one of my lessons. I got behind the kit and have played with Wilson Pickett, Peaches and Herb, Lloyd Price, and the last 15 years of James Brown. I even worked with Chuck (Brown) for a little while. Chuck said, 'I don't want all those rolls. Just give me the biscuits!' Rick was the man! He's left a presence with what's going on in Go-Go. He's the seed."

John "JB" Buchanan, who played alongside Wellman in the Soul Searchers, adds, "His background in jazz and improvisation strongly influenced where that innovation came from!"

In full circle, just as Wellman was the first drummer to play with Chuck Brown while establishing the Go-Go sound, Kenny "Kwick" Gross was the final drummer to play with Chuck Brown prior to Brown's passing in May of 2012. On meeting Wellman, Gross described, "It was the first night I had ever shaken Ricky Wellman's hand. I felt the power and love; he really is a drummer because he grips your hand. He set the foundation for a lot of us. I am taking care of my family because of the foundation that he set. Chuck took me to Japan, but Ricky got me to Japan."

Mike "Go-Go Mike" "Hardstep" Taylor, trombonist, relays an incident regarding Wellman. "In 1981, I was fresh out of high school. I had been playing with E.U. for about 3 or 4 months. We were playing at the Moonlight Inn, and our regular drummer wasn't there. I asked, 'Who is this pretty red guy behind the drums?' I really tried not to like him because he wasn't our regular drummer, but he started playing 'Drummer's Beat,' and I started dancing, and since that day, Bear called me 'Go-Go Mike,' so he inspired my name."

Gregory "Sugarbear" Elliott, front man and bassist of Experience Unlimited, also recounts of Wellman, "I've had some powerhouse drummers, but when I saw him with Chuck... I gave Rick freedom to play what he wanted to play and that made me better. He taught me about discipline. There's only one Sugarfoot Ricky."

"Chuck kept Rick in a pocket, and they fought and fought. Rick taught me to tune my congas to his two toms so that the sound could be unified. He's inspired me," clarifies Roland Smith, who played with Wellman in Chuck Brown and the Soul Searchers.

Kiggo Wellman, another drummer from the Wellman dynasty of musicians, relates, "I have to thank my cousin for the business factors he gave me when I started playing professionally. He said, 'Don't get star struck and get your money. They can't play without the drummer.' That took me a long way because I always get my money."

William "Ju Ju" House, a prominent drummer locally and nationally that Wellman also admired greatly, stated, "We were in the dungeons and wars together for so many years. I owe my whole career to this man. The Madonna, the Grace Jones, David Sanborn- all of it."

During Wellman's illustrious career, he played with Miles Davis, Carlos Santana, Quincy Jones, Herbie Hancock, Joe Zawinul, Chick Corea, Wayne Shorter, David Sanborn, Chaka Khan, Paolo Rustichelli, George Clinton and Parliament Funkadelic, Experience Unlimited, Slug-go, Bits n Pieces, Little Benny and the Masters, Frank Hooker and the Positive People, Trouble Funk, the New Breed, Dynamic Corvettes, the Headliners, the Pharaohs Band and in 1994, Wellman auditioned with rock act, Steve Perry and Journey.

Wellman reiterates, "Go out and spread your wings. There are different genres. The more you take advantage, the more will come your way."

Sadly, Ricky Wellman died of pancreatic cancer on November 23, 2013, at 58.

Spotlight: Malachi Johns

I'm trying to remember what my first experience managing was. The first one that I would call. Quasi-managing stuff before the first legitimate management that I can think of was I was playing for NE Groovers, which happens to give me a bit more cache with the band from Annapolis that started playing with my first, Go-Go band called Occupation. A lot of members in other bands, you know, they're out now, played with including NE Groovers, Mambo Sauce, Still Familiar. The band was getting back together, as I recall. Oh, I think we were doing a reunion, as you know Go-Go bands want to do and I don't remember if they asked me to manage or I just kind of started doing it or what. But anyway, I was managing them. That was probably in 2001. Maybe 2000 or 2001? And I wasn't managing at all, but I was sort of in the business meetings of Northeast Groovers, if you will, like the marketing meetings and stuff. At that time, I was playing with them. I wasn't making any decisions or anything. So, I wasn't really managing Northeast Groovers, but I was more involved in the business side, but not a decision-maker. I was just in the conversations, and I gave my 2 cents. And I guess when NEG turned into SOULO. When NEG turned over to SOULO, I was in the same situation where the managers were Dig Dug and Ron Moten, and Marlon Clark for a little while. I was again in on the conversations but not a decision-maker. I was in college in Montana in 1998, and some college friends and I put together a band that I guess you could say I managed because I did everything from the booking to the scheduling to pretty much everything. It was not a Go-Go band, although there was another guy in the band from Alexandria, so since we both knew what Go-Go was, we tried to throw some Go-Go stuff in there. We had this hippie dude that had a Djembe drum and some congas, so we made him listen to Go-Go CDs so he could try to learn how to play. He never did, but I remember we played one night at the club that I DJed, and the Harlem Globetrotters were there and other guys from D.C. They were like, "What're all these congas for? You got a Go-Go band?"

My next experience was with Mambo Sauce, but I was never supposed to be the manager. The way Mambo Sauce started was I started a record label. The purpose of starting a record label when I moved back from LA when I lived there the first time was to try to globalize Go-Go, if you will. There was no band that existed that was doing what I was trying to do or that even had any desire to do what I was trying to do. I had to put a band together myself so I put Mambo Sauce together piece by piece with the intention of turning them into the No Doubt of Go-Go if you will. Basically the group would do what No Doubt did for Ska music. That's what I was trying to do. I didn't really ever plan on being involved in

218

whether the band made it to rehearsal on time or wrote songs all the time or anything like that. I was just trying to be the label to release the music, but because they weren't able to handle these things on their own and needed someone to sort of babysit them, I don't want to make it seem like they were children, but there were a lot of childlike activities that occurred. I kind of became the de facto manager because nobody else was doing it or even having exploratory conversations with other people about taking a management role. Knowing more now than I did then, it was probably not a good idea for the label to be doing it and have the artists doing it themselves, but again, getting them to do anything was easier to do it myself. I became the de facto manager, and then at one point, the guitar player called me like 2 days before a show in Baltimore and said, "Hey, I can't do the show. I'm going on tour with Mya."

I had to go put a guitar amp on my credit card. I hadn't been playing guitar for a long time, and I had to learn all the songs in 2 days. I ended up playing for a few years, and that's me playing on the whole album. Like 98% of the album. And then I played with the band when they were hot. I played with the band almost the whole time. So I was the record label, the manager, the booking agent, the graphic designer, the van driver, the everything for Mambo Sauce the whole time I was there. Then after that situation kind of fell apart, I decided that instead of trying to achieve my goal with a band, I would try to do it with a solo artist basically like Chuck Brown. Chuck Brown is an artist who performed with the Soul Searchers and performed with the Chuck Brown Band.

He performed with them and recorded with them, but Chuck Brown is the artist. He's the one who makes the decisions. Stan Cooper recommended me to this kid who was friends with his son in school named Nick Hakeen. I started working with him and started developing him into a Go-Go artist, and someone called me about a show for Mambo Sauce at the 9:30 Club and just put Nick on it instead. So, his first show was at the 9:30 Club with the band that is now Wale's band, his backing band, and we started to get some songs submitted. I got a song submitted by the lead singer of the reggae band Soulja who just won a Grammy last year. He submitted a song for us, and we were going to record it, but as I was putting all of these pieces into place, he got accepted to Berkley College of Music. He ended up going to Berkley, and so we had to stop that project, and now he's one of those hipster neo-soul type artists. He's fairly successful, so he did ok for himself. Then at that time, I was being courted heavily by this kid, who used to go by the name D.C. the Loverboy. He used to come up to WPGC when I worked there, and he would try to get his songs played. Then he got my information and trying to get me to manage him because everybody in the whole city was trying to get me to manage them after Mambo Sauce because they thought I just pressed a button and made them successful.

I said no to all of them (the rappers) because I just wanted to work with Go-Go. So, then David Cory's (D.C. the Loverboy) mother campaigned to a friend of my family to take on David. He had one song that was kind of Pop and I told him that we could put a band behind him, and he was excited. He coined his genre, "Urban Rock," and he is actually a very good singer. And because of my relationship with Wale's band, UCB, I put these guys behind David, and I ended up replacing people. I'm not sure what happened, but I basically ended up with the Chuck Brown Band when Chuck was alive. It was Kenny "Kwick" on the drums, Ice on the bass, Marcus Young on the keys, and Anthony, the guitar player that used to play with Black Alley. But then Tom (Goldfogle) came and basically stole my whole band to go and play with Chuck.

I did some other stuff with David, and then David didn't want to do Urban Rock anymore and wanted to do straight up Hip Hop and R&B, and I just wasn't interested in that. At that time, Northeast Groovers had started to play again, this was Northeast Groovers sans Rapper, it was when 32 was the lead vocalist. I started playing with them again. I think 32 had asked me to manage because Pearl, Ms. Pratt, had passed away, so I managed a severely handicapped version of Northeast Groovers- Northeast Groovers without the star. So that was an exciting ride, and then I just stopped managing, and I just started promoting shows in Annapolis. I started bringing Go-Go bands down starting with Faycez U Know, and I think I brought Secret Society and that kind of stuff. I brought Black Alley down; it was the first time I had seen them in this form. When they started, they were more like L! SSEN. It was not all these cool sneakers and stuff they do now. We were trading members between Mambo Sauce and Black Alley. So after seeing them, I started another band called Lipstick and Congas which had a lot of good musicians that I could draw from, but I didn't have any vocalists. My formula for doing things is that I don't really go after traditional Go-Go vocalists. I go after vocalists like Black Boo was a rapper. It was not just a neighborhood band concept. My goal was always to move this thing up about 10 notches, so I didn't know of any vocalists who fit the bill, so I held a contest to find a vocalist called "Are You the Lipstick?" I got all these people to create drops. "Are you the lipstick?"

A friend of mine, funny enough, started telling me that she applied for a job at a casino that was just about to open, and I applied for the job because I was just about to get married and maybe I needed to get a real job so I got the job at the casino. I was not able to have them both at the same time. It was disappointing because starting a creative project is never a straight line, but it was a little bit of a relief. We were opening the casino, and it was 80 hours a week of craziness. I was still at the casino in maybe 2012 or 2013, and BJ (Mickey's son) started calling me asking me to manage this band, LOUD. I said I wasn't doing that anymore, and then he put Kendell on me to try selling me on this band. I said I would give it 6 months. I started managing them and learned one of the biggest lessons I ever learned in management and I cut half the band. They just weren't reliable, whatever the reason. To me, at that point, it just seemed like a good idea. It screwed up the gel of the band a little bit. I came in like a corporate raider, and you can't really take that approach in music. In the end, it ended up kinda cool, but there was just a lot of ego and dysfunction in that group. I am a believer in having the least amount of people in the band.

Malachai left after 6 months.

I'm a booking agent now. A manager in Go-Go is essentially a booking agent because booking agents book shows. That's it. There is no black-and-white description. In the greater, wider industry, the manager is essentially the CEO of the artist's business. They're not the owner but run it and they are responsible for the team. The booking agent, the publicist, the business manager who handles the money, maybe the social media manager/digital marketing, all of those things. In a Go-Go band, there are primarily 2 things- a financier is atypical in the larger music industry. Managers are not required to put up money at all, although it is a fairly regular occurrence in Go-Go and has come to be expected. It's also become expected that the manager becomes the financier and never gets any of that money back just for the privilege of babysitting 11 grown-ass men, so that's kind of become the expectation in Go-Go. But that's not really the function of a manager in the greater music industry, although some managers in the greater music industry have bankrolled their clients. Typically they get that money back, but sometimes…. It's different in every situation, but typically the manager's job is to be the CEO of the artist's company. I also think there is a misconception that the artist is just supposed to make music and the manager is supposed to do everything else and that's not how it is in successful partnerships. It's a partnership.

In the Go-Go world, I am defining this as your primary goal is to get multiple weekly shows on a recurring basis in perpetuity. The job of a manager should be to work with their artist, make that artist desirable and figure out a way to connect that artist (a mechanism for the artist to connect / communicate with their fans). The band's brand becomes desirable so that people will want to pay to come and see that band. Anything that fits within that model. The manager's job should not be to make sure that you come to rehearsal and learn your songs. As a musician, just be an adult.

Make sure there is a good video of the band performing and a website where all of the band's shows are. If you can't do that, at least submit it to gogotix.co. It's free so that people will know where you are playing.

Spotlight: Backyard Band

Backyard Band, which started in about 1988, is one of the great musical products stemming from Uptown NW D.C. around 14th and Girard St. NW. More than 30 years later, the band is still playing throughout the region, and their impact and legacy only continue to grow.

In April 2023, I interviewed Anwan "Big G" Glover and Earl Vincent of Backyard Band, along with former manager Terrance "Coop" Cooper, who managed the band from the late 80s until 2013, to discuss the loyalty, growth, and development of the band over the past 30+ years.

Anwan "Big G" Glover, or as he is sometimes known as "The Ghetto Prince" or "Genghis," is the remaining founding member of the Backyard Band. He is also known for his movie roles and most notably as the character "Slim Charles" from HBO's The Wire.

Anwan reflects, "Officially, at the start, I would be the only "original" band member [left]. There were all the other band members at the start. As we took form, I brought on EB [Eric Britt] and Los [Carlos Chavels]. We were all teenagers."

When discussing the original sound at the band's inception, he continues, "At the start, it was a gritty, more of an underground sound. We changed the sound during our era with NE Groovers, Young Impressions, Huck-A-Bucks, etc. However, our sound has evolved."

Cooper elaborates, "The style of music was Underground, more hardcore hiphopish and as they got older and trying to get out of that stereotype, they were trying to play more sophisticated venues, so they had to change their style. They were always flexible. They even played jazz back in the day because Chucky Thompson [Producer extraordinaire- Chuck Brown, Mary J. Blige] had worked with them. He was helping direct the music and the vision of the music they played. He wasn't a member, but he was a close friend of mine. I took them down to Chucky's basement and said I needed help grooming these guys. He started helping, and then he even played with them- played in the back, just making sure they were learning. He was teaching them while they were playing. He would sit in on a lot of shows just back there with EB and Mike [on the keyboards] and play the keyboard so Chucky would play when they had reunions and stuff because he was a part of creating that sound."

Anwan states, "We had our own identity. We changed the sound of Go-Go during that time. I was always more accessible, being a people person, so that helped us stand out as well. I always listened to our fans and incorporated what they were interested in. As a band, we would always

223

check out the older bands and pay homage, ensuring we created our own lane. I would recognize different neighborhood fans and create different ways to put them on display, as we would say back then, or shout them out. I would do this by creating a neighborhood crew their own chant."

Earl Vincent, who has been with the band for 16 years, shares his thoughts, "The only thing that I can see that's really changed is we have matured over the last... I would say since I've been here. Once upon a time, we were considered the Bad Boys of Go-Go, and I don't think people give us that stereotype now. We have proven that we have been able to play in all forms of entertainment venues. At one time, I guess they were scared to let us in certain venues because maybe they thought our crowd was too rowdy. I think that would be what has changed. Everyone has grown up, and the crowd has matured. Everyone is older now, so I believe the party is much better."

He continues, "I would like to say that even though we are a D.C. band- a band from D.C., which many people would view as a traditional Go-Go band, I believe that we would be what you would consider the true definition of a band meaning we can play all genres of music. Now because many of the venues that we play at, we are not able to express ourselves in many of the genres depending on what show it is, but you know the great thing about Backyard? Backyard can play any style of music so I like the fact that we're not, in my opinion, a Go-Go band meaning that we don't just play Go-Go. We play all genres of music."

CDs include Real Niggaz, We Like It Raw, On the 95 Tip, Hood Related, Skillet, and many, many live CDs directly from their shows, as is customary in the Go-Go tradition of releasing "PA" tapes/ CDs.

The band also did a remake of Adele's "Hello," which was notable.

A rarity in Go-Go, the Backyard Band has kept most of its members intact for 30 years.

"We have become stronger and managed to keep our band members at least over 25+ years, give or take," remarks Anwan.

Currently, the band consists of Anwan "Big G" Glover (lead talker), Tiffany "Sweetthang" White (vocals), Carlos "Los" Chavels (rapper), Leroy "Weensey" Brandon (vocals), Earl Vincent (vocals), Mike Dunklin (keyboards), Eric "EB" Britt (keyboards), Paul "Buggy" Edwards (drums), Keith "Hot Sauce" Robinson (congas), Bob Terry (guitar) and Nate Field (bass guitar).

Coop adds his thoughts on keeping a band together with most of the same members for decades: "Loyalty first and great leadership. Sometimes at rehearsal, we used to just talk about life. Just being a brotherhood to each family when times were hard, we always picked each other up, and they rallied off of that. They rallied off of, Hey! This is my brother, and I can't let my brother down. Now, have they played with other groups periodically? Yeah, because that's the nature of the beast, but it's known that they aren't going to pick [another band] over Backyard. It's a family. It's just a loyalty thing. We always cared about how can we, you know, we needed each other to make it. It's just getting the right people and putting them in your band. We had been through band members that might not have been as loyal, but that was from Day 1. They've grown up with each other. When I came in, they were growing up with each other. They were kids from the same neighborhood, like Rare Essence and Junkyard. They're from the same neighborhood. Nowadays, you may have somebody from Rockville who has to drive all the way over to Landover and somebody living in Laurel having to drive all the way to Landover, and they didn't grow up with each other. There's no real tie. It's just business. Hey, I need a guitar player. Ok, I have this cat from Baltimore. He's going to come down for the show. He's not going to be invested. These guys are invested in life- in each other. Times have changed."

"I know I've only been there 16 years, but the band is very family oriented. We try to keep things family-oriented, having a true brotherhood along with our sister that's there—understanding that we have something. When you have something, and everyone has really bought into the gameplay- everyone can do their job and do their position, all things run very smoothly," offers Earl.

He continues, "We love each other. We really have genuine love for each other. We care about each other's well-being, we care about how each other is doing, mentally, physically, financially, so with that being said, when you have guys around you that are very family oriented, we really care for each other, so when you are doing what you love to do, it's not work. It's more of a great advantage and opportunity that you have to come by. We really love each other."

"You look at a lot of the bands – things happen- people go through things in their own private lives. A band is a collective situation, and singularly you have to be able to take care of yourself to be in the collective situation. I think the guys overall have an understanding singularly, which helps us to be better members when we come together collectively. I've seen a lot of bands, we're not the only band still playing from back then, but we are one of the few bands that still have, maybe the only band that still has most of the members [for 25+ years]. So, I tip my hat to Ghengis for keeping a lot of us together. Ghengis has gone through many things, and to be able to keep the band together for so long. That's a great attribute to him as the leader," confirms Earl.

Glover assures, "We ensure we stay tuned into our original fans as well as ensure we stay grounded enough to bring on newer generations to enjoy our music. We still have many more things to accomplish and achieve to keep go-go alive."

Earl also conveys, "In my opinion, I believe that we have always been a band that was not biased, and when I say wasn't biased, we have been willing to work with any and everyone willing to work with us. Backyard covers a lot of ground with the music that we play, so I think we can play with some of the younger bands because we've always tried to stay relevant. We try to play music that would cater to all lifestyles, all walks of life, and ages."

As far as Glover's other passion, acting, he thinks that his involvement in music and acting has been a win-win for not only himself but also the fans.

"I believe it has helped because our fans would follow me, support my acting, and genuinely show their support at our shows and tune into whatever project I was working on. In turn, it helped both ways."

In summation, Vincent, Glover, and Cooper share the following:

"Backyard prides itself in being prepared to entertain the people. There has been an epidemic, and I will say very cautiously, in the music genre of Go-Go, where bands are no longer practicing. They feel that they can use the stage as an audition. I really appreciate Backyard continuing to rehearse and practice honing our craft so that we can continue to try to elevate and be as best as we can be for the people. Our shows are not free. Many times people are paying – I'm not saying a couple hundred dollars to get in our shows, but they pay decent amounts to get in our shows and we don't take it lightly just because it's a local situation. We really try to give them the local situation, a national experience. When we play, we don't take it lightly. There are a lot of bands that have 'x'ed out practicing. Even after 30 years, we pride ourselves on practicing as hard as we did back in the day. You can't cheat people. We play three times a week, normally on the weekends, and all our shows are packed. We appreciate the people coming out, but we also want them to know that we don't take the fact that they are coming out and that we know that they are coming out. We don't take that lightly. We rehearse for them. We are in the process of putting out new music, so it's not one of those situations. We don't do this for money, even though the money comes, and we do it because we love to do what we do. Backyard is not a band that's going to take advantage of you. We are going to try to give you something that you are going to enjoy and that you're going to move to every time we click the sticks."- Earl Vincent.

"I did my part. I created one of the greatest bands in the history of Go-Go! They felt it was time to move on. That happens when you get older, and your kids move out of the house. I love them to death, but we don't do business together anymore; that's just life. The kids move on and get older. A manager's decision isn't always the popular decision, and as a manager, you have to make some hard decisions to keep the business going however you do it; sometimes, they might not like how you do it, and that's ok. They've grown from boys to men, and they're doing a great job."- Terrance "Coop" Cooper.

"Always know I will keep go-go on my back for life."- Anwan "Big G" Glover.

Chapter 14: Rest In Peace, Rest In Pocket

Many musicians, managers, promoters, club owners, and others have given of themselves to push Go-Go forward who are no longer with us. Although the people will never be forgotten, I thought it was also important to record their contributions to the culture. I asked a few members of the Go-Go community to speak about some of the people we've lost, and they shared their gifts to Go-Go and stories about their lives outside of music. Sadly, we've lost too many Go-Go luminaries over the years to pay tribute to each one here; these remembrances are primarily focused on band members, but so many more people could be mentioned as well, and their contributions are in no way overlooked or unappreciated. Without them, Go-Go could not have moved forward.

Chuck Brown, *Godfather of Go-Go, guitars and vocals, Chuck Brown and the Soul Searchers*

Mark Lawson, *keyboardist, Rare Essence, and Godfather and Friends*
Chuck taught us and took us under his wing. Chuck allowed us (Rare Essence) to be called the Baby Soul Searchers. That's how we were identified. He took us to Philadelphia. He shared the knowledge.

Gregory "Googie" Burton, *bassist, sound engineer*
The name speaks for who he was. The realist, humblest person I've ever worked for. He would say worked with, not for... He would never put himself above anyone else.

Jaime Lawson, *drummer, fan*
I was his next-door neighbor when Chuck moved to Wheaton on Parker Avenue. I was 12 at the time and he let me cut his grass and would pay me $20. I never forgot that because he was the only person I have ever seen drive his own limousine. Fast forward 12 years later, I'm on stage. I look to the right, and who do I see but Chuck Brown! The best part about it? He remembered me and said didn't you hear the shout-out I gave y'all on Go-Go Live? That just cemented how much I love Go-Go because I used to go around telling everybody he was talking to me at 3001 Parker Avenue. Chuck Brown lived at 3005.

Nekos Brown, *son of Chuck Brown*
The biggest lesson I learned from my dad, and I learned so many from him, but I think the main thing in my daily life is that I continue to stay humble. The biggest key in life is to remain humble and remain confident in yourself and understand that you wake up every day for a reason. There's no reason for us to stress really because once you wake up in the morning, you really have nothing to worry about at all. There's always something to do on a daily basis and stay humble and focus on the now, and everything will be fine.

"My father didn't like for anyone to be sad around him, so if there was anyone going through anything around him, he would always try to change their energy. He would always tell me, ' Life is what you make it, Son. The energy that you give is the energy that you get. If you continue to give the energy you want to receive, it will come back tenfold. However you want your life to be, that has to be the focus that you walk. That was one of the main reasons that he treated people the way that he did. It was a natural thing. He didn't hold any grudge. He was constantly cleansing. He didn't want any negative energy."

Wiley Brown, *son of Chuck Brown, guitarist, Chuck Brown Band*
I learned something new every day. The main thing my dad would say is 'Whatever you do, big or small, do it well or don't do it at all.' That's his main saying, but it's instilled in me. Whatever I'm doing, I make sure I'm doing it the best I can.

Milton "Go-Go Mickey" Freeman, *congas Rare Essence, Reality Band, and MANY other Go-Go bands*
A lot of things definitely wouldn't be happening right now. Chuck went to set me in my place one day. I'm in the studio, and he was trying to figure out how something should go. He said it out loud. So me, I said something. "I think you should do this." He said, "Son, you don't tell me nothing about my music." I ain't never had a problem. I didn't say nothing no more if he said something out loud. He put me straight, and Chuck was another one. He would call me in. A song could be finished and he would pay you... Chuck would pay you, and he'd want to do the same song again, and you'd tell him that he already paid you, and he'd say, "Naw. Take this." And he'd pay you again. "I want to make sure it's right." That type of thing. He'd call me in- him and Chucky (Thompson). A lot of times, Chuck would always say if he couldn't have whoever his conga player was

at the time, he wanted me to play.

Donald Tillery, trumpet, Chuck Brown & the Soul Searchers

"Chuck came a long way too- from jail and working on the chain gang, preaching. Chuck was a preacher. He would preach on the streets when he got out of jail. He knew the bible. He would be on the street preaching the gospel and people would throw money in a hat. That's how he wound up feeding himself to survive. His rapping skills were always there because by being a preacher and being out in the street, that's how he survived. So all he did was take what he was surviving on and put it into the music scene. He just blew my mind how he would get people to talk, and that's what you need to do."

Macdonald Carey, *Drummer, Trouble Funk, The Peacemakers, Chuck Brown*

Remembrance by Timothy "Teebone" David, percussionist, Trouble Funk

Macdonald Carey, better known as Mac, was a 100% Go-Go drummer. Of course, he could give you what you wanted, but his specialty was Go-Go. He played the Go-Go feel like no other drummer I played with. Mac and I were great friends. I would pick him up and take him to all the shows. We rode together and hung out together with his family. When Mac first came into the group, he played rototoms and cowbells. With his style, he brought a loudness to the group. I always watched Mac play when he was with the Peacemakers. I always liked the way he played. Oddly, Mac was left-handed, but he played right-handed.

Mac's contribution to Go-Go was that he created a sound on the cowbell rack, which gave Go-Go the hop, and he also did a speed roll on the record "Arcade Funk" which was his identity. When Mac switched to the drums, I developed the 1/16 swing feel, which makes Go-Go "Go-Go", and it was because of the way Mac played. His style gave you the right space to make all those percussion patterns fall together just right. Mac was killed in an auto accident in Southeast D.C. I'm not sure about the details, but speed was a significant factor in the accident. At the time, Mac was playing with Chuck. I really miss Mac on stage and off. Before his passing, he recorded a record with Reo (Edwards) called "Mac Attack." It was a percussion track where he played everything- drums, congas, cowbell, roto toms, and timbales. It was a great recording. Mac was the other half of Double

Trouble when Trouble experimented with two drummers. The live Go-Go Album Saturday Night Live was Mac and Slim on the drums and was recorded at The Paragon Two on Wisconsin Ave., Northwest, which was our weekly spot-on Thursday nights. However, this recording was done on Saturday. I'm not sure about the dates, but Mac played with Trouble Funk in the late 80s. I'm not sure of the year he died.

Derek "House" Colquitt, *Bassist and former Manager of Junkyard Band*

Remembrance by Vernell "Wink" Powell, *percussionist, Junkyard Band*
House was my man. He was like my confidant. He helped me keep a whole lot of my mental in order. House helped me a whole lot with that.

Quentin "Footz" Davidson, *Drummer and founding member* of Rare Essence

Milton "Go-Go Mickey" Freeman, *congas, District Kings, Rare Essence, Reality Band, and many others*
Quentin Davidson was a bowling buddy of mine, but Footz was a pocket drummer, which is now hard to come by. You've got a lot of drummers out there now that's in the way of a lot of conga players. He was a drummer that stayed back—laid back. He always used to tell Funk or Andre to let me get my solo and let me get it out of my system in the beginning. I could do whatever I wanted because he was such a laid-back drummer, and I was so wide open. Same as when Tyrone (Jungle Boogie) was playing if you listen to any of the old Rare Essence tapes. Footz was a humble dressing guy. Many guys have broken drumsticks and cymbals, but Footz always made sure he went to Chuck Levins and kept some stuff with him. A lot of drummers today study Go-Go, but there are a lot that aren't studying. They hear it, but they're not studying it and they really need to study. They need to study Footz, and they need to study Sugarfoot (Ricky Wellman). I would love for drummers to study Footz, Sugarfoot, JuJu, the drummers that were here before them- and Butch Lewis. All those guys had a different style.

As time went on, Footz and I got tighter and tighter onstage and you can hear that on a lot of tapes. A lot of people say it was the perfect combination, but I can say yeah to that, but before me, Jungle Boogie,

231

David Green, and Footz was the best combination in the style of Go-Go I like. Footz started to pick his game up. He was the first one to use the open high hat and you can hear that on that Doug E. Fresh song. He started implementing that with his Go-Go drumbeats. You can hear that today with other drummers still doing it. He started to do more things until we lost him.

David Green, *percussionist, Rare Essence*
Footz had stamina. He was a driving force of Essence and could switch a beat better than anyone. He would lock the pocket with the best.

James "Slim Jim" Harrington, *percussionist, Prophecy and Hot Cold Sweat*
When I was at Kolossal Records, we were in Ned's basement all day working on a Go-Go rap joint. I arrived at noon, and it was going on 6:00 pm when Footz and Donnell walked in with Chinese food. Silently, I was happy as hell to see they brought food. Footz and Donnell pulled out forks and started eating that shyt out the box until it was gone. Needless to say, I had to take my hungry ass to the Eastover Burger King.

Gregory "Googie" Burton, *bassist, sound engineer*
He was the man with the plan. He was always trying to find a way to make everything better. He was a great friend and musician.

Dwayne Lee, *Recording Engineer, Music Producer, and Drummer for Redds and the Boys*
Footz was the Originator. I wanted to play that *Body Moves* beat so bad on a gig back then, but Redds would lose his mind and wanted Danny ("Disco" Danny Peete on congas) and I to only play our own beats. ú   ℣
He also played traditional grip as I did along with "Sugarfoot" Ricky (Wellman) and only a few others.

Kato Hammond, *founder TMOTTGo Go, guitarist, author*
I used to love it whenever I could stand behind the stage because I used to love to watch Footz play. I would be standing right behind him. His timing was so emasculate that it was just so cool watching him in action. And I swear I don't recall ever seeing him miss a cue. And that's wild because there would be so much going on back there. He and Mickey joking around back there, him reaching in his bag for another stick or anything else that was almost seemed like he wasn't paying attention. But I swear every time something was called by Funk on the frontline, regardless of what it was,

Footz would be right on it without missing a step. At least, that's the way it would always appear to me. And it would always astonish me.

Mark Wade, *fan*
His rolls and use of the high hat was the best ever...

Devin Davidson, *son of Quentin "Footz" Davidson, rap artist*
I remember one time when I was little, my Dad took me to the Ringling Brothers and Barnum and Bailey circus, and I spilled my nacho cheese on his shirt. That was my first-time eating nacho cheese, and instead of cleaning it up, I grabbed a chip, wiped the cheese off his shirt, and ate it. He was kind of pissed off because it was a brand-new rugby shirt, but it was all good times." (Davidson lost his father at age 3).

Glenn Ellis, *Bassist, Chuck Brown and the Soul Searchers, Little Benny and the Masters, Bits n Pieces*

As told by Karen Franklin, vocalist

Born and raised in Washington, D.C., Glenn Ellis (November 2, 1956 – December 21, 2013) was a gifted bassist, musical director, songwriter, arranger, producer, and one of the funniest people with the biggest smile and an even bigger heart.

Growing up in Northeast D.C., Glenn was Go-Go. Born into a musical family and under the tutelage of his uncles, he pursued music at an early age, first learning to play guitar.

Glenn later collaborated with such groups as D.C.'s own Slug-go and Proper Utensils, but it was his 25-plus year tenure with the Godfather of Go-Go, Chuck Brown, that etched his place in Go-Go history. My first recollection was that of him with Chuck Brown and the Soul Searchers in the iconic 1987 concert Go-Go Live at the Capital Centre. I was in awe of his musicianship.

Glenn left an indelible print on the music industry by lending his talents to such acts as Hip Hop artists Afrika Bambaataa and Family, Questionmark Asylum and R&B group SWV.

I not only had the pleasure of sharing the stage with him during his years with Washington, D.C.'s Wildflower Band and Let It Flow Band, respectively, but I shared daily laughs with him and his side-splitting commentary. He was not only a musical comrade to me but also became my family... my brother, protector, and friend. He is missed dearly.

Rory "DC" Felton, *Saxophonist, cowbells, stepper choreography), Rare Essence, and Godfather and Friends:*

Terry Lambert, *bassist, drummer, Little Benny and the Masters, Godfather and Friends*
It was fun. When you were working with "DC," it was just fun, and we would laugh and joke a lot. Sometimes when I was playing roto toms, there were certain times when I would play the cowbells when he wasn't playing, and then we would cue each other- he's gonna play, or I'm gonna going to play. But he was a bunch of energy and a bunch of fun. He just was that guy who just enjoyed life. When you think about him, you think, "This joker here just loved to have fun."

David Green, *percussionist, Rare Essence*
DC, was hardworking and self-taught. He was a pure showman and a beast on cowbell.

Mark Lawson, *keyboardist, Rare Essence, and Godfather and Friends*
"DC" would do anything for anybody. He was a great dude. He was a great guy. He would always bring joy and happiness and wanted to get something done. He was very creative.

Milton "Go-Go Mickey" Freeman, *congas Rare Essence, Reality Band, and MANY other Go-Go bands*
I use to hide my bell from him when playing with Benny...He will break a cowbell...bad man.

Gregory "Googie" Burton, *bassist and sound engineer*
DC was always a cool, down-to-earth dude... Whenever wherever he would see me, he would make a U-turn just to speak and make sure I was good. And that was mutual with us. He was a great entertainer and musician as well.

Kato Hammond, *founder TMOTTGo-Go, guitarist, author*
My man!!! Another cat who was always fun to be around... and always

made the stage fun to perform on. He never had a bad thing to say about anyone. And always wore wild and sometimes crazy-looking hats.

One of my most significant memories with him was the time he and I was working on a song he had written called "Uptown." This was back somewhere around 91/92. We recorded a demo of the joint in a home studio that I had set up in the living room of my apartment. He recorded the vocals of what he wrote, and I laid all the music tracks. But we never got a chance to finish the joint.

Leroy Fleming, *Saxophonist, Young Senators, Chuck Brown and the Soul Searchers*

As written by Jill Greenleigh
LeRoy Fleming, the well-known saxophonist of the Young Senators and Chuck Brown and the Soul Searchers, passed away on March 8, 2013.

Fleming was one of the original members of the Young Senators, a band formed in 1964 in upper Northwest, Washington, D.C., along with Derrick Davis on organ, Warren Smith on bass, Frank Hooker on lead guitar, and Ronald Worthy on drums.

The Young Senators were referred to as the Emperors of Go-Go and captured the attention of critics with the single "Jungle." Appearing with the Young Senators, Fleming entertained at functions for the late Governor Rockefeller and the late Senator Kennedy.

In 1971, Fleming and his bandmates in the Young Senators joined Eddie Kendricks, who had recently left the Temptations to embark on a solo career and recorded with him as the first group outside of Motown to record with a Motown act.

Many reviews of the Young Senators' performances with Kendricks nod more to the success of the band rather than Kendricks' performance, including one by journalist Dennis Hunt who wrote in the Los Angeles Times on November 30, 1973, that "Eddie Kendricks' robust band, The Young Senators, played impeccably on 'Keep on Truckin' and 'Boogie Down.' These seven musicians were so good throughout the show that I often found myself listening more to them than to Kendricks."

Jimi Dougans of the Young Senators recalls, "I met LeRoy in the early sixties during the formation of our group, The Young Senators, and we remained friends throughout the years. LeRoy was a phenomenal guy blessed with a talent to play any instrument but was known for his unique style of blowing his horn."

"LeRoy had a quiet demeanor but was very fun-loving. His favorite quote was, 'Don't ever do that.' This kind of humor gave us much-needed stress relief while traveling on the road. He was always a lot of fun to be around and pulled a surprise prank on us at certain venues."

"At a point in our musical career, The Young Senators were blessed to tour and record with Eddie Kendricks. During that time, we performed at sold-out shows nationwide and at certain venues, like The Apollo and Madison Square Garden. LeRoy decided he would conduct the band and would step out of his usual position on stage and place himself front and center to be seen. But this position put him right in front of our drummer, James Drummer Johnson, and although Drummer and LeRoy were close friends, Drummer wasn't crazy about the new unplanned development and would say, 'LeRoy, move man! You're blocking my view," adds Dougans.

He concludes, "We had a fantastic musical journey, and even after The Young Senators disbanded, and LeRoy played with other bands, he always carried the spirit of The Young Senators because he was a Young Senator for life.

In 1978, Fleming joined Chuck Brown and the Soul Searchers and can be heard on the 'Bustin' Loose' album released that year and several other Chuck Brown and the Soul Searchers albums.

With the Soul Searchers, most notably in the song "Bustin' Loose," you hear Brown shout, "Hey LeRoy! Gimmie some of that horn right here!" Fleming then bursts into a soaring saxophone solo. This soulful style can be heard throughout all the songs on which LeRoy plays.

Soul Searchers Lloyd Pinchback, John "JB" Buchanan, Curtis Johnson, and Steve Coleman have many memories of sharing the stage with Fleming.

"LeRoy was very outgoing and always a dapper dresser since the first time I saw him perform onstage. He had much more 'flash and flair' than I, and he was a party animal, to put it mildly. LeRoy is well known for his ability as a saxophonist, but he also played the flute and bassoon, and, surprisingly, the brother was also an adept drummer. We shared a mutual respect for each other's musicianship," states Pinchback, one of the original Soul Searchers.

John "JB" Buchanan recounts, "He was a real musician in every sense of the word. Our relationship pre-dates Go-Go, going back to high school in the 60s, where we both played in the D.C. Youth Orchestra. He played bassoon and was a clarinet soloist. One of my fondest and funniest memories was hearing LeRoy play Junior Walker's 'Shotgun' solo on the contra-bassoon, two full octaves below."

"Another flashback took place on Eastern High School's field right after the DCPS JROTC Cadet Drill Competition in 1967, where LeRoy, Donald Tillery, and I hooked up for the first time to exchange notes and jazz licks. Who would have guessed that we would become the Soul Searchers 'Bustin' Loose' Horn Section 11 years later? Don't forget that LeRoy was also a writer, singer, and played harmonica," Buchanan continues.

Curtis Johnson, who remained in touch with Fleming off and on, spoke with him in the months prior to his death. He relays, "LeRoy called me and said that he was going to have a cabaret. This was to be one of his last gigs, and he wanted to do this one just like he wanted and asked if I would work with him. I said, 'hell yeah,' just let me know what you want me to do! LeRoy was fun to work with, always had a smile, and was always someone I could talk to. LeRoy's soulful saxophone style was truly a factor in the Go-Go style of music created by Chuck Brown and the Bustin' Loose Crew, aka the Soul Searchers."

"When I joined the band in 1986, I was in awe of LeRoy. I was always the leader of the horn sections in the previous bands I had performed with. LeRoy was extremely kind-hearted and gracious in welcoming me to the Soul Searchers. For the first time in my musical career, I found myself being led by LeRoy. It didn't take long for me to realize just how much I didn't know about being a consummate professional musician. Through his impeccable talent, LeRoy taught me the many nuances that transform a very good musician into a great musician. Musically speaking, his phrasing, tone, balance, and, most importantly, his musical confidence revealed itself in every note that came out of his tenor sax. I often teased him that he sounded like Dexter Gordon. LeRoy never overplayed and taught me to concentrate on blending intimately to create the sweet sounds of our horn section. There were times during performances, specifically during his solo, when LeRoy would close his eyes and blow his horn, and the magic that flowed out was breathtaking. After gigs, I would often ask him how he came up with a particular musical passage or 'run.' He would always just shrug his shoulders (a true sign of a God-gifted musician), unable to explain his gifted musical prowess," reminisces "Too Tall "Steve Coleman.

In February 2002, the Young Senators were inducted into the Go-Go Hall of Fame. Fleming, along with his Young Senators band mates Jimi Dougans, Frank Hooker, James Drummer Johnson, Calvin Charity, Wornell Jones, and David Lecraft, was honored by Former D.C. Mayor Anthony Williams when he issued a Proclamation that June 11, 2002, was Young Senators Day in the District of Columbia. Another Proclamation was issued by Mayor Adrian Fenty on June 11, 2009 also for Young Senators Day in Washington, D.C.

On February 1, 2011, the Council of the District of Columbia presented Chuck Brown, Donald Tillery, John Buchanan, LeRoy Fleming, Curtis Johnson, Jerry Wilder, Ricky "Sugar Foot" Wellman, and Gregory Gerran with Soul Searchers Band and Chuck Brown as the true originators of Go-Go Recognition Resolution of 2011. It was Resolution number CER 19-4.

In addition to recording with The Young Senators, Chuck Brown and the Soul Searchers, and Eddie Kendricks, Fleming also released a solo project, "Easy Livin'"/ "Come What May," under the single name LeRoy, on Dream Machine Records, which Fleming and Al Johnson produced.

Willie "Heavy One" Gaston, *Drummer, Junkyard Band*

Daniel Baker, *keyboardist, Junkyard Band*
What got us real tight was us performing together, clicking together. I liked that right there. It was a good time right there. He would say, "I was getting ready to come over to your house," and I would say, "I was getting ready to come over to your house." We were still young. Teenagers. His mother had moved out and gotten married. She moved out of Barry Farms and let me and Heavy One have the house. We still were going to school

and still stayed in the band and that was good too as teenagers especially during those times. Everybody and their mother at our age was out there, and everybody wanted to do what everybody else was trying to do. But we went to Georgetown or 19th and M and made some money. And we'll come back home, and everybody had been shooting around here. They were gambling. Somebody got killed. And we'd miss all of it.

Vernell Wink Powell, *percussionist, Junkyard Band*
My best memories of Heavy One were all of them. From Day one. Man, Heavy was like a young Oracle. If anyone knows the meaning of the word Oracle, he was that. That big boy was like that. He was educated, and he loved the way Go-Go was formed. He just was; he always had energy. His energy was crazy. He was an all-around smart dude who knew how to put everything together. It was a natural thing for him.

Brad Farmer, *Avid Fan*
I saw Junkyard play at the Calvert County fairgrounds in 92. Heavy One kicked the entire show with Tims on! Gone way too soon. Jaime Lawson, *drummer, Young Ecstasy, Domination Band, and Inner County Crank (ICC)*- Watching Heavy One on GO-GO Live is the sole reason I play drums and Go-Go for 35 years.

Timothy "Shorty Tim" Glover, *Percussionist, EU, Trouble Funk, The Peacemakers*

Vic Vanison, *Avid Fan*
I remember hooping with him at the rec. He was a fast lil dude and would hustle his ass off.

Jay Solis, *Music Collector and Avid Fan*
In my eyes, Shorty Tim was the most exciting Roto Tom/Timbale player I have ever seen. His energy was something to behold.

Darrin X Frazier, *keyboardist, Rare Essence*
Just seeing somebody my height and size do what he was doing, and he was good at it. I always liked talking to Tim. He was the first real Go-Go person I'd hung around on that level who was actually a legend in the making playing roto toms. David (Green) had left RE before I got there but Tim, right before meeting Quentin "Shorty Dud" Ivey, was my first exposure to that level of Go-Go percussionist.

Whop Craig, *saxophonist and band leader of Wisdom Speeks*
Shorty Tim is the best AUTHENTIC percussionist IN Go-Go, along with
David Green (RE). They stood out amongst the pack and are still talked
about. That's legendary.

Bones Simmons, *photographer, and videographer, owner of The Big Picture*
I remember when Tim said to me, "I'm tired of you taking pictures! Let
me take yours!"

Marc Lewis, *trumpet, Redds and the Boys, Maniac Soldiers*
The 1st time I (really) met Tim, he and Ju-Ju were down at the Monument.
They were still with the Peacemakers then. One of my boys and I were just
starting a lil band. We wanted to see them up close. I was trying to go see
(Garry) Clark and Loose Booty. Tim spotted us watching and called us
'shortys' over. Tim and Ju-Ju were so cool. (I'd first met Clark through
either Terry Lambert or Steady Eddie) They let us chill with them. We
were 11 or 12. They weren't arrogant. And they cranked like *ish that
day. I don't even remember what the event was. Go-Go was very rarely
allowed down at the Washington Monument. We stayed cool after. Tim
even taught me a few principles about playing rototoms and timbales. As
I moved up through the ranks over the years, he was always cool. He was
always down to earth, no matter what band I was with or location. He and
Benny were both like that. It's a shame many of the 'so-called' Go-Go
legends weren't that way.

Gregory "Sugar Bear" Elliott, *bassist, founding member of Experience Unlimited (E.U.)*
Tim was a great, great percussionist. He was what I call a hype
percussionist. Because when he was with EU, he was always and even
with The Peacemakers, although he wasn't as vocal as he was with EU. I
let him have some shine. That's why I put together (Bear singing) "Hey
Shorty Tim? " "Yeahhh" It was a fan favorite. Shorty Tim was definitely
a great dude. A great guy. A great contributor to Go-Go. A great
percussionist. He was excellent all the way around.

Ron Duckett, *band manager and promoter, G-Swagg*
I first met Tim at the Glenarden apartments on the basketball court. He
was with the Peacemakers. That's the day Juju House introduced me to
him and that began a 35+ year relationship. He was a good dude on and

off stage. My last memory of him was on December 19, 2021, with him playing at my birthday party which turned out to be his last show.

Chuck Vinson, *avid listener, fan*
My best memory was walking to Nalle Elementary with him, my man Eggshell and Glenn. They were older than us, but they use to let us tag along.

James "Slim Jim" Harrington, *percussionist, Prophecy and Hot Cold Sweat*
His stage energy molded my style of play in the early 80s. To this day, Dave Green's style of cowbell play has moved into Bojack's style, and I would say, "the majority are doing the style Bojack brought back to light"... I still use Shorty Tim's style overall.

Ivan Goff, *Record Producer, Keyboardist for E.U., Redds and the Boys and More*

As told by Ju Ju House, Drummer Extraordinaire, E.U., The Peacemakers, Chuck Brown, David Sanborn
A lot of people have no idea that the connection that was made between me and Becky (Marcus) and Tom (Goldfogle) (of Liaison Records) was through Ivan. Ivan introduced us. I was the producer, and I wrote most of the songs that Ivan was putting out, but Ivan borrowed the money, and we went to New York to see (record executive) Wes "Party" Johnson- Ivan got the Misty record done for Chuck, he got the Cat in the Hat and the Go Ju Ju Go albums for Little Benny and EU. Ivan was the connection of the Liaison Tom and Becky. Ivan Goff was the connection for the original Familiar Faces with Stephon (Woodland) and David Gussom. Ivan was the connection for a lot of the groups that were out then. Ivan was actually distributing and putting records in the Mom-and-Pop stores when nobody else would even touch them. Ivan Goff was the one running around in that broke-down Mustang with no heat.

He had Big City Records. Ivan was doing a hell of a job. This is the reason why a lot of these records broke and actually got introduced into D.C. was because of Ivan Goff. Ivan wasn't just a keyboard player. Ivan was a production manager, a producer, and a store- Ivan Goff store out of his trunk, he actually introduced a lot and connected a lot of people. I don't think Chuck would have even ever met Tom or even Eva Cassidy because

Ivan was the one who actually put out "Misty," and he brought me over. I kind of knew Chris (Biondo, Black Pond Studios), but Ivan introduced me to Chris Biondo. We did the Cat in the Hat and Go Ju Ju, Go albums with Chris Biondo. That's how Chris got introduced into the Go-Go thing and ended up going to California with EU and Kent (Wood).

Ivan taught me how to do it, and that's when I came out with my own Ju Ju Jada and all that other stuff that I was putting out Ivan taught me. So, Ivan played a crucial part in this community; many young people don't know that. I don't think they even do the research or know the history, and it's so embarrassing that when you go to other countries, how in the hell do they know this? And the people you play around. You know what? If you go to Japan, they know everything about you- when you started, who you've played with, where you've toured.

Around 85 and 86, Ivan had many of the young groups coming out. Nasty Band, Go-Go Lorenzo, Pure Elegance, and the Pumpblenders.

Milton "Go-Go Mickey" Freeman, *congas Rare Essence, Reality Band, and MANY other Go-Go bands*
For some reason, we were out at the Capital Center, and Ivan had to bring me home. I think we were both playing with Redds and the Boys; whatever the case was, Ivan wouldn't drive me all the way home. Ivan dropped me off on New York Avenue – New York and Florida, and I had to run home. He wasn't coming this way. Back then, you had Orleans Street and all of that by Galludet- that's the crews that used to get into all the fights, so I ran all the way down Florida Avenue to my house. Ivan was a quiet dude, but he made a lot of stuff. He made a lot of stuff that I didn't even know.

Gregory "Sugar Bear" Elliott, *bassist, founding member of Experience Unlimited (E.U.)* Ivan was the maestro: another great keyboard player, a friend. I miss him so much- I miss both of them. Ivan played with me the longest. When I had both of them together, he and Kent, we didn't need any horns. We had them. You know what I mean? Because they played so good. They played very well together, and they complimented our sound so much, and they played very aggressively. That's what I like, and you can watch Go-Go Live I and see. Kent is actually playing percussion on keyboards as fillers. Nobody really caught that, but I did, and it sounds good. And they did it on "Da Butt," too. He and Ivan. God just put them in my life, and we had like 10 or 15 years together. Ivan was definitely my man, 50 grand.

Benny Harley, *Trumpet, Band Leader, Rare Essence, Little Benny and the Masters, Proper Utensils, Suttle Thoughts*
As told by Milton "Go-Go Mickey" Freeman, congas Rare Essence, Reality Band, and MANY other Go-Go bands

That guy... there's so much I could say about him. There were days that Benny and Rick (Wellman) had me in the studio. I couldn't believe the things they had going on. I would call BoJack, and BoJack would call Buggy, and they would head out to Chris Biondo's studio (Black Pond). I have seen Rick play on a 2 piece, 3-piece drum set and make it sound like 10 drums. And Benny would orchestrate everything. He'd put it how he wanted it, where he wanted to go. If he was still here, a lot of things wouldn't be happening right now. I can tell you that. I say that about him and Chuck Brown. Benny was the one who showed me how to, you know, how everybody's jumping stages? But one thing Benny said was you can't let nobody stop you from getting your money. If they want you, they want you. If you're hot, you're hot. You have to go after it to take care of yourself and your family. Benny could always call you out of the blue and make a band up. You could be asleep, and he'd call, "Get up! I've got something to go play." And one time he called me and we played at a jail. I was on the drums. It was just me, him and somebody else. And we played for one of the juvenile jails. He would call us and say, "Let's go over to Sursum Cordas. They want a band over there." He'd call BoJack, Buggy, whoever. We had fun whatever we did. We hung out all the time, went to my mother's house, and went to eat. He loved to eat crabs. I just miss him. I go celebrate him every year for his birthday and sometimes Christmas.

Me, Little Benny and Big Wally, we always park over at Benny's house, so we get in the car and go down MLK to see Chuck Brown somewhere down on "I" Street downtown. Anyway, we're coming home, and that's a park. Benny made a turn and went over the yellow lines, and the Park police pulled us over. So, this white police pulled us over, and me and Wally are in the car and just sitting there waiting to see what's going on, and you see Benny moving his hands, talking ... so I'll never forget this. It's my first time with a cell phone, and I called somebody and I was like "Ummmm, when you get locked up from here, where do they send you?" So anyway,

243

we look back out of the window and see Benny doing the Roll Call step outside on the sidewalk. I said, "Wally! Wally! We're going to jail!" So, the next thing, a black police officer pulls up; of course, he knows Benny. They end up checking everybody's eyes, and they let Wally drive. That was the craziest day of my life with Benny. We looked out the window, and he was doing the Roll Call step. They must have told him, you know how they tell you to walk? He started doing the Roll Call step! Right downtown. This was at the monument. Right Downtown. As we drove off and got halfway away from them, Benny made Wally get out of the driver's seat and said, "Switch! This is my car. I can drive my own car home!"

Me, Rick (Wellman) and Little Benny used to put all our money on the table and play this game called 500 (a card game). We would just sit there and watch the money go down the pockets of whoever was winning. We did it all the time.

Terry Lambert, *bassist, drummer, Little Benny and the Masters, Godfather and Friends*

I think Benny looked at me like one of those guys with a good head on his shoulders. I think he talked to me the way he talked to me was because he thought that I was always going to say the right things. I spoke with him about a week before he passed. Benny knew what type of voice he had. He knew that he had a powerful voice. We would be at practice sometimes, and he'd know how to bring out that bass in his voice. You knew that he knew that his voice was legendary. And then, when it came to him learning his parts, he was very serious about making sure that he learned his parts.

Sometimes they wouldn't come out exactly the way that he would want them to, but you've got to figure, by being on the stage and you're doing all the showmanship stuff. You know that when he's doing his steps, there's no body that ever came through Go-Go from Day One, and I've been here since it started, that can step like Benny. The only folks that came close to him were Go-Go Mike (Mike Taylor) and DC (Rory Felton). When the three of them were playing together, and I was playing drums, I could sit back and watch them step, and they were like a perfect pair of folks stepping. Stepping was like breathing for Benny. It was so natural to him. He was great. No one could step like Benny. No one. You've got to call that a work of art.

David Green, *percussionist, Rare Essence*

Benny had energy! He was dominant, a leader, and a firecracker!

James Funk, *lead talker, Rare Essence, Proper Utensils*
I never could dance, well I could dance, I never was the routine guy. Benny was that. He was the James Brown. The Prince. The Michael Jackson. I give him all of that because he did all of that.

Mark Lawson, *keyboardist, Rare Essence, and Godfather and Friends*
We formed Little Benny and the Masters. Me and Benny used to always perform things together. He was my Godbrother. Benny wasn't just a musician. Benny was real talented with dancing and choreography. It went on as we got older. He was very creative. I miss him every day. Every day he would call. We kept in touch. He listened to me, and I listened to him. We always shared ideas. We always prayed together. We always told each other to have a blessed day every day. Me and Benny worked with Verdine White of Earth, Wind and Fire.

Mike Hughes, *Recording engineer, keyboardist, producer, AM/FM, Experience Unlimited, Rare Essence, Proper Utensils*

As told by Jacques Vaughan, percussionist, manager, AM/FM, Chuck Brown, Trouble Funk, Proper Utensils, Wisdom Speaks
I had always heard of "OUTTA SITE MIKE" but got the pleasure to meet him back in 1987 when I got back from the Army.
After a few years passed and my many visits to his studio... We actually formed a friendship, and he became a music mentor of mine early on. I was always blown away by his multi-faceted gifts as a producer, writer, arranger, manager, engineer, and musician!

I knew he was an Icon in GO-GO but was taken back once I realized that he produced music for many national artists as well but was so humble that you would never know unless you walk into his studio and see all the proof on the walls in the form of awards & Silver, Gold or Platinum albums.
One day, we spoke after I had stopped playing for a year or so, and he said he was hand-picking musicians and wanted me to come audition for the next phase of his AM-FM project. The kicker was, rehearsal was that same day, he told me. I said, "HELL YEAH!" However, he didn't know I didn't have any equipment because I sold it, thinking I was done playing

at the time! I quickly went to Chuck Levin's that day and purchased ALL NEW EQUIPMENT with cases and bags. I showed up at his rehearsal and told him I was late because I was buying new stuff! Lol

He said, "Well, hell, I gotta let you in the band just because you got all this new stuff!"

Mike had the coolest personality ever! He was always pouring into people without reservation or hesitation. As a teenager, just being able to sponge off such an incredibly humble guy was a blessing for me.

I never forget our talks & his vivid vision to create a sound called "GO-HOP," which would have been a hybrid between GO-GO & HIP-HOP, way back in 1990!

We went on to play together with PROPER UTENSILS and also got to travel abroad, playing with CHUCK BROWN, which was an awesome experience.

Some years had gone by, and I was now playing and managing Wisdom Speeks, a.k.a. "Whop n Em," and he was supposed to collaborate with Brian Craig, a.k.a "Whop," to help us cultivate the new sound and similar concept of "GO-HOP!"

Shortly after, I heard the devastating news of the freak accident that happened, which took his life. I could not believe that he was gone! He was such a great guy who was quick to always asked, "HOW CAN I HELP?" I couldn't believe he was gone just like that!

His many contributions to music and all of the people that he touched while he was here have not gone unnoticed. He is someone that I think about often because he became a BIG BROTHER to me... I always think about what he would be doing now if he were still here.

David Green, *percussionist, Rare Essence*
Mike Hughes was brilliant and super talented! He could play multiple instruments on a high level. He would set the sound as an engineer and then get on stage and perform with us. He was greatness, for sure.

Gregory "Sugar Bear" Elliott, *bassist, founding member of Experience Unlimited (E.U.)*

Mike Hughes came from a different band when I met him. He and I were both Leos, and Mike was also a great keyboard player, and he recorded on our first LP. That's how far we go back. "Peace Gone Away," "Free Yourself," all that! Once Mike left us, he put together another band, AM/FM. And they had success. Look at that. They had a Go-Go hit- "*You Are the One*." See. That shows you that people accepted it. And after that band broke up, he started doing sound and learned that from William Benjamin. William Benjamin was the best soundman in Go-Go history, in my opinion.

Derrick Ingram, *Percussionist, Junkyard Band*

Daniel Baker, *keyboardist, Junkyard Band*
Derrick was a good kid. He was fun. He had 2 dogs, I think they were Doberman Pinschers. And we used to tell him to go get his dogs and make them chase us, and we used to have fun as long as we didn't get caught! They weren't gonna bite. Nobody ever got caught. We used to have little parties, little gatherings. We used to have them at the Scout House, where we would practice. That was fun.

Vernell "Wink" Powell, *percussionist, Junkyard Band*
That was the original Dog. That was the kid of the band, for real. He was like a crazy little kid. A crazy, spoiled little kid. He was like Dennis the Menace. Little Derrick was Dennis the Menace for real. You talk about always wanting to do something crazy that was fun. He was like a white boy in a black body. And he lived in the ghetto. He did everything adventurous like white kids and he is in the middle of the f***in' hood. Dirt Bikes, he did all that rock climbing. He did all that stuff that a lot of us are just learning about now. He was doing that s**t back then. He was the first one in the neighborhood that had the laser disk that you could watch the movies on, everything. All the new BMX bikes, trick bikes. Shorty used to have all that s**t before anybody. That was our white boy of the hood. He was wearing that Fresh Prince of Bel-Air hairdo before anybody in the city. He had a high-top fade before anybody. As a little kid, we were about 12, 13, 14 years old, and there wasn't anyone rockin' the high-top fade back then. He was on the front line. That was Buggs' first front line. I had gotten pushed to the back. I was playing the tin cans.

Byron "BJ" Jackson, *Keyboardist, vocalist, bassist, writer, producer, Rare Essence, Team Familiar, 911*

Kato Hammond, *founder TMOTTGo-Go, guitarist, and author*
BJ was a child prodigy who played many different instruments and whom I was highly influenced and inspired by musically my entire life. I even wrote a children's book about him called "I Want To Play Too."

Darrin Frazier, *keyboardist, Rare Essence, 911*
BJ came up with the keyboard rhythm for *"Lock It."* His finger coordination was elite.

Michael Benjamin, *keyboardist, Reality Band*
We went to Largo High School together, and sometimes we would skip school and sneak into PG Community College. They had piano rooms. Man, we would go in there and play all Essence grooves. The first two bands I was ever in, BJ was in them. He was my first mentor on Keys.

Gregory "Googie" Burton, *bassist, sound engineer*
Whenever I would see BJ, he was always a humble dude. With the multitalented skills he had, you would expect some arrogance. Never a day when I was ever around him. Young Brother Gone too Soon…

Ron Duckett, *band manager and promoter, G-Swagg*
Our daughters were on the same cheer team, and when I managed GSwagg, he was always willing to sit in either on Keys or Bass extremely Humble Guy. I sure miss his presence.

Pam Ward- Godbold, *vocalist, Let It Flow, Pink PaLish, Push Play*
One of the most talented, humble, and coolest individuals I had the privilege to work with for many years and befriend. I love and miss him dearly.

Donald Barnes, *vocalist, EU*
I did a wedding in Baltimore, and BJ was my pianist!! It was in the hood, and we didn't wanna park! We laugh so hard!! But the wedding was fantastic! He accompanied me magnificently, and my car still had all the tires when we came out!! We B-lined back to the DMV!!

Harold Little, *trumpet, songwriter, producer*
Unbeknownst to me at the time, BJ was sick but still showed up for the gig!!

Milton "Go-Go Mickey" Freeman, *congas Rare Essence, Reality Band, and MANY other Go-Go bands*
My roommate on the Road with RE...ALL AROUND GOOD DUDE.

Chester Reis, *producer*
BJ was as good as it gets. He was the epitome of generosity...

Dwayne Lee, *Recording Engineer, Music Producer, and Drummer for Redds and the Boys*
BJ was my Co-Broducer, friend, and fellow FUNKATEER.

Tino Jackson, *Guitarist, Experience Unlimited-*
As told by Vincent Coleman, percussionist, vocalist

Valentino Jackson - I first got to know Tino in the late 70s when he came to my grandparents' garage in Fairmont Heights. He would jam with my uncle Maurice "Ghost" Wellman on drums and Louis "Foxx" Pough on bass guitar. They would play mostly hard rock/funk songs by Rush, Black Sabbath, Funkadelic, Van Halen, and others. I gotta say Tino was always on point with his guitar playing. One week I brought my cassette player and recorded them. I still have those tapes. When my brother Steve and cousin Ricky joined EU, me and my friends/family would go see them perform all the time. Over the years, I would ride to some gigs with Tino and hang out going to see other bands perform. We always had fun discussing and discovering new music, mostly fusion rock like guitarists Greg Howe and Yngwie Malmsteen. Sometimes we would ride up to the Fish Market and he would sit in with the band, usually on the song "Purple Rain." The constant jokes, wisecracking, and joaning about everything and everybody, are what I miss the most. But, his good-natured spirit will always be with me.

Gregory "Sugar Bear" Elliott, *bassist, founding member of Experience Unlimited (E.U.)*
Tino was the greatest guitar player that EU ever had and a great vocalist, if you don't know. Tino could sing just as well as he played. I would let him shine on our stage. He could sing *"Taste of Your Love"* better than Junie could. And, of course, a guitar player was right up my alley. I'm the left hand, and he's the right hand. That's how we worked. We played together so much that we knew where each other was on stage, with no keyboards. We filled it in with that rock flavor, and that's what separated

249

us from Essence, Chuck Brown, and all these bands, and that's what separated us because everybody knew our sound. These days, you hear one band and you never know who's who until you walk in the building. Back then, and I always try to do that now. I always tried to keep EU's sound with that rock edge, so you knew it was us. You can't duplicate everything you try to do, but I try to keep that rock element.

Maxx Kidd, *Promoter, Innovator*

As told by Darryll Brooks, Concert Promoter, Record Label Executive, Tiger Flower, G-Street Express, CD Enterprises

Maxx was a true soldier. And Maxx had a way about him that was interesting. Because of what he believed in, he supported, and those people who didn't understand that mentality were probably a little bit intimidated by it. But also, if you tried to bullshit him, you might have gotten hurt by it. And he introduced me to the Gap Band. He had me go up to a convention in New York. And he introduced me to the manager of the Gap Band, and we did some Gap Band dates back in the day. He was very accommodating. But at the same time, he was... I went to a convention in California, and Maxx was working the record "I Need Money" by Chuck Brown. So, I'm in the hotel room at Century Plaza, and everybody's screaming, and I hear all this noise. I heard Chuck Brown's record, but it was so loud, it was like out the window or like somebody put speakers outside of the window, so I looked out the window of the hotel, and Maxx was throwing money out the window- "I Need Money" so they were making it rain in front of the hotel. And people were going bananas. But, my point is, everybody knew that record. Everybody knew Chuck Brown and Maxx Kidd. He was a hell of a promotion guy, and he was THAT person. I guess that's my best Maxx story.

Milton "Go-Go Mickey" Freeman, *congas Rare Essence, Reality Band, and MANY other Go-Go bands*

Maxx took RE to do the *Jimmy Lee* video with Aretha Franklin. We recorded Live at Breeze, then hit the bus that was waiting to take us to Detroit. We learned steps on the bus, but when we got there, they said, "We don't need all that." Maxx had me and Derek Paige drinking the good stuff going up. We had the cheap coming back because Maxx stayed in Detroit.

David Green, *percussionist, Rare Essence*

I just remember walking downstairs in my underwear, and Maxx Kidd was sitting there with my mom, Miss Sis, and Ms. Mack booking a show!

Randy Kilpatrick, *bassist, Redds and the Boys*
Maxx took us to dinner at Gallagher's Steakhouse in NYC before recording the Billboard charting hit, "Movin' and Groovin'" in 1985 with Redds and the Boys. The best steak in the world! Seeing the bill after feeding the band a top-shelf meal. Maxx brought Verdine and Fred White of "Earth Wind and Fire" to the DMV to do a recording project with the one and only "Sugarfoot" Ricky Wellman on drums! What an amazing recording experience with the best band in the land! Maybe one day, those songs will be released!

"Too Tall" Steven Coleman, *trumpet, Redds and the Boys, Experience Unlimited, Chuck Brown and the Soul Searchers*
Maxx introduced us to the national music scene. So many great memories that most wouldn't believe it to be true. Case in point: We traveled to NYC (The Palladium) to perform. We're backstage warming up, and in walks Madonna. She took the stage with us... joined in on the choreography and stayed with us on stage for about ten minutes. Incredible experience long before cell phones, so there's no videos or photos. Salute, Maxx Kidd!

Melvin "Butch" Lewis, *Drummer, Experience Unlimited, Little Benny and the Masters*

Terry Lambert, *bassist, drummer, Little Benny and the Masters, Godfather and Friends*
Butch was one of those guys we all looked up to before I even knew him. He was playing drums with EU. Butch played in an era when you could hear maybe 10 seconds of a clip and know that's Butch playing drums. Back then, I could listen to 10 seconds of any band and say, "Oh, that's EU. Oh, that's Trouble. The sounds were so distinctively different. The drummers had distinctly different styles that you knew who it was in 5-10 seconds. And Butch fit that. Nobody had a style like Butch when he was playing, and anybody that listened to Go-Go back then will tell you that-true listeners. Butch was a guy that would give you the shirt off his back. Just very, very calm. He's another guy that joined the band, and then he and I became really, really close. We talked all the time. I still have text messages on my phone that I never deleted.

251

Milton "Go-Go Mickey" Freeman, *congas Rare Essence, Reality Band, and MANY other Go-Go bands*
Butch Lewis used to be a dynamite drummer, too, back in the Coliseum days back when he was playing with EU. I was going to see them play at the Coliseum.

Gregory "Sugar Bear" Elliott, *bassist, founding member of Experience Unlimited (E.U.)*
"EU Freeze," That's Butch. Butch was there before Ju Ju and Butch recorded *EU Freeze* and *Rock Your Butt*. Butch was a great asset after our original drummer Block. Block was the second drummer, and then Butch came.

Lloyd Pinchback, *Saxophone, Cow Bell, Flute, Chuck Brown and the Soul Searchers, Proper Utensils*

Charles Vinson, *avid listener, fan*
I met Lloyd when he was performing With Proper Utensils. We would kick it before shows and at halftime. We would also chat through text messages. One night I noticed how worn out his cowbell was and brought him a new one. He lit up like a Christmas tree. That night he gave me the one I replaced along with the stick. Oh yeah, I dubbed him "The Cowbell King" and started the "We need more cowbell" chant at Takoma Station Tavern.

Ron Duckett, *band manager, and promoter, G-Swagg*
Lloyd Pinchback, very humble soul, 1st guy I saw breakout the flute & harmonics at the Go-Go.

"Too Tall" Steven Coleman, *trumpet, Redds and the Boys, Experience Unlimited, Chuck Brown and the Soul Searchers*
G.O.A.T! Lloyd set the standard for the reedmen of the original generation of horn players. His influence was so dynamic that if you were a saxman but didn't also play flute, you were not qualified to even join a local band. Lloyd was also a great writer, literally and musically. Ashley's Roachclip is an all-time favorite.

Maiesha Rashad, *Vocalist, Maiesha and the Hip Huggers*

As told by Cherie Mitchell-Agurs, vocals, keyboards, Chuck Brown, Be'la Dona, Maiesha and the Hip Huggers Maiesha was very motherly to me.

> *When I first met her, she invited me into her home and treated me like her sister/daughter. She was very talented. She sang very well in the jazzy style of Phyllis Hyman. She could also get down dirty and funky like Chaka Kahn and Betty Wright. I think Go-Go was her alter ego. I've played numerous jazz clubs, cruise lines, and private events with her, such as Takoma Station, the O Street Mansion, the Odyssey, etc., with her Jazz Quartet. She also created an all-female jazz group called Lavender Rain-me on keys, Errica Poindexter on bass, and Darci Scaringe on drums.*

Robert Dyke Reed, *Music Director, Instrumentalist, Songwriter, Trouble Funk*

As told by Timothy "Teebone" David, *Percussionist, Trouble Funk*

> *Robert "Dyke" Reed was an extremely talented musician. He was the music director for Trouble Funk, played the guitar, trombone, keyboards, and was also a vocalist. He was a music teacher at HD Woodson High School and Howard University. Along with being a big factor in creating all the music for Trouble Funk, he also did some music with the Two Live Crew and many other artists. Dyke was a big-hearted young man, and he would do anything in the world for you. He had a style like no other musician that I've ever played with. There's only one Dyke, and no one else can replace him. In 2008, Dyke was taken away from us as he lost his bout with pancreatic cancer. He never told us that he had cancer, but eventually, we could see as his appearance started to change. Dyke was truly a genius when it came to creating music. He would often bring a tune to the rehearsal hall, and we had to tell him that the tune was too much. He had created four songs in one, but we would break it down and make 4 grooves out of it. His contribution to Go-Go was phenomenal and legendary. He left a lot of music behind. His son carries on his legacy. I, too, learned a lot from him. He taught me the correct way to play rudiments as I struggled with my left hand. Again, he was a good-hearted guy.*

Marguerite Rice, *Assistant Manager, Backyard Band and Band and Fan Mother*

Bobbie Westmoreland, *writer, advocate*
Everyone called her either Miss Marguerite, or simply "Ma." If you ever went to a Backyard show at the Hot Shoppes, the 501 Club, the Met, or any of Backyard's weekly shows, then you saw her at the door. In addition to raising her own four girls, Miss Marguerite became a mother to many of her daughter's friends, with her house serving as a refuge for those who had problems at home.

She assisted Backyard's former manager Terrance Cooper with bookkeeping and payroll and provided administrative duties. If Coop was unable to be somewhere, she acted in his stead. She was a second mother to many of the band members and organized birthday dinners and celebrations for band members, security, and club employees. She didn't forget anyone. I watched her buy clothes for band members and slip money to them between paydays. And always with a smile. Her spirit is greatly missed.

Dewayne Morris (BAM 640), *host*
Ms. Marguerite was like a Mom to me. Every time at the Black Hole, Eastside, and Tradewinds, she was always good to all the Backyard Band fans and when you acted up, you were banned from a Backyard Band show for a month. Her talks and her leading the way for the youth and Go-Go are unmatched.

Kapri Monique Curtis, *hostess*
She was a family friend. We called her "Auntie." She was one of my favorite faces to see when I entered the club. She was hip and she knew what was what... and she was not for any foolishness in the events! Outside of the club, she was indeed one of the sweetest and realist people I ever met. She told me years ago that whatever I wanted was mine... I just had to work as hard for it as I want it... Definitely missing her.

Alonzo Robinson, *Drummer, percussionist, Trouble Funk, Rare Essence*

As told by Timothy "Teebone" David, Percussionist, Trouble Funk
Alonzo Robinson was a drummer/ percussionist with Trouble Funk.

Lonzo came to us as a percussionist when Mac was moved to the Drums.

Lonzo was the backup percussionist with Rare Essence before joining Trouble Funk. He got his training at HD Woodson High School, being part of the Marching Band. Lonzo was an outstanding drummer. His style was different from Mac, but his style fit perfectly when he joined the band. We went overseas, and he was able to adjust to the different tempos. Lonzo was quite a character keeping everybody laughing all the time with his jokes while we were on the road. Lonzo and I also were good friends. Lonzo struggled with diabetes, and he died from complications of that disease. He, too, is truly missed on stage and as a friend.

Clarence "Boolah" Roper, *Guitarist, Ayre Rayde, Little Benny and the Masters, 911*

Terry Lambert, *bassist, drummer, Little Benny and the Masters, Godfather and Friends*
Clarence "Boolah" Roper and I used to hang out a lot. We would go to Haines Point and wax our cars and we would practice together a lot. We had a lot of fun.

Darrin X Frazier, *keyboardist, Rare Essence, 911*
Anything with Him, Donnell and 911…

Gregory "Googie" Burton, *bassist, sound engineer*
He was one bad man on his guitar.   He is missed by many. Malachai Johns, *guitarist, manager, booking agent, Northeast Groovers, Mambo Sauce, Allive Entertainment*- He was like the best guitar player I've ever seen.

Mark Lawson, *keyboardist, Rare Essence, and Godfather and Friends*
Sanchez was a great guy. We used to call him Sanchez. Ron Duckett, *band manager and promoter, G-Swagg* - Next to Tino, hands down one of the great Wire pullers James "Slim Jim" Harrington, *percussionist, Prophecy and Hot Cold Sweat*- I met him when I was a kid. They were called "The Roper Brothers." He played lead and Tony Roper was on the bass—two of the best in the region to perform.

Kato Hammond, *founder TMOTTGo-Go, guitarist, author*
Boolah was a beast on that lead guitar without a doubt— he and his brother Tony Roper. I first met him during his days with Ayre Rayde. And then later, when I replaced him as lead guitarist for Little Benny & The Masters,

I knew good and well that I had impossible shoes to fill, so I didn't even try. I just did me and the best that I could to make my mark in my own kind of way as well.

Although Boolah was a wild dude sometimes, he and I always got along real cool. One of the biggest performances of his that stands out in my mind was during the period he was playing with 911 and the gig they had at the 9:30 club for Chuck Brown's birthday. Tony Sharpe sang India Arie's "I Am Ready For Love" as Boolah accompanied him on the acoustic guitar.

Dave Rubin, *Concert Promoter*

As told by Alona Wartofsky, *Journalist, Author*

Dave Rubin was born and raised on Long Island, New York; David Rubin fell in love with Go-Go as an undergraduate student at George Washington University in the early 80s. A business major, he was eager to prove himself in the real world. He began promoting Go-Go concerts during his sophomore year at GW, working with Trouble Funk and other bands, including Chuck Brown and the Soul Searchers, Experience Unlimited, Rare Essence, the Mighty Peacemakers, Petworth, Class Band, and many others. Dave was convinced that Go-Go, like other music genres before it, could help break down barriers between races and cultures. His early shows brought Go-Go artists to the predominantly white GW campus.

He promoted shows at the Washington Coliseum and at dozens of other area clubs and concert venues. He brought Chuck Brown and James Brown together on the same bill, as well as Trouble Funk and punk band Minor Threat. He also brought Go-Go to RFK Stadium. He advocated tirelessly for the music, bringing Trouble Funk to play the Ritz in the early 80s.

He also produced Class Band's "Welcome to the Go-Go."
In later years, he moved into producing theater.
Sadly, Dave Rubin passed away in 2005 at the age of 42.

Andre "Elmoe" Smith, *Percussionist, Little Benny and the Masters*

256

Terry Lambert, *bassist, drummer, Little Benny and the Masters, Godfather and Friends*

I just think that there were 2 Elmoes. And that's the truth with a lot of people. There's a street version of the person and then a personal version of the person. There's a street version where they are into things and doing things. When you know the person, they're fun, creative, and talented; and that was Elmoe. I think that the Elmoe that was on the outside of that-he couldn't get rid of that guy. And if he could've gotten rid of that guy right now, he would be a successful person. He could draw. He could rap. I still have the CD he gave me a week before his death. It's just unfortunate because he had that other side to him. He knew he was gonna die because he told me. It was unfortunate.

Mark Lawson, *keyboardist, Rare Essence, and Godfather and Friends*

I had a closeness like Benny with Elmoe. Same with "DC." We worked well together. Elmoe was a very talented young man. He and Byron Jackson, and I worked on projects together. He was a young producer.

Vic Vanison, *avid fan*

10th-grade drafting class down Anacostia. This was way before he played in a band that I know about…anyway, he used to play congas on the desk and sounded good. Fast forward many years later, I'm in the military, and I see him on stage with Lil Benny on the Go-Go live VHS tape, and I was in Korea at the time…

Gregory "Googie" Burton, *bassist, sound engineer*

Elmoe was a real cool dude. He came through to play with Reality Band while Walker Redds went to college.

Milton "Go-Go Mickey" Freeman, *congas Rare Essence, Reality Band, and MANY other Go-Go bands*

My man was crazy fun to be around…never planned it, just did it…Lets go… Remember, his van broke down on Suitland Parkway. We had just got crabs… instead of looking to get help, he was like, bust that bag open… so we started eating the crabs... funny thing is Mark, Godfather, saw the van and got us off of there... Remember, no cell phones then...

Carl "Chucky" Thompson, *Renowned record producer, keyboardist, congas, Petworth, Chuck Brown*

Milton "Go-Go Mickey" Freeman, *congas Rare Essence, Reality Band, and MANY other Go-Go bands*
The songs that Chucky would do for Chuck, he would always call me to come in the studio. Me and Chucky go way back era-wise. Chucky was playing with Petworth… Chucky was a keyboard player and then he switched over to congas with Chuck Brown—Hell of a producer. Chucky would always call me to come to his studio out there off of 210.

Maurice "Moe" Tillar, *keyboardist, Class Band*
James "Slim Jim" Harrington, *percussionist, Prophecy and Hot Cold Sweat*- The most musically talented street brawler I knew. He can have you dancing or running. It depends on the circumstance!!!

William Lansdown, *Avid Listener, Fan*
Definitely a classic guy. I miss those days at the Cheriys.

Miles Simmons, *keyboardist, Wisdom Speeks*
Moe taught me how to warm up the keyboards in a groove.

Sheldon "Shorty Pop" Watkins- *Vocalist, keyboardist, Junkyard Band*
Daniel Baker, *keyboardist, Junkyard Band* - Pop was real funny. When we were going out of town, like when we were going up to New York, we'd be in there and just be joking and joaning on each other, and Pop was a good boy then. A good guy. There were some good times then. I taught him how to do the keyboards, and he learned pretty fast.

Vernell Wink Powell, *percussionist, Junkyard Band*
Me and Shorty were so close, we were like brothers. I get emotional just thinking about Shorty. I don't know how to explain him. When Pop was in the band, he was funny. He was always smiling. You would never catch him with a frown on his face. He always was happy. He was playful as a mug. And his energy on the stage when he was on the front line because he started on the keyboards with Bake doing steps with Mike Strong and them. One time, it was Lil Pop, Shorty Dave (32), Mike Strong, and Buggs. I can't call him 32. That's not a Junkyard thing. He was Lil Dave.

Ricky "Sugarfoot" Wellman, *Drummer Extraordinaire, Chuck Brown and the Soul Searchers,*

Experience Unlimited, Miles Davis, Carlos Santana

Milton "Go-Go Mickey" Freeman, *congas Rare Essence, Reality Band, and MANY other Go-Go bands*
I loved Sugar Foots because of everything he could do on the drums. That was unheard of in D.C. for Go-Go drummers, anyway. Ju Ju was second, I guess I could say on that. Sugar Foots was my man, too, because a long time ago, when I used to go to drum lessons, I used to want to learn what Sugar Foots used to do.

Lawrence "Maniac" West, *Vocalist, Songwriter, Rare Essence, Maniac and the Soldiers, Godfather and Friends*

Gregory "Googie" Burton, *bassist, sound engineer*
Maniac was a musician 1st. In the mid-late 70s, he played keyboards and sang with The Peacemakers. He was very talented. Continue to Rest, Brother. David Green, *percussionist, Rare Essence* – Maniac was witty and slick. He could adjust quickly and create off the fly! He was a great vocalist!

Mark Lawson, *keyboards, Rare Essence, and Godfather and Friends*
Maniac was a good guy, very creative. He was a young businessman about making things work. He came from The Peacemakers.

Ron Duckett, *band manager and promoter, G-Swagg*
I first met him in Glenarden when The Peacemakers played on the basketball court. One of my fondest memories was hanging out at the Big Mouth club at a show with him, Michael Muse, Mark Lawson, and friends.

Terrance Cooper, *band manager, Top 5*
Maniac was one of my favorites on that mic – Legend.

Chester Reis, *producer* - It was that handheld spotlight that everybody waited for . £

Mark Ward, an *avid listener, Fan*
Maniac came up with some OG Go-Go Hook masters! Classic joints like "Camay All Over," "Take me out to the Go-Go," and "Workin' up a Sweat. You ain't seen nothing yet," "at the Howard short kids fat kids," "Ooh we look what Essence has done to me!"

259

Patrick Wise, *keyboards, Redds and the Boys, Petworth, Physical Wunder*
Showed me how to play "Game 7" by Chuck Brown on the keyboards.

Benjamin "Scotty" Haskel, *keyboardist, Rare Essence*
Making up the first part of "Take Me out to the Go-Go" "We want u grooving, want u really moving, and you know you can't deny that she told u she was shy, but she's not your girlfriend when she calls you on the phone when she thinks your all alone, what do you do when you're home doing nothing?"

Anthony "Redds" Williams, Vocalist, guitarist, Redds and the Boys, Rare Essence

As told by Carl "Blow Your Horn CJ" Jones, *Saxophonist, vocalist, Redds and the Boys, Experience Unlimited, Little Benny and the Masters, CJ's Uptown Crew*

During the early 1980s, Anthony "Redds" Williams captured the city's imagination as the charismatic leader of Redds and the Boys. Redds was an early member of Rare Essence, and his fans and fellow musicians considered him to be the funkiest guitar player around town. But it was his oversized personality that attracted the attention of the DMV's Go-Go audiences. Redds masterfully created irresistible chants, and one of his best-known was the title of the band's hit single, "Put Your Right Hand in The Air Put Your Left Hand Down in Your Underwear." His music was fun, and the audience participation was engaging.

When Redds and the Boys entered the Go-Go scene in 1981, Redds' goal was to lead a band that would eventually become known nationwide. Throughout the 1980s, many Go-Go bands sought the national spotlight and played original material that reflected their distinct personalities. Redds surrounded himself with talented local musicians, including his cousin "Blow Your Horn CJ" Jones on saxophone, Reginald "Lil Beats" Daughtry on congas, Randy "Hollywood" Kilpatrick on bass, Derrick Pearson and Reggie Baker on keyboards, Steve "Too Tall" Coleman on trumpet, and Wayne "Sugar Foot" Mickle on drums.

In 1981, Redds and the Boys released Hitt'n & Holding, which eventually led to his smash hit "Movin & Groovin," which captured the attention of audiences across the U.S. Released on Island Records, it was one of the handful of Go-Go songs to chart on the Billboard Hot 100; it was also released on London Records in the United Kingdom and on Metronome in Germany. In the U.S., "Movin & Groovin" reached #25 and was featured on a 1986 episode of the television series Miami Vice.

Redds and the Boys were one of several groups signed by Chris Blackwell's Island Records, and the label's commitment included promoting the 1986 film Good to Go. Redds, Lil Beats, and CJ all appeared as fictional characters in the film. Unfortunately, for various reasons, including its violent aspects, the film was released and hugely panned in Washington, D.C.

The early '80s local hit, "What You Say-Love Boat, Love Boat," was released.

In 1997, Redds passed away.

During his life, Redds was undoubtedly a gift to the city's emerging Go-Go scene, and his contributions to the culture are indisputable. Audiences move and groove to the Go-Go beat because Redds told us so.

Milton "Go-Go Mickey" Freeman, *congas Rare Essence, Reality Band, and MANY other Go-Go bands*
One that sticks with me… We were playing at the Washington Coliseum Shacks the trumpet player had no horn stand... so he had his case on stage… Redds tripped over the case... just going to say... it is a good thing Redds had a guitar cord. It was funny but not funny. "You Fired Shacks. You fired."

Marc Lewis, *trumpet, Redds and the Boys, Maniac Soldiers*
Funniest, at rehearsals. We stayed arguing. Redds (later) loved playing everything in 'C' No matter what—another one. I think we were opening for Backyard (bad combo. I know) at Bumpers. We had to turn his mic off (low). In the middle of a groove, he came out of nowhere and started yelling, 'Funk your body Redds' while strumming C major chords. Miss that dude.

Patrick Wise, *keyboards, Redds and the Boys, Petworth, Physical Wunder*

261

Marc Lewis You ain't lying with everything being played in the key of "C." Don't forget about his favorite turn-around/reset in the key of "D." Regardless of what grooves we had lined up for a particular show, he always wanted almost everything in those two keys! LOL

David Green, *percussionist, Rare Essence*
Redds was super talented, creative, and crazy as hell! He was a showman on stage and so full of life.

Dwayne Lee, *Recording Engineer, Music Producer, Drummer for Redds and the Boys*
The most fun I had in the early days of Go-Go was with Redds and the Boys. We got to create our own style individually and laugh at Redds' corny jokes even when he tried to be a James Brown-type tyrant. ● ⰰ* By the way, some of these drummers and bands are still playing our beats and chanting our sayings and stuff. Most don't know it or realize where it came from.

Brian "Slick Rick" Williams, *Vocalist, Central Groove, Hot Cold Sweat, Crossover Band, Sweat Band*

Hosea "Heartbeat" Williams, *congas, Gerardo, Chuck Brown, Ayre Rayde, Central Groove*
Chuck was someone who always had a sidekick. My brother was the first one to do it at the Kilimanjaro. He was the only one never to ask Pops for money. Pop was always like, "What do I owe you, son?" And Rick never took a dollar from Chuck. Never. Rick was sitting in our apartment bedroom when we were with Central Groove, and Rick had that gravelly voice and he would say, "Say What?" Class Band was out, and Tidy was one of Rick's inspirations. Rick's got that gravelly voice, and Hot Cold Sweat needed a rapper, and they brought Rick in for an audition and Rock Steady, and everybody approved it. We grew up sharing the same bedroom. No one had a bad thing to say about Rick. Rick was always uplifting. He was always smiling. When he thought I was doing wrong or whatever, man, he would cuss my ass out. With me, it was like, he looked up to me and didn't want to see me fail at anything. Rick always thought I was perfect; whenever I made a wrong move, he would come at me 100 miles. Everything I do from now on is dedicated to my baby brother.

Kent "Hot Dog" Wood, *Keyboardist, E.U., Rare Essence*

Ju Ju House, *Drummer Extraordinaire, E.U., The Peacemakers, Chuck Brown, David Sanborn*

Kent was probably one of the most amazing keyboard players ever. One of the most creative cats. That was my partner in crime. Kent Wood. He was another one. He was definitely overlooked when it comes to the Go-Go thing being introduced and pushed in D.C. Now Chuck had that foundation, absolutely, and we all came off of Chuck Brown, but Ivan, Kent, and I pushed these records- getting them to the stores- cassette tapes and wax then, there were no such thing as a CD or a download. They didn't exist. This was before "Da Butt." This was the Go Ju Go album and Cat in the Hat- way before "Da Butt."

Gregory "Sugar Bear" Elliott, *bassist and founding member of Experience Unlimited (E.U.)*

Kent, was the greatest keyboard player we ever had. That man was talented, but he was so quiet! It's funny because Kent came to EU, but he loved Rare Essence. So, he finally got a chance to go and play with them, and I was happy for him. But while he was here, we recorded a lot of stuff. He recorded a lot of songs with EU. And a whole lot of shows, a lot of tours, and Kent Wood was just multi-talented. He was a good arranger. He could play the funkiest lines on the keyboards. I have nothing but all "A"'s for Kent.

263

Conclusion

In conclusion, again, what you've read here only scratches the surface of Go-Go as it discusses more of the "Golden Age of Go-Go." With this book, I hope to bring you the voices of the people who have created this music- what makes the music "tick," so to speak. The music tells the story of D.C., the "other" Washington. When people think of Washington, they think of the politics, the monuments, and such, but D.C. is the people, the city, the hopes, the triumphs and tragedies, and the music. Go-Go is the heartbeat of the culture.

Over time, alternative styles have been created in the Go-Go genre that people love to debate about. Bounce Beat is one such classification. Many more bands have sprung up over the years, appealing to younger crowds. Some bands to check out would be Suttle, UCB, TOB, TCB, and MAB.

A lot of the pioneering bands have also reinvented themselves as well. One such band would be Rare Essence. Andre "Whiteboy" Johnson is the single remaining founding member of the band still playing with them and has recreated and reinvented the band many, many times as the members come and go. Trouble Funk, Experience Unlimited, and Junkyard Band are still around, with legions of fans crossing generational lines. And then there's the Chuck Brown Band. The band is still going strong, along with some members who played with him before his passing on May 16, 2012. His son Wiley and daughter KK are heavily involved in performing with the band, and Tom Goldfogle is still managing the band.

Backyard Band is still one of the hottest, if not THE hottest, bands out here and is worth the price of admission. You will undoubtedly recognize band leader Anwan "Big G" Glover from his role as Slim Charles of The Wire or any of the other characters he has played on the big screen.
Other bands that I would recommend would be Blacc Print Experience, Prophecy, Proper Utensils, Bela Dona, Sirius Company, Godfather and Friends, Wisdom Speeks, Crank Caviar, and Still Familiar. Push Play is also a great group featuring many Go-Go Veterans, although they aren't a Go-Go band.

Venues come and go, but one of my favorite places is still Takoma Station Tavern. You can usually find a Go-Go band playing somewhere in the DMV any night of the week. It's always a party and is truly something that must be experienced at least once in your lifetime in its proper form-LIVE.

We have Go-Go bands from D.C. traveling to perform on festivals-Something in the Water, Floydfest, and South x Southwest. There are also "Takeovers," where a group of bands will go down to Miami or some other city, and people from D.C. will flock down there to see their favorite bands in a different setting. Hopefully, some people from those cities will come out to see what Go-Go is about, and it will continue to grow, spread, and stay alive.

Go-Go has spread to other cities as Go-Go bands have popped up nationwide. Jus Once from North Carolina is one that I have personally checked out. Some other bands are DCAF, Alter Egos, Project 919, Uptown Swagga Band, and Raw Deal Band 954, but there are more.

There is a Go-Go Museum in the works which will open in Southeast Washington, D.C., complete with a mobile museum that will travel around. The Martin Luther King Jr. Memorial Library also has an extensive collection of Go-Go artifacts comprising a permanent exhibit. The library is at 901 G Street NW, Washington, D.C. 20001.

There are many resources for those who want to know about this genre, which means so much to so many. As you can see, the people involved have dedicated their whole lives to this culture. My hope is that the D.C. Government will one day treat Go-Go the way that New Orleans treats its jazz. Tourists flock to Preservation Hall in New Orleans to soak up the vibes and see the live show to see the music in its true form. I hope that D.C. will do that too.

Hopefully, this book will inspire someone to write about the younger groups still growing, thriving, and participating in the Go-Go culture and give them their "shine." Go-Go has been around, bringing people together and fostering community, and I hope the younger bands and the younger fans will continue to embrace it and that it will continue for years to come.

GALLERY

Redds & The Boys: Anthony "Redds" Williams, "Too Tall" Steve Coleman,
Randy "Hollywood" Kilpatrick and Carl "CJ" Jones

Photo Credit: Private Collection of Carl "CJ" Jones

Drummers JuJu House and Ricky Wellman at the Lifetime Achievement
Award Celebration for Ricky Wellman presented by
the Heartbeat Conga Hour

Photo Credit: Jill Greenleigh

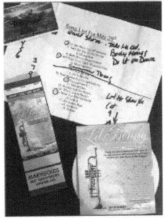

Set List from Little Benny Tribute, May 2011

Photo Credit: Jill Greenleigh

Jungle Boogie, The Blueprint

Photo Credit: Jill Greenleigh

Trouble Funk Pioneers James Avery, Timothy "TeeBone" David and "Big Tony" Fisher

Photo Credit: Jill Greenleigh

The Official Music of Washington, D.C.- Go-Go!

Ron Moten, Gregory "Sugar Bear" Elliott, Michael "Funky Ned" Neal, Salih Williams, Moe Shorter, D.C. Mayor Muriel Bowser, Anwan "Big G" Glover, Kenyan McDuffie Ward 5 Councilmember and Jas. Funk in Feb 2020 at Bill Signing

Photo Credit: Jill Greenleigh

The Icons of Promotions- Darryll Brooks, Gerald Scott and Carol
Kirkendall on the Heartbeat Conga Hour

Photo Credit: Jill Greenleigh

Little Benny Harley and Jill Greenleigh, 1988

Photo Credit: Jill Greenleigh

Soul Searcher John "JB" Buchanan, keys and horn at a rehearsal to re-establish the group.

Photo Credit: Thomas Sayers Ellis

Rory "DC" Felton at Little Benny Tribute. DC was a Triple Threat with his steps, sax and cowbell, May 2011

Photo Credit: Unknown

271

Powerful Percussion- Bojack, Buggy, Mickey, Sali Marky, Foxy Rob and
Vincent Coleman

Photo Credit: Jill Greenleigh

Jill Greenleigh with the Godfather of Go-Go, Chuck Brown

Photo Credit: Private Collection of Jill Greenleigh

The Original Familiar Faces

Photo: Personal Collection of Ivan Goff

Junkyard Band

Photo Credit: Unknown, Personal File of Junkyard Band

Curtis Johnson, Donald Tillery, Chuck Brown cut out, "Ken Boy" Scoggins, John "JB" Buchanan

Photo Credit: Jill Greenleigh

Rory "DC" Felton, Mike "Hardstep" Taylor and John Cabalou at Little Benny Memorial Show May 2011

Photo Credit: Jill Greenleigh

Angie Green and Jill Greenleigh

Photo Credit: Carl Hylton

Busey Brothers

Photo Credit: Private Collection of Keith Busey

Vincent Coleman and Tino Jackson at Go Go Radio

Photo Credit: Jill Greenleigh

John Cabalou, Terry Lambert and Greg "Googie" Burton

Photo Credit: Unknown

Go-Go Flicks

Photo Credit: Jill Greenleigh

Timothy "Shorty Tim" Glover

Photo Credit: Jill Greenleigh

Proclamation

Photo Credit: Jill Greenleigh

AM/FM Promo Photo

Photo Credit: Unknown

Junkyard Band

Photo Credit: Unknown

Lifetime Achievement Award

Photo Credit: Jill Greenleigh

Anwan "Big G" Glover at Go-Go Bill Signing

Photo Credit: Jill Greenleigh

Jill Greenleigh and Nathaniel "GoGo Bouncey" Lucas -
Legacy Band vs. High Potential (MoCo's 2 Best)

Photo Credit: Unknown

PA CD (Evolved from the PA Tape) Rare Essence Highland August 5, 1982- Most sought after PA Tape/ CD Truly a Classic

Photo Credit: Jill Greenleigh

Donald Tillery with two horns at once- his trademark!

Photo Credit: Thomas Sayers Ellis

Maxx Kidd & Randy Kilpatrick

Photo Credit: Private Collection of Randy Kilpatrick

Hand drawn logo by Elmoe of Little Benny & The Masters, circa 1988

Photo Credit: Jill Greenleigh